Online Marketing Heroes

Interviews with 25 Successful Online Marketing Gurus

Online Marketing Heroes

Interviews with 25 Successful Online Marketing Gurus

Michael Miller

WILEY

Wiley Publishing, Inc.

Online Marketing Heroes: Interviews with 25 Successful Online Marketing Gurus

Published by
Wiley Publishing, Inc.
10475 Crosspoint Boulevard
Indianapolis, IN 46256
www.wiley.com

Published simultaneously in Canada

ISBN: 978-0-470-24204-9

Manufactured in the United States of America

10 9 8 7 6 5 4 3 2 1

For general information on our other products and services or to obtain technical support, please contact our Customer Care Department within the U.S. at (800) 762-2974, outside the U.S. at (317) 572-3993 or fax (317) 572-4002.

Library of Congress Cataloging-in-Publication Data

Miller, Michael, 1958-
  Online marketing heroes : interviews with 25 successful online
marketing gurus / Michael Miller.
    p. cm.
  Includes index.
  ISBN 978-0-470-24204-9 (cloth)
  1. Internet marketing. 2. Internet advertising. I. Title.
  HF5415.1265M554 2009
  658.8'72--dc22
                                2007051406

To Sherry, a hero in her own right.

About the Author

Michael Miller is a former marketer and a prolific writer and has authored more than 75 non-fiction books over the past two decades. He is known for his casual, easy-to-read writing style and his ability to explain a wide variety of complex topics to an everyday audience. Collectively, his books have sold more than a million copies worldwide. More information can be found at his Molehill Group web site, www.molehillgroup.com. He can be reached via email at heroes@molehillgroup.com.

Credits

Contents

Introduction

"Marketing is not an event, but a process"

—*Jay Conrad Levinson*

I've always thought of marketing as a big tent. There are lots of different pieces to the marketing puzzle, from research to product development to advertising to public relations. I know this from personal experience; in my two decades of marketing prior to becoming a full-time author, I did everything a typical marketer does, including copywriting, advertising placement, direct mail, trade shows, publicity, product development, branding, you name it. That's the way marketing works.

The big-tent aspect of marketing is even more apparent when you're marketing online. An online marketer has to deal with all the traditional marketing disciplines plus a few new ones, such as search engine optimization and social networking. As with traditional marketing, it's all in service of the brand, the product, and (most importantly) the customer.

Pieces of the Whole

The concept of the big marketing tent informs the book that you hold in your hands. In spite of the title *Online Marketing Heroes*, there is no single discipline known as "online marketing;" instead, it's a collection of different disciplines, which added together paint the entire online marketing picture.

Accordingly, I've interviewed 25 different people, each representing a different aspect of online marketing. There are interviews with people who do email marketing, blog marketing, search engine marketing, online retailing, web copywriting, Internet PR, and more; whatever aspect of online marketing you're interested in, there's at least one interview that should pique your interest.

While each interview is interesting and informative in and of itself, taken together they provide a complete overview of today's state of the online marketing art. To be successful online, you need to know a little bit (or more) about all the topics discussed here. And what better place to learn than from the experts in each discipline?

Meet the Heroes

While there might not be a single discipline known as "online marketing," there most certainly are heroes involved in marketing online. An online marketing hero is an expert in his or her field, someone who has mastered that discipline in the service of customers, clients, or companies. These are people who have done or are doing cutting-edge online marketing; their activities are worth examining and emulating for anyone interested in becoming a successful online marketer.

The online marketing heroes interviewed in this book represent a range of marketing disciplines, from copywriting to public relations to direct marketing. The list of interviewees includes folks in cubicles and folks in corner offices; there are people who get their hands dirty every day, executives who manage large marketing teams, and consultants who provide their advice and expertise to companies both large and small.

If you're a savvy marketing professional, you'll recognize some of these heroes from their past and present work in the industry. Even if the names aren't familiar to you, the companies they represent surely will be; the interviewees in this book represent companies and firms the like of Circuit City, Edelman, Google, Overstock.com, Travelocity, and Yahoo! And, to provide a big-picture overview, there's even a marketing professor from Northwestern University's Kellogg School of Management.

Some of these folks have been around since before there was online marketing—before the Internet became the Web and, in some cases, before the advent of personal computers. Other interviewees are newer to the trenches, with a history that goes back no further than the rise of Google. That's reflective of the state of online marketing today, however, which requires a mix of traditional marketing with technological savvy.

How did I pick these particular people to be showcased in this book? My overriding goal was to cover each particular aspect of online marketing, which meant selecting individuals from each discipline. I wanted a mix of viewpoints, so I avoided choosing all executives or all consultants. I tried to choose individuals who had a history of sharing their expertise, which meant seeking out marketers who spoke at industry conferences, wrote blogs and magazine articles, and so forth. Over the course of setting up the interviews, I often found that one interviewee led to another; the experts in our field are often well known, especially to one another. It helped if they or their companies were also known to the general public.

In the end, I assembled a list of interviewees that, to me at least, represented the big-tent aspect of online marketing. I tried to avoid duplication of skills as much as possible, although some duplication of information couldn't be avoided; good advice is good advice, after all, and not limited to a single marketing discipline.

Fortunately for me—and for you, the reader—all the interviewees were gracious with their time and their expertise. I truly enjoyed my talks with each of the people included in this book. It's always fun to talk shop, and that's what this book ultimately is: a series of marketing shop talks. As a marketer yourself, you should appreciate that.

Read—and Learn

Not only are the 25 individuals featured in this book successful in what they do; they're also willing to share the secrets of their success with others. As we all learned from reading Spider-Man comic books, with great power comes great responsibility—and the online marketing heroes know it's their responsibility to help others in the marketing community.

This book isn't a collection of stale biographies; it's a compendium of information and advice of value to any current or aspiring online marketer. Want to learn how to optimize your site for search engine placement? Or utilize blogs and social networks as part of your marketing mix? Or create a compelling online retailing site? Or write an effective online press release? All that information—and more—is here, courtesy of the online marketing heroes.

Who better, after all, to talk about search engine advertising than the head of Yahoo! Search Marketing? Who better to talk about online PR than the SVP of Edelman's me2revolution practice? Who better to talk about email marketing than the founder of ExactTarget? Who better to talk about blog marketing than the person who runs Southwest Airlines' Nuts About Southwest blog? And who better to talk about online retailing than the heads of marketing at Circuit City, Overstock.com, and Travelocity?

In other words, *Online Marketing Heroes* lets you learn from the experts. Yes, it's interesting to read about how these marketers got to where they are today, but there's ton of practical information beyond that. Whether you want to learn more about social network marketing, mobile marketing, search engine marketing, or online PR, the online marketing heroes have the information you need.

So whether you're an experienced marketer looking to hone his online skills or a marketing newbie just now learning the ropes, there's something in this book for you. Just remember where you picked up the newfound knowledge—and thank the online marketing heroes for sharing their expertise.

Joan Holman: Joan Holman Productions

"You need an information-rich web site and a web site that responds to [customer] needs, whatever they are."

—Joan Holman

A business' presence on the Internet isn't the result of just one or two things; it's a combination of everything the business does or doesn't do online. No one knows this better than Joan Holman, who brings a holistic approach to web marketing.

Joan is that rare consultant without a specialty. She's a broad-based marketing consultant whose expertise includes marketing, business development, branding, and public relations. But online marketing isn't the only thing Joan does—she also created and produced the PBS documentary *The Legacy of Achievement*, founded The Legacy of Achievement Foundation to document the lives of successful and inspiring people, and wrote the biographical book *Hands That Touch, Hands That Heal* (Sister Rosalind Christian Ministries, 2003). Not surprisingly, Joan is also an in-demand motivational speaker.

> **FACT SHEET: JOAN HOLMAN**
>
> Chief Enlightenment Officer, Joan Holman Productions
> (www.holman.com)
>
> Founder, The Legacy of Achievement Foundation
> (www.legacyofachievement.org)

Improving a Company's Web Presence

By looking at all aspects of a company's web presence, Joan Holman is about to offer advice that other narrowly focused consultants might miss. In this interview she discusses everything from web site design to the use of humor online—and why you don't want the artists or the geeks driving how your web site looks.

How has the whole concept of marketing changed with the advent of the online world?

We are having a convergence of public relations and marketing online. You are able to bypass gatekeepers. You can go direct to the public now, direct to the consumer. It used to be that you'd have to use advertising, you'd have to use the media, to get your message out. The Internet allows you to bypass all these people who have been in control before. If you are creative and if you understand the medium, or if you have somebody working with you who does, there are powerful things that you can do for yourself with marketing—for a fraction of the cost of what it used to take to build a brand or become a celebrity. It's just amazing, the opportunities that are there for people who know how to do this.

> *"You need to get feedback from your target market."*

There are some people who've been very, very effective with this, like Dane Cook, the comedian. In the year 2000, he took $30,000 of his own money and he launched his web site (www.danecook .com) to further his career. He had been on Comedy Central and he had a fan base, but he understood the power of the Internet. He became one of the first celebrities to really harness the Internet to catapult himself to a much greater degree of success. He was the first person to get two million fans on MySpace, listed as his friends. So when he came out with tickets to his events, and with products—DVDs, CDs—there he was, in instant contact with a worldwide audience who could come buy his stuff and support him. Things like that were not possible before we had the Internet.

Can you talk a bit about how a company might use the Internet to go directly to their customers?

You are probably aware of PR Web (www.prweb.com), where you can post your direct-to-consumer, direct-to-public news releases. Those news releases get permanently archived online. You can select target markets for your releases and it's a great way to get information out there, to get your name out there, and to have visibility online.

As far as reaching your existing customers, you need an information-rich web site and a web site that responds to their needs, whatever they are. If they want to buy online or get customer service or read frequently asked questions, then you set that up for them. People are also going to do their research for their product purchases online and you need to help them with that process.

A lot of the big corporations have used advertising agencies and people with an advertising agency consciousness to create web sites that are based on traditional broadcast television advertising. They have tried to take TV advertising and put that online. But that is not what is really effective online. What is effective online is great content and authentic information. That's why people will go to consumer sites, to actually see product reviews, rather than go to a large corporate web site, which they may not trust to give them the real picture.

It's very important for a company to monitor what is being said online about their products and services, about their brand. It's important to be on top of that and be responsive. When appropriate, a company may open up its own web site for some honest dialogue and interactivity with its customer base, in order to respond to customer needs and to improve its products and services.

So if a company already has a web site, what would they look for in trying to improve that site, with online marketing in mind?

First of all, they should conduct some sort of usability testing. Extensive usability testing can be very expensive, but you can do some limited or informal usability testing on a small budget. You need to get feedback from your target market and also find out who is coming to your web site and what is their experience of your web site.

I personally have seen so many web sites that do not function well for their target audiences. I recently evaluated a web site of a real estate developer who is building expensive condos and much of his target market is an older population. My recommendation to him, or to anyone building a web site, is to know

> *"What are these people working with and how can we make our web site user-friendly for them?"*

what kinds of computer platforms his prospective buyers are using and how this impacts the usability of his web site. His home page and much of the web site was created in Flash—and to view it, you must have the latest version of Flash. This could be a major problem with an older population, which may not have the latest and greatest technology One solution is to provide an alternative version of specific web pages, or even the entire web site, for those people who do not have the most current version of Flash.

According to research from early 2007 by the Pew Internet & American Life Project, 71 percent of American adults are now online. Internet users access the web from all kinds of computers, devices, monitors, browsers, and connection speeds, which impacts how they can view or use any given web site. Although high-speed Internet is pervasive in the workplace, Pew research indicates that as of early 2007, only about half of U.S. adults had high-speed connections at home. And there's a lot of businesses creating web sites that try to force their customers and prospective customers to adapt to the parameters of the web site—instead of saying, "What are these people working with and how can we make our web site user-friendly for them?" These businesses don't have the knowledge of all the technicalities of the web, the different platforms, and they don't understand what it takes to create a truly effective and usable web site. They may get a phone call one day from someone who says, "I can't use your web site." Then the assumption is made that, well, there's something wrong with that person's computer, and that just may not be the case. It just may be that the user is on a platform that limits the use of the web site. Some people, because of security issues, won't allow ActiveX or pop-up windows. So they're screening out a lot of stuff that you want them to view and you may not even be aware of this. If you want to be effective, you need to know what's really going on with your web site and you need to develop a web site that is usable for your target audience.

Why do you think companies create bad web sites? Like you, I see a lot of these web sites using Flash and other technologies that aren't going to be visible on some people's computers. Why do companies gravitate towards that?

Well, because of the people developing the web site. Mostly these are young techie people and this is what they're being trained in. They're either taking courses in it or they're self training, and this is what's fun for them. This is what's trendy and cool, and since they are techies, they love technology and want to use it. Quite frankly, they're not marketing people. So many web sites are being designed and developed by these techies and also by graphic designers. The designers want to create artistically and they are used to designing for print, which is a completely different medium than the web. And such constraints as ease of use, download time, and functionality can seriously spoil their fun. I don't mean to say that all techies and designers are inept at producing effective web sites; however, both of these groups have a really different mindset and background than marketing people.

There needs to be a really close integration among the techies, the artists, and marketing people who understand usability and online marketing. That's something very important. In fact, an online marketing specialist should be directing the development of the web site.

An online marketing expert can help businesses and organizations leverage the potential of the Internet for marketing in a number of ways. This includes creating a user-friendly web site for target audiences; optimizing a web site for search engine market-

> *"It is not about art or technology; it is about providing information and services."*

ing; enhancing the design and layout of the site to achieve marketing, sales, communications and branding goals; and creating compelling content that attracts and retains the interest of target audiences. An online marketing expert can also help write and present content in the optimum way for the unique web environment and create content-specific web pages or stand-alone web sites to target specific groups of buyers. The online marketing expert should also have knowledge of the multiple online tools available for marketing and public relations, and should be aware of the newest marketing tools and trends in the ever-changing online environment.

I've had to direct projects with the graphics people, the arty people, and the techie people. Their talents are a valuable part of the development of a web site; however, one should never lose sight of the real goals of a web site. For most businesses and organizations, it is not about art or technology; it is about providing information and services.

Jakob Nielsen, the usability expert, talks about the clash between the engineers and the creatives. The engineering approach is to try to solve a problem for someone. The artistic approach is about self-expression. There has to be some sort of a balance. But I'm all about marketing, and I want to see results.

I had somebody come to me who had spent a very large sum of money on a business web site. He had used an advertising agency, and his web site—even on a high-speed connection—took a very long time to download. The entire web site was done in Flash and was set up so it could only be viewed after the whole web site had downloaded first, which took anywhere from 58 seconds to a few minutes, depending on the type of computer and connection. I told him, "People are going to be gone," and, "You have about four seconds, maybe seven seconds, to engage your site visitor." To prove to him that there was this problem, I did some informal usability testing and gave him feedback, which confirmed the problem. But this guy was young, aggressive in his business, a young entrepreneur, and I think he didn't want to hear it—because it worked fine on *his* computer and because my feedback revealed that he had wasted a great deal of money on a web site that was basically unusable for many, if not most, people.

See what I'm saying? It's like, you better get this, folks. People in business better get this. Because if you don't get it, whoever does get it is going to have a competitive advantage over you. And if you don't get it, you are going to waste a lot of money and a lot of time.

I'm surprised more companies don't take the lead from the most popular web site out there, which is Google—which has probably the simplest home page on the web.

Look how popular it is.

And that's one of the reasons why it's popular—its simplicity.

That's right.

You know, people have these Flash intros, these Flash splash pages. It's like, why? What is the point? Whoever puts these up does not understand what people really want. And web design is about giving people what they really want, not what you think they want, or what you want.

If people want to be entertained, let them go to YouTube. But for a company doing business, trying to sell products and services, it's not about the entertainment—it's about the information. It's about the content. This is not to say that entertainment cannot be used to help build a brand, or to create awareness or be used for marketing purposes; however, that entertainment should be user-friendly and should supplement and not supplant other useful content.

Obviously, the web site is just one part of the online marketing mix; publicity is another part. How does a company get publicity on the Internet?

There's a lot of ways to do it. There are direct-to-consumer news releases that can be loaded with keywords that are going to make you visible on the search engines. These online news releases can generate interest not only from buyers, but from bloggers and online news sites and offline media as well.

Then there's doing something remarkable, doing something fun or interesting and putting it on YouTube. Have you seen the video with the Diet Coke and Mentos experiments, where they put them together and create eruptions? It's so entertaining and it has been viewed over three million times on YouTube. In public relations they oftentimes will say there's no such thing as bad press—because even if it's bad, you're getting your name in front of people, you're creating awareness and visibility.

You can get publicity through the search engines, getting mentioned in blogs, doing creative things (like on YouTube), and word of mouth via email and social networking web sites. Everybody has their email lists of their friends, and if you do something really special and interesting with a web site, oftentimes people will send it around.

Recently a friend emailed me a link to something called the Color Quiz personality test, which reveals your current emotional state. I was familiar with the Color Quiz from years ago through a book called the Luscher Color Test, which contained this quiz. As soon as I got the email I thought, this would be great fun to take again. So I went to the web site at www.colorquiz.com and took the test. And of course, I told all my friends by sending it out to my email list.

Now if a company is creative and does something that's fun, it creates an opportunity for people to do the marketing for you, through their

> *"Get young people involved."*

word of mouth online—emails and blogs and social networking sites like MySpace, Facebook, Gather, Zaadz and LinkedIn. There's just a lot of opportunities for companies that are creative and willing to try out these different things.

A lot of what you're talking about are very nontraditional forms of marketing. How do you get a company to think outside the box?

You share with them examples of success stories of how other companies have done it, or how individuals have done it online. You tell them if they want results, if they want prospects, if they want customers, then they need to open themselves up to being creative and nontraditional.

I also would tell them to get young people involved. Young people are living online; this is their medium. They're very creative. A lot of them come up with really fun things. I think every company should have a young intern, or a few young interns, and listen to their ideas. Be open to it. In my job as director of tourism for the city of Minneapolis, I brought in a 15-year-old intern I called my "wandering child prodigy." He was just great.

Should these efforts supplement traditional marketing or replace some of what a company's doing?

I think it can supplement. Not completely replace, but in some cases you might even go to 80 percent online marketing and 20 percent offline, depending on your type of business.

I'll give you an example. A couple of years ago, a client of mine bought an old apartment building to convert to condos. The market got very competitive here in the Twin Cities, very rough. There was a glut of condo conversions and new condos on the market. He said, whoa, what am I going to do? I'm going to have to sell these. So I did a mix of online and offline marketing.

> *"If you really know how to use online marketing, you're going to have a competitive edge."*

I created a web site for his project. Then I put a large and colorful sign in front of the building that showed some interior photos and directed people to the web site. I made the web site address very large and prominent on the sign. The sign was on a fairly busy street, so a lot of people saw the sign.

I designed a content-rich web site with a lot of photographs, because people want to see what they are getting. I also featured a virtual tour on the web site and testimonials and information about the neighborhood. The web site was very easy to use and compatible with the lowest common denominator of user platform. The web site was up for nine months and the building completely sold out, which was a great success in such a tough market. We had 9,000 visitors to the web site during that time, and 1,000 of those people who visited the web site came to the open houses, which were held every weekend. I kept sign-in sheets that asked people how they heard about the condos. And most of them heard about the condos online through my ads on Craigslist and through the web site.

Craigslist is great and it was very successful for getting prospects. But it was only one part of a three-step process. First, I put up the ad on Craigslist. Then I included a link to the web site from that ad. The web site created interest for viewing the condos at an open house, and the last step was prospects attending an open house.

There are all kinds of different ads that people put up on Craigslist, and you're competing with that. But if you really know how to use online marketing, you're going to have a competitive edge. You can use Craigslist to drive people to a dedicated web site to sell your product or service. If you know HTML markup language, you can also use that to dress up your ads on Craigslist and make them stand out from the crowd.

> *"You have to be really mindful of what kind of images you are putting online."*

Selling this condo project involved both online and offline marketing, and we would not have sold those condos without all that online marketing.

How is the Internet changing the whole business of real estate?

According to a 2006 survey by the the National Association of Realtors, over 80 percent of home buyers now use the Internet to search for a home. Realtors will tell you that people don't even ask to see a property until they've seen it online first. They want to see a lot of photographs, and also a virtual tour. If your photographs are really good, they will draw people to visit your property. But if your photographs are bad, or if you don't have photographs, people aren't going to come and visit your property. Most buyers are doing all their preliminary looking online.

Now here's the thing about the Internet: You have to be really mindful of what kind of images you are putting online. These images should be creating credibility and selling you and your products or services. Be careful with all the photographs you put up on your web site, including photos of yourself and your staff. Just know that these photos are going to project a positive or negative image to people who don't know you. Images are very important online.

> ## "It's important to have a personality and a point of view."

A number of years ago, I got a fabulous speaking engagement through a woman entrepreneur in Washington, D.C. who was putting on a conference there for women entrepreneurs and women leaders. She was going to hire a woman—I believe the woman's name was Diana Holman—to be a keynote speaker about the Internet. She typed holman.com into a browser window thinking she would find this woman and my web site came up instead. She said the minute she saw my photograph, she knew I was the one she wanted to hire, even though I was not her original choice. She had to substantiate it with my background and my abilities, and she had to have it approved by a committee that was working on this event. But I got that speaking engagement and today I still have clients who hired me because they saw me speak at that conference. So the photograph you have online is really important. It has the power to magnetize opportunities, so make sure it presents you in the best way possible.

The other thing is, I think it's important to have a personality and a point of view online. It depends on what type of business you have, but for a lot of companies, especially professional services companies, it's great to share some personal information, which can help to build a relationship.

There are a lot of web sites I go on where I want to see who the key players are in a company or organization. I want to see their faces; I want to get a feeling for them. When seeking professional services, a photo can make all the difference for whether I contact someone or not. And if there is no photo, I frequently will just keep searching to find people who do have a photo on their web site.

Do you have any general advice for a company wanting to improve their online presence?

First of all, get feedback. Get honest feedback about your web site, from the types of people who would be your customers. And be open to criticism and suggestions.

Finally, get creative. I'll tell you what really sells online, what engages people online, is humor and human interest. If you have people on staff, have them share their favorite jokes, favorite web sites, or their favorite humorous

YouTube videos. Have something enjoyable on your web site that makes it interesting, so somebody can say, you know what, you should go to this web site because they have this one section that's just hysterical, or remarkable, or amazing. Something so that people will do some word of mouth about your web site.

Sound Bites

I agree with Joan Holman about the state of web site design today. Too many sites are flashy (or Flash-y) for their own sakes, without regard for usability. I've also experienced the situation of a web site redesign being led by an artsy-fartsy design firm who only cares about an edgy style, or by a group of techies infatuated with the latest web programming technology; in fact, I've resigned from projects that didn't have the proper input from the company's marketing people. Focusing on the customer is what matters—not the style or the technology.

So here's what you can learn from Joan Holman's holistic approach to online marketing:

- Use the Internet to go directly to customers, bypassing the traditional gatekeeping media.
- Develop a web site that's information-rich and that responds to the customer's needs.
- Before you take your web site live, do usability testing to get feedback from your target audience.
- Avoid technology for technology's sake; take your customers' technology level into account before you add all sorts of tech-heavy features to your site.
- Be mindful of the photos you use on your site; friendly and attractive photos of company principals help build a relationship with customers.
- Get creative and use humor to engage site visitors and create a buzz about your site.

Greg Hartnett:
Best of the Web &
Hotel Hotline

"Focus on the user, build for the long view, and the money will come."

—*Greg Hartnett*

G reg Hartnett is a "serial entrepreneur." That means he has
started one business after another—
and they've all been successful. On
the web, his businesses include
Hotel Hotline, a travel-oriented site,
and Best of the Web, an editor-dri-
ven online directory, both very popular sites.

> **FACT SHEET: GREG HARTNETT**
>
> President, Best of the Web
> (www.botw.org)
>
> CEO, Hotel Hotline
> (www.hotelhotline.com)
>
> Blogger (www.greghartnett.com)

Greg is also a prolific blogger and something of an online activist. He has
a passion for both the Internet's commercial and social networking possibilities, and has vast experience in search engine marketing. His latest venture is
the Best of the Web Blog Directory, which attempts to organize the blogosphere in much the same as his Best of the Web directory organizes the web.

Launching an Online Business

Based on his record of success, Greg knows what he's talking about when it
comes to launching new businesses online. He has some very practical advice
for anyone thinking of starting an online business—from getting your house
in order before you start to the best ways to market and advertise your site.
Any budding Internet entrepreneur would be well-served to take Greg's words
of wisdom into account.

I've seen you described as a "serial entrepreneur." What exactly does that mean?

I've gotten to where I am, ultimately, through trial and error. I realized pretty quickly in my professional career that corporate America was no place that I wanted to spend very much time in. I do have more than a handful of years' worth of experience in corporate America, and I have always known that working for somebody else just wasn't going to cut it for me. I grew up in a below-average-income household, so I had a natural distaste for and distrust of authority, which always led me to do things a little bit my own way. That attitude got me in trouble frequently when I was younger, but most certainly laid the foundation for a career of doing my own thing.

I fist took a stab at an entrepreneurial effort back in high school, walking the beaches during the summer with coolers of soda, selling them for anywhere from two to three dollars a clip. Back then I was 16, 17 years old, and I made $250 to $300 cash a day walking up and down the beach.

That's good money.

Yeah, for a high school kid it was all the money in the world. I still say, to this day, that was the best job I ever had.

So I got an early taste of successful entrepreneurship back in high school. After leaving college, I poked around corporate America for close to ten years, working primarily in the financial industry. My first real entrepreneurial effort came in 1999, when my business partner (who was my next-door neighbor at the time) Brian Prince and I decided that we were going to stake our claim in the new online world. At that point, we just knew we wanted something on the Internet, [but] we had no idea what it was.

We decided we were going to start a holding company. The name of the company was eBusiness Holdings, and the plan was that we were going to be kind of like an IdeaLab. We were going to start 15 or whatever different projects, and one of them, we figured, was bound to take off.

> *"Yahoo!'s biggest flaw was...that the price was out of reach for most web companies."*

It just so happened that the very first one that we started, which was in the travel space, took off like wildfire. So our whole holding company/big portfolio concept kind of evaporated, and we pounced on the travel end of it.

A few years later, eBusiness Holdings, from a corporate standpoint, changed into Hotel Hotline. We figured, all right, we're not really a holding company; we're an online travel company, so we might as well have a name that reflects what we're doing. So in early 2001, I think it was, we changed from eBusiness Holdings to Hotel Hotline.

Where did the Best of the Web come from?

Basically, we saw a void in the marketplace and decided that we could fill it. I had been frustrated with directories. At that point there were basically two directories. One was Yahoo! Directory; the other was the Open Directory Project. Both of those, I felt, were fantastic directories, but I felt both of them had very big flaws.

Yahoo!'s biggest flaw was, I thought, that the price was out of reach for most web companies; a small site owner has a tough time spending $299 a year on the product. And the Open Directory—it took forever to get reviewed, if you did get reviewed at all.

I thought to myself, I would be very willing to pay a reasonable review fee to have my site listed in a solid directory. So if I would, other people probably would, as well.

So in the year 2001, Brian and I purchased Best of the Web from a handful of university professors who had started the project but just let it die. We made them an offer on it, purchased it, and spent the next few years transforming it. They had it as kind of a directory structure that was honoring the best sites online. We changed it from that to a more general, comprehensive directory. We spent the next couple of years doing that transformation, and launched it to the general public in 2003.

These days, companies spend a lot of money on search engine advertising. What role do directories, such as Best of the Web, play in online marketing today?

Directories can play a pivotal role in where marketers can start. A directory that's doing its job well focuses on providing quality content to its users— sort of a general interest and general level of resources for the average user. As a by-product of focusing on adding quality resources for the user, they serve a greater purpose, which is providing the search engines with a trusted spot for quality content.

As the search engines continue to grow and there is more and more content online, and as the stakes of the game get higher for search engines, [the search engines] need to make sure that they can provide their users with the most relevant results to search queries. A good place for them to find relevant resources is a trusted web directory. If Google, Yahoo!, or MSN need to know of quality sites that are relevant to real estate, a good place to come and look for that would be a trusted web directory that has real estate categories containing relevant sites.

> *"The landscape has gotten dramatically more competitive."*

A new marketer, or even an established marketer, can benefit from the relevancy of a listing within a web directory. A web directory will send direct traffic relevant to your web site, but you also get the added value of increased visibility in the major search engines.

That's something a lot of businesses probably don't know.

Most don't. We spend a lot of our time trying to let the general population of site owners know that. That's why we go to the conferences, why we spend money on the booth and everything, to get that word out there.

You started your businesses in the relatively early days of the web. How much harder is it for an entrepreneur to start up a web business today?

Barriers to entry remain relatively the same as they did back in the mid- to late-'90s. Depending upon the niche that you're going to target, though, the landscape has gotten dramatically more competitive. From terms of just advertising dollars, pay per click, back in 1999, was 25 to 30 cents to be in the top spot of the most popular terms. Now those terms go for anywhere from 12 to 15 *dollars* per click.

Starting off and becoming successful in a competitive environment is much more difficult now that it was ten years ago. The marketing departments at the major corporations have finally realized the value of search engine marketing, which has created more of an uphill battle for the small site owner.

So I think that today, the average webmaster who's starting to get into online marketing needs to pick more specific, targeted, niche-type applications and market there rather than to the broad base and go for massive amounts of people.

For instance, in the travel market, instead of building a web site thinking that you're going to compete with Expedia or Hotels.com or general travel-type queries, I think it would be a much better idea for somebody to go after a specific niche within the travel market. Family travel or adventure travel or business travel—or to take it one step further, business travel for lawyers, something like that. If you can identify the niche and target them properly, there's still plenty of upside potential for new site owners.

> *"The rush of corporate America…to capitalize on search marketing has completely changed the landscape."*

That advice sounds more similar to what I would give someone starting a brick-and-mortar business today. You don't want to go after Home Depot directly; you want to find a niche outside of the big shadow. Does this mean that online business is becoming more like traditional business?

Absolutely. As the industry matures, we're seeing more consolidation, which follows the same patterns of brick-and-mortar businesses. In a lot of markets that used to be completely fragmented, you have a handful of major players who are rising up to the top and garnering the vast percentage of the users.

Ultimately, it boils down to the large corporate dollars finally realizing that there is gold in them hills. The rush of corporate America, over the last handful of years, to capitalize on search marketing, has completely changed the landscape.

That said, why might someone decide to do an online business as opposed to a traditional business? What advantages are there to doing it online?

It's funny, because now that I have almost a decade of experience in online marketing, I'm routinely dumbstruck when I go into a brick-and-mortar business. I stand there and wonder, how do these people pull it off? With the amount of overhead that goes into a brick-and-mortar operation, and their geographically limited audience, it's no surprise that most businesses fail in their first few years.

Typically you've got a dozen or so employees working your corner drugstore or hardware store, and the amount of revenue generated per employee is minimal compared to an online company. Starting an online company you are able to get much more revenue per employee. At Hotel Hotline, we're going to do probably close to $15 [million] to $16 million in sales this year, and that's with a staff of six people. That's roughly $2.5 million in revenue per employee. I'd be amazed if you could show me *any* brick-and-mortar store that that's doing $16 million a year in sales with six people managing the entire operation.

You're going to have six people working at an average travel agency, doing a fraction of that revenue.

Right. The average travel agency probably doesn't have the biggest benefit of an online presence, the global marketplace. My stores are open 24 hours a day, 7 days a week. They're open to people that are in Portland, Oregon all the way over to Portland, Maine—and overseas, as well. Even if a company had prime real estate at their local mall, how can they compete with that kind of audience? It's just two separate worlds.

> *"Do you want to portray that small mom-and-pop-type feel, or do you want to give yourself a bigger size?"*

That's something I've always grappled with a little bit. As a business owner, you want a buyer to think that you have the infrastructure in place to support their transaction. You never want somebody that's going to give you their credit card information to think that it's just you and one other guy sitting in your house.

But on the flip side of that coin, it's always struck a chord with me as a consumer to do business with the small guy, as opposed to the Wal-Marts or the giant faceless corporations. I think it's really a matter of a personal choice of the business owner. Do you want to portray that small mom-and pop-type feel, or do you want to give yourself a bigger size?

We've typically chosen more on the larger side. I can't imagine that anybody that comes to one of our hotel sites thinks that there are six people that are responsible for the operation.

If you're looking to go bigger, to make yourself appear bigger than you actually are, some things to do would be to make your emails come from a general customer care–type email [address], rather than from an actual person; *info@yourcompanyname.com* would get that across pretty well. An

> *"You need to hire the absolute best people that you possibly can, in every aspect of your operation."*

"about us" page that speaks about the company in terms that would make it appear to be larger than it actually is. Of course, I'm not recommending that people falsify their information at all. But break out your thesaurus when you're writing that "about us" page, and tailor it to give the impression that there's an entire organization, that you're a "real company," and it'll help put your buyer's mind at ease.

I would imagine that another place to spend the money would be on web site design. I'm looking at Hotel Hotline, and it's a very sophisticated site. I wouldn't expect this to be run by a half-dozen people.

I guess it's true with any business that you run, but I think even more so with an online business, especially if you're going to run it with six people; you're really only as good as your weakest employee. So you need to hire the absolute best people that you possibly can, in every aspect of your operation. I like to say that when I'm meeting with my guys, I always want to be the dumbest person in the room.

When it comes to graphics and design, stuff like that, we hire people to do that because there's nobody within my organization that can produce graphics to the level that I would like it done. We saw that as a weakness in our organization and rectified it with an expert from the outside who could do it better than anybody that we had internally.

That brings up another point. If you're a small organization online, you're not meeting the customer every day, you don't have to do everything yourself. You can outsource various parts of the equation, right?

Sure. I think the majority of successful online operations do just that. The pool of talent available today is drawn from a global marketplace which has created a business owner's dream—higher quality at more competitive rates. You can find vast numbers of people to do really anything that it is that needs to be done for your business for a fraction of what you would expect to pay.

How difficult is it to manage the outsourced services?

It can be tricky. If you are outsourcing work to people in another country, there's a lot of stuff that gets lost in translation. You need to be very, very specific about what it is that you're looking for. Leave as little open for interpretation as possible.

> *"You have to be focused on the long view."*

My job has morphed over the years from doing a lot of this stuff myself to managing other people to do it for me. It's much better to have a handful of different people working on different projects and managing them, rather than trying to do everything myself.

It's gotten tricky, especially as we take on more and more outsourced people. Especially if you're working on a project where one piece depends upon another piece to be done, it can get tricky in that regard. But I can't imagine doing it any other way.

That's probably a bigger issue with Best of the Web, where you have all the editors looking over all the web site submissions.

With Best of the Web we have different groups of people that work on it. So we've got the editors that are working on it 24 hours a day, 7 days a week. By having our editorial teams located throughout the world we have created a company that never stops introducing new content.

But most of the stuff that we have accompanying development we do in-house. With Best of the Web, we outsource the more menial-type tasks. The heavy lifting and the coding and the development, stuff like that—we do that in-house. Fortunately, very rarely are we held up in-house by anything that any outsourced program might be working on.

What advice would you give to a person who's thinking of starting up a company on the web today?

My first piece of advice is to get your shop in order beforehand. We learned that the hard way. Make sure your accounting is in place, your books are in place, make sure you have good legal representation. Get all that stuff before you go out and start your venture. That's just basic Business 101, but you'd be amazed how many people I meet in my travels now that completely forget about any of that stuff. So returning to the basics of Business 101 would be my first recommendation.

Then I would recommend, and arguably most importantly, is to realize that it's a long haul. You have to be focused on the long view. There is no magic bullet. There's no trick that's going to make you be number one in Google or Yahoo!

> *"You have to focus on providing users of your web site with A-plus-type content."*

tomorrow morning. It's a long, steady process. You have to do the dirty work, day in, day out. You'll see modest gains over a long period of time. And those modest gains will eventually lead you to top listings, and those top listings will eventually lead to increased revenues on a month-over-month basis. So you take the long view. And hopefully you're not just going to quit your job today and start your online business tomorrow, because there's very little chance of making any kind of livable wage off online marketing for a considerable period of time.

That's one of the things that have become apparent to me as I've done these interviews; I'm not talking to people who've been in business six months and become billionaires. These are all businesses that have been around for five or even ten years. This is a real thing now.

Well, the days of throwing up an HTML web site and making ten grand a month in two months are long gone. That can be done—I know of plenty of guys that use less than white hat methods to have their sites attain top ranking. They make a killing for a month or six weeks, and then the engine sniffs out what they're doing and bans them or devalues their site, and all of a sudden they're making no money.

If you're looking to build something that will endure, there is no substitution for a focus on quality. You have to concentrate on providing users of your web site with A-plus-type content. And in time the engines will recognize what it is that you're doing and view you as a valuable resource to their users.

More often than not I find that webmasters have an improper view of their relationship with the search engines. They're always viewing the search engines as, what do search engines do for me? How can I get my site to the top of Google? What do I need to do in order to trick Google into thinking that I'm a great site?

> *"There should be a proper balance between pay-per-click and organic search engine marketing."*

What webmasters need to do really requires a bit of a paradigm shift, a realization that we live in a symbiotic relationship with the search engines. If you're doing your job properly and providing your users with valuable content, then the search engines need your site as much as your site needs the search engines. Without quality sites, Google and Yahoo! are worthless. So if you produce quality content, then the search engines will never leave you alone.

So focus on the user, build for the long view, and the money will come.

I think that's it right there. There aren't any tricks—just solid business sense.

Yeah. There used to be tricks, but not anymore.

Do you have any more tips for online marketers?

Some other tips might be not to rely 100 perecent on organic search engine listings. There should be a proper balance between pay-per-click and organic search engine marketing. If you can run your pay-per-click advertising campaign profitably, then you have insulated yourself from the tweaking of the algorithms. If you are completely reliant on organic search engine rankings, then you've set yourself up for what could potentially be a devastating Tuesday morning. You could spend three years working on the organic rankings and you're number one, number five, number eight for all these great keywords, and then the search engines change their algorithms, and you're nowhere. And now you have an entire business that has absolutely no traffic because you put all your eggs in one basket.

I've read about that happening.

It's very important to get a mixture of traffic to your site. We spoke earlier about how it's more difficult in some aspects, but in other aspects it's much easier. In contrast to earlier days, there are now many other ways of driving traffic to your web site, outside of just search engine marketing. There are a lot of Web 2.0–type sites that can drive huge visitors to your site. For instance, there's the blogosphere. Eight years ago there wasn't a blogosphere, there was nobody online talking about your product or service. So there are additional avenues available to the webmaster now, to manipulate and exploit results, which anybody thinking of getting involved in online marketing should consider.

Should you rely exclusively on the search-type advertising, or are we talking about banner ads and other types of advertising, as well?

I was speaking particularly about pay-per-click advertising, using Yahoo! Search Marketing or Google AdWords. If you're looking for

> *"People just don't click on banner ads."*

actual visitors to your web site, banner advertising is not the way to go. If you're looking for branding of your web site, then banner advertising might be a good option.

People just don't click on banner ads. They see them, and it'll register with them that you're there, but very, very few of them actually click on them to check out what you have.

So it doesn't have the immediacy that the pay-per-click does.

I think pay-per-click, those little text-link ads, I think they still register with some people as more trustworthy, less of an advertisement. People see those banners and that's all they're thinking about, is that's an ad. They see the text links and they think, maybe here's a resource for what it is that I'm looking for. I think Google's brilliant to use the text-link format as their advertising model. I think today it's more trustworthy to the average user than a banner.

Is that going to change over time, as people become more familiar with it?

Well, click-through rates for AdWords definitely have dropped since they first produced it. There has already been a lessening of the click-through for text-link ads. I think that there are a lot of people that are beginning to mentally filter them out. They see them and they immediately know that they're an ad, and they avert their eyes from them and look for the content on the page. I do think that that's going to be an issue that Google and Yahoo! are going to have to deal with, going forward.

Sound Bites

Greg Hartnett knows what it takes to successfully launch a new online business, and to use the Internet to market that business. You can benefit from what Greg has learned over the years, including the following:

- Do your homework before you launch your business—establish an accounting system, obtain legal representation, do all the typical Business 101 stuff.
- Focus on the long haul—don't expect to get rich quick.
- Incorporate web directories into your marketing mix, along with traditional search engine marketing.
- Strive for a mix of pay-per-click and organic search engine results.
- Hire the best possible individuals—and don't be afraid to outsource nonessential activities.

Jacob Hawkins: Overstock.com

3

"Every year the marketing landscape changes, every year the customers become more demanding, every year they're wanting more things. You have to always be sprinting to stay ahead of the competition."

—*Jacob Hawkins*

Overstock.com is great online success story. There's not really a brick-and-mortar equivalent to what Overstock does online; it's kind of like a complete outlet mall under one virtual roof. Founded by Patrick Byrne in 1999, Overstock has since gone on to become one of the largest online-only retailers on the Internet, registering almost $800 million in sales in 2006.

Jacob Hawkins is senior vice president of online marketing for overstock, responsible for all online marketing and customer-acquisition activities. He joined the company shortly after its founding, in 2000; before that, he was a consultant for Professional Marketing International.

At least part of Overstock's success is due to Jacob's online marketing skills and experience. He knows what works and what doesn't, and how to turn web surfers into profitable customers.

Creating an Online Megaretailer

Anyone looking to move into online retail can learn a lot from Jacob. In this interview we discuss everything from basic positioning to customer acquisition and retention to the importance of online customer reviews. Read and learn.

Let's start with positioning. How do you position a company on the web—and, particularly, what positioning do you take with Overstock?

That's a great question. At Overstock, we realized the online world is not far different from the offline world. You have different stores that meet different niches. There are stores that compete on quality, stores that compete on price, stores that compete on service, and stores that compete on a mixture of these points. If you asked someone on the street to recommend a place to buy a book, TV, or a pair of pants, they would be able to name a store or two for each product. Each store is there trying to fill a consumer niche.

Patrick Byrne, our CEO, realized in the late '90s that the value niche had not yet been fulfilled on the Internet. He saw Overstock.com as an opportunity to fill that niche.

At Overstock, we sell name-brand products at discounted prices. We have a best-price guarantee for every product we sell, ensuring that customers get the best price online when they shop our site. Additionally, we work very hard to ensure that customers who shop our web site are highly satisfied.

How difficult is the fact that you compete in so many different product categories? Is that a plus or a minus for you?

It's a plus. In the offline world, the stores that are thriving are the big-box stores like Wal-Mart. People shop these stores in part for the convenience of finding many products they're interested in at one location.

> *"We work very hard to have the best prices online for the products we sell."*

In the online world, although your competitors are just a few keystrokes away, consumers are still looking for stores they trust and that offer many products they're interested in.

While we currently have over 750,000 products, we believe we have only scratched the surface of the many categories we can compete in. You can expect us to continue to grow our product assortment and bring on additional product categories that our customers are interested in.

How do you attract new customers to the site?

Ultimately, we attract customers by offering compelling products at bargain prices, and then offering world-class customer service. To get the word out about the deals at Overstock, we employ television commercials, email campaigns, and a variety of online marketing campaigns.

The other way people find out about Overstock.com is by word-of-mouth marketing from our existing customers. Sixty percent of our site visitors are female. Many of these visitors are very vocal about where to go online to get the best prices on name-brand products.

Do you make a conscious effort to keep your prices below your competitors'? Do you track that on a regular basis?

Absolutely. We work very hard to have the best price online for the products we sell. We love when people compare prices, as we generally have the lowest price, which reinforces our value proposition.

I would think, when you're looking at price comparison, that the shopping engines, like Shopping.com, would be an important part of your marketing mix.

The comparison-shopping engines are an important part of our marketing mix so far as they make it easy for potential customers to compare prices. Most people who visit a comparison-shopping engine do so with the intent to buy something. They typically have already researched the item and are looking for a store with a competitive price that they would feel comfortable buying that product from.

When you talk about the promotions to grow your business, how are people finding you? Is it the email promotion or advertising or something else that's working for you?

The answer is, yes. It's all of those things. We'll advertise anywhere we can economically do so online, so far as the web site is not illegal or will not upset our customers.

In the marketing world, you have brand marketers and direct marketers. Brand marketers, like Ford or Visa, don't measure which advertising dollars are driving which

> *"The Internet is a direct marketer's dream."*

revenue dollars. Direct marketers, like Overstock.com, do measure which advertising dollars are generating which revenue dollars.

The Internet is a direct marketer's dream. Very early in our company's history, we developed an in-house tracking system that allowed us to track the performance of each online advertisement we did. We would track how much revenue and gross profit a campaign generated versus how much that campaign cost. In a short amount of time, we were able to weed out the dogs and invest in the great campaigns.

We were one of the first companies that was able to do this. It gave us a great advantage over our competition. Our CEO gave the analogy of living in a city full of cash machines where you put a dollar in and they each spit out a different amount. One machine might spit out a quarter, another $0.50, another $1.00, and every now and again you would find one that spit out $1.25. When you find the machine that spits out $1.25, how much money do you put in to it? As much as you can for as long as you can.

Our job, as marketers, is to test each advertising cash machine to find the ones that spit out more than you put in to it. We found many such deals in the early days and advertised as much as we could in those areas. Sooner or later, our competitors would come along and see us huddled around a cash machine and would come over and take advantage of the same deal. As competition for the machine increased, the opportunity decreased. We constantly have to test new machines to stay ahead of the competition.

> *"The key is to help them find what they are looking for as quickly as possible."*

In addition to finding advertising deals that were underpriced, we also have spent a great deal of time optimizing our advertising campaigns and web site to stretch our marketing dollars further.

The online advertising space continues to dramatically change. It's gone from a game where advertisers were buying eyeballs, to where they were buying clicks, to where they were buying revenue, to where they are now buying profit on the present transaction and the future lifetime-value of that customer. Every day the level of sophistication and experience of the advertisers increases and becomes more competitive.

Much of the dumb money that came into the online game early is gone. The companies who survive long-term are the ones that discover how to best meet the needs of their customers. The customer rules.

Let's talk about that a little bit. Once you attract someone to the site, what are the things that turn lookers into buyers?

People come to your web site for a reason. The key is to help them find what they are looking for as quickly as possible. The longer it takes for a person to find what they are looking for on your site, the less chance there is that they will continue looking.

In the offline world, every person who walks through the door of a store sees the same thing. In the online world, we have the advantage of being able to personalize our web site store for each visitor. If we have the right data, when Sally visits she will see bedding products while John sees plasma televisions, if that's what they're most interested in.

We test top sellers, top categories, new products, and recommended products based on collaborative filtering and other algorithms. It

> *"Customer reviews are very important."*

becomes a game of how quickly we can determine what a person is looking for when they visit our web site.

Once you determine the right product, then you need great product information and competitive pricing so the customer can make an informed buying decision. After they decide to buy, then you need an easy-to-use check-out process.

You have to optimize all parts of your business. In every piece of the business, you must ask yourself how this area of your business impacts your customers. Figure out how to meet your customer's needs and you win.

In this process, how important are customer reviews on your site?

Customer reviews are very important. Many customers pay more attention to the customer review than they do the other information that we provide the customer about the product. Customers view information provided by other customers as less jaded and a better indicator of the experience they will have with the product. Customers believe that reviewing only information that is provided by the person trying to sell you a product is like asking a barber if you need a haircut—they're always going to tell you what benefits them the most.

We believe [customer reviews] really help round out the buying decision. This is key because customers can't see, touch, or feel a product in the online world. The reviews also act as a surrogate way for customers to have an idea of what type of experience they will have with a product by reading what types of experiences other customers have had with that product.

It always surprises me how helpful some customers are. Malcolm Gladwell, in his book *The Tipping Point*, talks about these "inherently helpful mavens," who can't help but be helpful. You have customers who buy products and then write very robust, meaty reviews to help other customers in their buying decision.

Do you monitor these reviews at all? Or do you have more of a problem with people putting deliberately bad reviews or deliberately good reviews on the site?

We absolutely monitor reviews to ensure the review is relevant, not obscene, and that it will add to a customer's buying experience, regardless of whether the review reflects positively or negatively on the product in question.

There was a time years ago where our reviews were controlled by the same people who were merchandising our web site. Can you guess what reviews ended up on the web site? Only the reviews that were highly positive for the products.

We then switched to a new review system that is managed by our customer care and marketing, where we put any review on site that actually enhances the customer's buying experience.

If a customer buys a lightweight desk, and then writes a negative review because it's more lightweight than she anticipated, then I hope they write a review about that. That way, future customers who are looking for lightweight desks can take this into consideration and customers who are looking for heavier-duty desks can avoid these products.

Do the product reviews also help you in managing your product mix? It would seem to me that if you have a product with bad reviews, that would provide feedback to your buyers.

Absolutely. We actually have a team of people who monitor product reviews. If a product has a large proportion of negative reviews, we'll pull that product offsite and we'll review it. There are products we'll actually liquidate because they just aren't good products, they're not satisfying our customers. There are other products where we just need to change out the image on the product, or we need to change out the description, to make it more accurate, so it better reflects what customers experience when they receive that product.

Once you've captured a customer, how do you market that customer to get more business from him?

We use emails primarily. In the past, we've also sent care packages to customers who have been very valuable to us. We've tried a number of other things, but the primary form of communication is through emails. If the customer comes and shops on our web site, we give them the chance to receive emails from us. Most people who come and shop our site actually accept emails. Then we start sending them emails.

At Overstock, we have so many products that come on and off site in any given week that we can always have fresh products to send to people. So we send a fair amount of email to our customers.

How targeted or personalized are the emails?

Very. We make sure with the amount of product that we're sending that we're not taking the old marketing approach, where you just throw hundreds of products to customers and hope that a couple of them stick. As people come and they move around on our web site, and as they buy things from us, we track that information and we work very hard to make sure that as we send information to them, that it's information that would be relevant to them, that's personalized to them.

We do that because our customers, just like everyone, are very busy. They have a finite amount of time and attention. If you don't send them something that's acceptable and relevant to them, they're not going to allow you to send them information for very long.

> *"If you're going to move online, you need to have a clear model."*

Do you also include loyalty programs as part of your marketing mix?

We do. We have a program Club O, where for $29.95 you can get a Club O membership for 12 months. It gives you $1 shipping on all of your orders from Overstock, and gives you a five-percent discount on those orders, as well.

We've got that, and then we also have a co-branded credit card, where people can get a credit card that's an Overstock.com credit card, and receive some points on that, as well.

So what advice would you give to a new company, a small firm wanting to move into the web for online retailing, based on your years of experience with Overstock?

One of the biggest things is, if you're going to move online, you need to have a clear model. Early on, a lot of the companies that went bust, they didn't have a viable business model. The online world isn't a special place; it's the same as the offline world. There are people, they are looking for things, they have a finite amount of time and attention, and you have to have a viable business model; otherwise you're not going to succeed longer-term.

Most offline companies that are out there, especially on the retail side of things, there's great opportunity to move online. If you look online, there are many ways you can service your customers better if you have an online presence.

Whether you're a brick-and-mortar store or a cataloger looking to go online, you need to ensure that you have a consistent strategy across the online and offline channels. There's a push for what people are calling multi-channel retailing. It's integrating all those different touch points to better service the customer.

> *"You've got to stop and think about how it all integrates."*

There are a lot of products where it just doesn't make sense to stock and sell at a store. So people are taking those products and moving them to their online store. If you go into the offline store and they don't have an item, in many stores they'll actually walk you over to a kiosk in the store and place an order for you right there in the store.

You've got to have a business model. You've got to stop and think about how it all integrates. If you've got brick-and-mortar stores, if you have an offline presence, you want to make sure that there's an incentive for those people who are working in the offline world of your business to integrate and accept the online presence. There are stores out there where if a customer places an order and they live right next to the retail store, the physical store might not get any credit for that sale. Well, what motive is there for a sales rep to ever send anyone to the web site if it's not there in the store? They're going to try to place an order for it, which might be several days and you might lose the customer. So you've got to think about how, if you've got an offline store, and if you've got a catalog, and if you have an online store, how do you mesh all three of those things together and create one business that is going to be agile and is going to be successful?

Is there anything else you'd like to add for our readers?

One of the things I would say is if you're going to get into this game, you don't want to just dabble in it. If you're going to get into it, you need to get into it seriously. You need to do your due diligence and see if you have a viable business model, that there's a chance to succeed. You need to see what your competition is doing, and make sure that you can be competitive. You need to make sure that you go out there and find what the third-party service providers are offering to help you better manage your business. You need to make sure you get the tools that will allow you to be successful online.

It really helps to have people who have experience—and they're not easy to come by. There aren't a lot of people out there who have great experience. If you can get someone

> *"The offline world is changing slower than the online world is."*

who has some experience in all of that, they can go through and do a lot of these things and put you light years ahead of where you'd be if you just tried to do it on your own.

I know that in the past, people have thought that going online would be a get-rich-quick sort of thing. But from talking to you and talking to others, it's as much work going online—if not more so—than doing a brick-and-mortar store, right?

There is a lot of work. I don't know if I would say that there's more work, because I also have family who do offline retail, and that's a lot of work, in and of itself. The thing that I think is different is, you have more people who've done offline retail than who have done online retail successfully.

The offline world is changing slower than the online world is. The offline world, there are more people who understand it than who understand the online world. So as you come onto the online world, you need to be prepared to have people who know what's going on, who can stay current with different trends.

I look at it every year; the space is changing. Every year the marketing landscape changes, every year the customers become more demanding, every year they're wanting more things. You have to always be sprinting to keep up with the competition.

It certainly seems like you guys have done that, over time.

I appreciate that. We're really working on it; it's not an easy thing to do.

Back in 1999 I was doing consulting, and I worked with a number of individuals from small businesses about going out and creating web sites and marketing their web sites on the Internet. It was always so hard to get people to understand everything that it took to do that. I walked a number of these people through this process.

As I came over to work with Overstock, starting in 2000, it's been absolutely fascinating for me to be in this space and see the changes that have occurred, and to see the work that's gone into keeping up with those changes. There are still a number of changes, and Overstock's still working hard to try to keep up with those changes. I'm sure that if I stay in this space another seven years I'll look back and say, man, little did we know what a ride we were in for over the next seven or ten years.

It changes quickly. It's a great and fun space to be in. You've got to have the energy, you've got to be willing to work hard. It's not an area where you're going to come in throw up a web site and become rich quickly. You really have to work at it.

Sound Bites

Whew—Jacob Hawkins just covered a lot of ground, all of it important. While it's hard to generalize from the experience of any single online company, Jacob and Overstock play the game by a set of proven rules, rules that other online marketers would also be wise to follow.

What do you need to do to establish a successful online retailing business? Here are just a few of Jacob's rules:

- Recognize that online retailing isn't that different from traditional brick-and-mortar retailing.
- Create a viable business model.
- Religiously track the performance of your advertising and promotions—and use that information to serve appropriate products to your customers.
- Help your customers find what they want as easily and quickly as possible.
- Optimize all parts of your business to provide the most efficient shopping experience for your customers.
- Incorporate customers' product reviews as part of the product information on your site.
- If you have an existing offline or catalog operation, integrate it with your online business.

Mark Oldani:
Circuit City

4

*"What we're trying to do is make sure that we are provid-
ing the most flexibility and the most convenient ways for
customers to shop, whether they start online and go in
the store, or start in the store and go online."*

—*Mark Oldani*

Mark Oldani has been doing
online retailing for some time
now. Originally director of marketing for Dell, Mark is now the VP and
general manager for Circuit City
Direct, the online arm of the giant
consumer electronics retailer.

> **FACT SHEET: MARK OLDANI**
>
> Vice President & General
> Manager, Circuit City Direct
> (www.circuitcity.com)

If you haven't visited Circuit City's web site lately, you should—especially
if you're in the market for a new TV or other home electronics product. The
Circuit City site is one of the best consumer electronics sites on the web, full
of useful information about each product, easy-to-navigate search and browse
functions, and a huge database of customer product reviews. It's those reviews
that I find particularly useful; it's great to know upfront what other consumers
think about a specific product.

Multi-Channel Retailing: The Best of Both Worlds

I wanted to interview Mark because Circuit City offers a unique multi-channel experience. Yes, you can shop on the company's web site, but you can also
pick up your online orders from the nearest Circuit City store. Just how does
Circuit City exploit the synergy between its online and offline channels? Does
the online site enhance or detract from the in-store experience? Those are just
a few of the questions I had for Mark when we conducted this interview.

There are a lot of consumer electronics web sites out there. What do you think distinguishes Circuit City from the competition?

There are a number of things that set us apart from the competition; some areas that we're trying to focus on to provide some differentiation.

> *"We're trying to help educate and support customers as they go through the purchase process."*

One, we're trying to provide a resource for customers, almost building out a community for customers, so that they can come learn about products and services, understand how they may be able to use these products and services, in their daily lives, and be more than a site that just sells product. We do a lot of things to build this type of community for customers, and have a lot of these features on our site that we get very positive feedback from customers on. Here are just a couple of examples that you may be familiar with.

We've got our customer ratings and reviews out there online. We've got tens of thousands of customer reviews on products that are unedited. Those are direct words from customers about the products that we're selling. Good, bad, or indifferent, you see it—and it actually helps guide customers through the purchase path.

We've got situations where we've got customers helping customers like that. We've got our online community forums, where customers are answering questions from other customers. We're building a site that does more than just sell a product; we're trying to help educate and support consumers as they go through the purchase process. As they're doing that, we are really trying to build out additional forms of convenience for the customer. So we want all this information at their hands. We're also providing third-party content and ratings and reviews. We were the first site to have a partnership with *Consumer Reports*.

We've got these things on our site to help customers. As they then learn about it, what we're trying to do—and what we've had some pretty good success doing, in the past—is make it easy for customers to get the full solution. So we want to make recommendations to customers: When they're buying a TV, what else might they need to consider? They need cables, they need a wall mount, they need help with installation, because these are all things that customers tell us they need help with. Our site actually allows them to walk through the things that are critical to the purchase.

That's what we call "solution selling," and trying to build out the full solution for customers. We've got some strong capabilities there today and we've got plans to make them even stronger as we go forward, around full solutions for customers.

When they do decide to move forward with their purchase, we offer them the flexibility and convenience of buying it online, so they can just go ahead and execute the transaction right there. If they want to talk to somebody and they don't want to go into the store, they can call into our call center; so we've got a call center that supports those customers in the same fashion, and we can execute the transaction that way. And if they want to go into the store and talk to an associate in the store, they can do that, too.

So we've got multiple ways for them to buy. What we're trying to do is simplify the process for customers, so that we lead them where they are interested in transacting the business that they're looking for.

It's that simplification process that we're really trying to drive. And that goes all the way to if you want to buy online and pick it up in the stores, you can do that. We're going to guarantee our performance on that, and we've got our 24/24 guarantee—which is just a reassurance to customers that if you want it,

> *"We want to try to provide the community that allows them to learn and build their own personal expertise."*

we've got it, you need it right now, you buy it online, and you can pick it up in the store within 24 minutes of your order confirmation. It's a great way for customers who want the immediacy of the purchase and the picking up the products but don't want to deal with trying to find it in the store and deal with the lines in the store. They can go right to our pickup counter—we've conveniently brought that forward, and can even help them with accessories that they may not have realized that they might need. It's continuing to expand on that convenience factor that we're trying to build up for customers.

The four key points that I'd point to, if I had to summarize, are:

- One, full solutions for customers is what we want to be helping them with.

- Two, we want to try to personalize the offers and the experience for customers, not just have a generic site that everyone has the same interaction with. We want to try to personalize it based on what customers are telling us they're interested in.

- We want to try to provide the community that allows them to learn and build their own personal expertise. Help them through the decision process and get support from other customers and other third-party organizations as they make some of these fairly significant financial decisions, when they're thinking about investing in some of these products that we're selling.

- Lastly, we really want to build out and are building out our multi-channel convenience for customers, where we are where they want to be—whether that's online, on the phone, or in the stores.

Those are some of the key things we believe differentiate us from some of the other online stores.

I want to talk more in-depth about the customer reviews, since that's one part of your site that I particularly like. You've been doing this for some time; has the customer review function changed at all, or do you see it changing in the future?

We have been doing it for quite awhile, and we have an extensive list of customer ratings and reviews. Some of the positive feedback that we've gotten from customers on those ratings and reviews is really the fact that they're unedited. We're not taking bad reviews off the site; we're putting the words that customers say about the products on the site, as a way to have customers help customers.

We're always looking for ways to improve on what we can do to help customers through their buying process. I don't know if it's as much changing the ratings and reviews capabilities that we have, but how are we supplementing that and providing new ways for customers to get information when they're considering their purchase—oftentimes from other customers.

We've expanded our community forums. We've got one for TVs, we've got one for imaging, so if customers want to know more about products, they can hear from other customers in those forums.

We are trying to provide multiple avenues for our customers to be able to get this unbiased feedback about the products and services they're considering. So we're really looking to supplement, not pull back or change in any way.

I've noticed something that I think is new for Circuit City—the concept of web shows. Can you talk about that a little bit?

We're really excited about that. We've got the Connect Home Webshow coming up [in November 2007], and the idea behind that is, when I was talking about building out the community and being a resource for customers, that's another example of how we're trying to help customers. So this Connected Home Webshow is us facilitating and bringing together experts to help customers with oftentimes very difficult questions that they have about the technology in their home. What we're trying to do is be a resource there; we're bringing trusted experts into our site and fielding questions from customers.

This is not a big sales pitch, if you've seen any of our previous forums or shows like this. We've done some of these before. Just a simple example: When Vista launched, we did a Vista live forum with customers and a *PC Magazine* editor to talk through what are some of the issues with

> *"We don't ever think we've captured a customer; we've got to earn their business every single day."*

Vista, what are some of the considerations. We have customers talking to customers, customers talking to experts, and all of that content is saved on our site, so people can go back and refer to it over time.

Whether it's that or whether it's having a live chat with [Tennessee Titans quarterback] Vince Young the day after Madden NFL 08 was released, which we did this year, we just want to provide ways for our customers to learn and enjoy and be a part of the technology. They're not really buying the product; they're really buying the experience. We feel that this is a good way to help them get the most out of their experience. So we're really excited about it.

After you've captured a customer, what kind of efforts do you make to get additional business from that customer?

We don't ever think we've captured a customer; we've got to earn their business every single day. We do that through the avenues that I mentioned before. That four-pronged approach is the approach that we're trying to take every single day with our customers.

Probably the most important thing we can do, as we make the first sale with the customer, is to try to personalize their experience for them, as they consider coming back to us. Maybe that's personalized email, based on things that they've shopped or browsed before that they may be interested in considering. It's making suggestions to those customers about things that can enhance their current experience that they're getting from the product, whether it's additional products or services.

And we do that online, we do that through email, we do that through our call centers. We really try to take a multi-pronged approach to continuing to earn customers' business every single day, by making it personalized and relevant—not just blanket. We're trying to target those communications with customers to be meaningful to them.

What communications do you have with them?

As I mentioned, we make phone calls to customers, after the sale, before their warranty is about to expire; we try to help them make sure they don't wind up in a situation where they've not realized that they may not have coverage any longer. We also try to support them in getting the most out of their experience. If they bought a TV, do they need additional products or services? Do they need help getting it installed?

> "The majority of our customers are not single-channel shoppers; they are multi-channel shoppers."

Many customers buy a TV and they think they'll hang it on the wall themselves. They don't realize how difficult it is. Three or four days after you have a TV sitting on the floor of your family room, with your spouse wondering why you spent that money and is it ever getting off the floor and you don't have a plan for that, we oftentimes are a welcome voice when we call the customer and say, "Need some help?" So it's things like that.

It's also targeted emails that we send customers. So customers who have said that they like to receive communications from us, we send them specific and targeted emails—whether it be post-purchase emails or ongoing inter-actions that we have through email with them. We also send some direct mail to customers, too, letting them know about new stores in their area, letting them know about special promotions that we may have for them.

Just to continue to earn their business every single day is critical for our long-term success.

One of the advantages you have is your retail stores. Do you coordinate your marketing activities and promotions between the online and the offline stores?

We absolutely work in tight coordination across the stores and the web and the call center. As you look at our major promotions and our key marketing messages, what we're trying to do is provide a seamless interface for customers, so that we're not confusing them based on which channel they might choose to shop or research at any one time.

What we find is, the majority of our customers are not single-channel shoppers; they are multi-channel shoppers. What we want to make sure we're doing is simplifying and streamlining the messages for customers, so that they are not confused. It's through that consistency

> *"We survey our customers regularly to hear what's working and what's not working."*

of marketing message cross-channel that we're able to bring one voice to the customer and help them as they are making their considerations for their next purchase. It's really a cross-channel simplicity that we're trying to drive.

You mentioned earlier about the option for in-store pickup. How popular is that?

Our in-store pickup is tremendously popular with our customers. More than 50 percent of our online purchases are being picked up in the stores. Customers give us tremendously popular feedback about one, having that available, and two, the way we execute. It's unique in the marketplace.

When a customer sees inventory online, that is inventory that's in the stores. As soon as they make that purchase, our store associates go pull that inventory and put it to the side, and have it waiting for the customer. All the customer needs to do is come in and pick that up. They can pick it up in 24 minutes, or if they can't pick it up right away, it'll be there waiting for them.

Customers love it. They absolutely love the flexibility that we're providing to them and the ability to eliminate the need to look around the store. If they're in a hurry, we have it waiting for them. It's a tremendously popular feature we have to offer in all the channels.

It seems to me that one of the challenges of having multiple channels would be tracking just where you're getting the response from. When somebody comes into the store, how do you know whether they came from a newspaper ad, from the web site, or what? How do you track all that?

We can track pretty specifically the customer behavior through our direct marketing efforts. What we're trying to do is make sure that we are providing the most flexibility and the most convenient ways for customers to shop, whether they start online and go in the store, or start in the store and go online. We survey our customers regularly to hear what's working and what's not working. We'll oftentimes get feedback from customers, and we have data on where did they start, what drove them into the store, what drove them online.

It's through talking to our customers every day that we actually know what are the primary motivators that brought them to the store or brought them to the call center or brought them online. It's really the direct interactions we have with customers that help provide that insight.

You've been doing this for a while. What particular challenges do you see coming up in the next year or two with your operations?

Competitively there are certainly a number of challenges with new entrants into the marketplace and more aggressive competition. But I think that what we've got is a great opportunity in front of us.

The four prongs that I mentioned earlier—solutions and personalization and community and convenience—I believe that to the extent that we can build on each one of those four prongs of our plan, we'll be able to differentiate ourselves from the competitors. It's only through that complete focus that we can continue to provide great value to customers.

I think there's continued growth. The online CE [consumer electronics] marketplace is growing rapidly as customers get more and more comfortable with buying online. What we want to do is be there for them at those moments of truth when they're making their purchase decisions, but also when they're doing their research. We really believe that those focus areas that I mentioned before are the ones that are going to provide us with great opportunity to meet the needs of more and more customers, going forward.

Sound Bites

There are many traditional retailers who have yet to go online in a big way. And they are many new-generation retailers who exist online only. Circuit City blends the best of both worlds, using its strengths in both channels to offer more flexibility to the consumer.

How exactly does Circuit City do it? The company's vice president and general manager Mark Oldani points to four key prongs of his operation:

- Provide full "solution selling," complete with all necessary accessories or services to satisfactorily complete the sale.
- Offer personalized experience and offers—not just a generic site with generic interactions.
- Provide a community that enables customers to learn from each other, via the use of customer reviews and forums.
- Offer multi-channel convenience so that customers can order and receive shipments from whichever channel best suits their needs.

One last thing: When the formal interview was over, I asked Mark to pick a winner in the Blu-ray vs. HD DVD high-definition DVD wars. His answer was that "technology is really going to be decided by the customers. We are trying to provide the options to customers to pick whatever they would like. You'll find us trying to meet both customer demand needs with both Blu-ray and HD DVD; at the end of the day, the customers are going to tell us what they want." A politically neutral answer to be sure, but one that recognizes the primacy of the customer in any business decision. (And I'm with him; it's too early to declare a winner in this particular format war!)

Jeffrey Glueck: Travelocity

5

"People are passionate about brands, not necessarily because they're getting some kind of buyoff. The best loyalty doesn't necessarily come from loyalty programs."

—Jeffrey Glueck

You might not think of Travelocity as an online retailer the same way you think of Amazon or Overstock. But Travelocity, like its fellow online travel sites, is one of the largest e-commerce companies

on the web, doing over $11 billion in global sales annually, substantially more business than the average online retailer.

That's partly because of the high average sale price of a plane ticket or hotel room, but it's also a factor of the huge number of customer transactions conducted on these sites each year. Travelocity in the US, for instance, handles over 10 million trips a year for its customers. Fueling all those transactions requires a lot of marketing activity, as Jeffrey Glueck well knows. Jeffrey is Travelocity's chief marketing officer, where he's responsible for all advertising, merchandising, customer experience, design, personalization, CRM, search engine marketing, editorial content, and business development for the brand. He assumed the role in January 2004, and promptly helped launch a new site design, new logo, new advertising campaign (the "roaming gnome"), and a new customer guarantee and bill of rights—the latter two were key to the site's subsequent surge in sales. That surge won Travelocity the "Turnaround Company of the Year" award from the American Business Awards; the gnome advertising campaign won a Gold Effie from the American Marketing Association for best retail advertising campaign. And Jeff himself was named to the *Advertising Age* "40 Under 40" list in 2007, a worthy personal accomplishment.

Customer Service as a Marketing Tool

The key to Travelocity's recent surge in sales is the company's renewed focus on customer service. Travelocity improved the visibility of its customer service, incorporating the company's customer focus as a key component in its marketing message. That's one of the things Jeffrey talks about in the following interview, along with the evolution of the online travel market, the importance of customer communities, and why many online advertisers are overpaying for search advertising.

When we're talking about various types of online businesses, what do you think makes online travel unique?

Travel is the consummate vertical for online—which is why, along with computers, it is the biggest category of online commerce, by far. If you look at travel companies, our gross sales are much larger than those of some of the big names in e-commerce, like Amazon.

Travelocity sells over $11 billion globally in travel, and we're the second-largest brand in the space. As a whole, we're seeing that because travel is so suited to e-commerce, up to 70 percent of Americans' leisure travel purchases are being made online now, either with online agencies or with supplier web sites.

> *"We put the old-fashioned values of trust and accountability and humanity back into this business."*

Because the industry is very digital (there's no delivery costs or warehousing) and information-rich (there are thousands of choices), it's very suited to the Internet. Choice, information, and electronic delivery are all things the travel industry is well set up to do. In fact, our parent company, Sabre, back in the '70s was the first to build a global electronic reservation system that originally served travel agencies; it's still the biggest travel network in the world. So the industry was already electronic and ready to go when the Internet arrived.

How do you think that the Internet, and your company and your competitors, have changed the travel market?

I think there were stages.

When Travelocity was founded in 1996, as the first online travel agency in the world, it was originally about price and choice for consumers—putting power of selection that was previously only available to travel agents in the hands of the consumers, at their desks, 24/7. It was just about price shopping, for the most part, for flights. That was the first stage of the Internet travel business.

It persisted and became quite commoditized as a lot of players entered, like Expedia and Orbitz, for the next four years. Americans started shifting their habits, particularly after 9/11; if they were going to travel, they looked for deals, and they turned to online sites to get those deals. Traditional travel agencies started shrinking, so business really was shifting channels to the online space.

I think the second stage of development was kicked off in 2005, when Travelocity was the first online travel agency to launch a service guarantee. The terms of debate shifted from advertising "hotels from $39.99 a night" to talking about things like customer service 24/7 and trust and accountability. Travelocity said we guarantee everything about your booking would be right or we'll make it right, right away, working with our partners. We put the old-fashioned values of trust and accountability and humanity back into this business that had become about software and commoditized deals. And, with the addition of the Travelocity roaming gnome, we added a personality and a voice to this kind of transactional relationship that existed before.

Our competitors, after initially disdaining that approach, have since sought to imitate it; particularly, they sought to imitate it after 2005, when Travelocity had several quarters of 30 percent growth when Expedia and Orbitz were growing at 15 percent or less. So that was the second stage, and it shifted towards service, trust, and personality.

I think a third stage is coming, and that's about experiences and relevance. Stage one was about tools and price; stage two was about brand affinity and being the customer's champion; stage three will be about relevance and experience. Online travel agencies will become your best friend in helping you plan all aspects of a great vacation or a great business trip—including the restaurants you should eat at, the parts of town you should stay in, the tours and activities you should take part in. We'll take every aspect of your trip—the price, the user-generated content, photos and videos—and allow you to fulfill a wish list and plan out your whole itinerary. Then we'll be available 24/7 in case some snags happen, all trip long. When you get home we'll have communities where you can share reviews of your experiences that will then enable the next traveler to travel smarter. That's the third stage, and I think we're just embarking on that.

Let's talk a little about the reviews and the communities, which appear to be a pretty important part of your site now. This is integrating social networking into the process, isn't it?

Yes, if you have a broad definition of community and social networking. One of the big areas of community on the Internet is user-generated content around travel. Sites like TripAdvisor or IgoUgo (a Travelocity company) allow people to share their experiences with people like them. And they're getting more granular.

> *"We put enormous effort into building a central data warehouse."*

On Travelocity this year we launched a way to search for reviews from "people like me." Consumers told us, over and over again, that they like reviews, but they don't know if the person reviewing the hotel or tour or restaurant is "like them." Obviously, if you limit yourself just to your close circle of friends, even if you have a couple of hundred friends, they probably haven't in sufficient numbers stayed in all of the hundred thousand hotels in the world—and probably not recently.

We just recently [mid 2007] introduced the ability to see only reviews from travelers in about 15 different categories—for instance, only show me business travelers, only show me travelers who are parents with teens, or parents with small children, or people with disabilities. All of these are categories you can use to filter the reviews on the hotels, just to find people like you.

How do you encourage more reviews? I was just looking at some hotels in Minneapolis; when you get into smaller cities, it's hard to get a wide body of reviews, isn't it?

I think there is a critical mass that you need to be useful, to be trustworthy. IgoUgo isn't quite as big as TripAdvisor, but it has this passionate community of over 300,000 members that like to share their thoughts and reviews. They just enjoy sharing what they've learned. That's a point of pride.

They'll take wonderful photos and write long journals, review restaurants and activities and nightlife and spots, say which places are tourist traps and which ones are insider secrets; it's just a pride point with them.

I think it's about making it easy, and it's about search engine optimization. There are people who are looking for information or have information; they need to find your site and become members and add their reviews. I think there are a lot of factors, but generally on all the sites that have gotten sizable, like VirtualTourist or IgoUgo or TripAdvisor, people aren't writing to get points or money or anything like that. They're just happy to share.

This brings us to another topic: How you retain your customers and market to your customers, as opposed to trying to attract new customers? Once you have 'em, what does Travelocity do to get more purchases from your customer base?

That's a big topic. There are a couple of different areas—CRM [customer relationship management], loyalty and rewards programs, and customer championship.

The first of those three is CRM. We put enormous effort into building a central data warehouse where we are able to track what things our members are looking for, and also track where deals are happening in the travel space—and look for the intersection between them.

I'll give you an example. We have this email program called Good Day to Buy. We monitor over a million routes around the world each day, and if fares go down by 20 percent or more in any market, we will detect that instantly. Then we will pull, automatically, any member who's been shopping, let's say, for Chicago to Seattle in the last 30 days. We'll send them an email saying, "Good morning, today is a good day to buy. Last night the airlines lowered their fares for Chicago to Seattle." Consumers love it. It solves a problem that existed for the consumer, which is "Should I wait? Should I not? Is today a good day to buy?" It's a paramount example of relevance, which we define as the mix of personalization and compelling offer.

You can be personalized and not give someone a great deal. You can offer a compelling offer but it's not something they're interested in. Relevance is the merger of the two—compelling and personalized. We do a lot of home page personalization, based on the fact that you bought a flight, let's say to Phoenix on October 22nd; when you return to the home page, you will be greeted with our picks for car deals and hotel deals in Phoenix on the exact days of your trip.

Those are some of the ways that we personalize the site. Even if you're not a member when you come to the site, we can personalize some deals by just knowing your IP address. If we find out you live in Boston, we can at least tell you a list of all the deals on flights leaving Boston in the next month. We find anything personalized to your home town has click rates that are four to ten times higher, with similarly higher conversion rates.

> *"In the end, loyalty is not about a loyalty program."*

The second thing that we're doing is working on things in the loyalty and rewards area. We launched a credit card, a Travelocity MasterCard, in partnership with Barclays bank, and it's a phenomenal product if you sign up for it. Every 20,000 points you earn, you get $400 to spend on Travelocity, with no blackouts, no seat restrictions; you can buy a hotel package, a flight, you name it. Unlike airline programs where if you try to redeem your 25,000 mile rewards these days, good luck finding a seat that's available. With this one, you just earn money. If you book a package you get triple points, if you're a member of our VIP program when you book on Travelocity, you get triple points; even if you're a regular member, you get double points for anything on Travelocity. Plus you still earn your frequent-flyer miles from the airlines as normal. It's a great rewards program; people are signing up rapidly. You also get $50 off your first purchase when you sign up for the card, right then and there online. We are so thrilled with that product.

Another area where we're pushing rewards is our VIP program. We sell about 10 million trips a year in the U.S., and we took about our top 1 million customers and enrolled them in a VIP program. It's about treating them special and recognizing them. We are giving them some discounts on high-margin products like vacation packages and hotel bookings, but more importantly we're also sending them free luggage tags with our 24/7 VIP Hotline, so they always get through to our top agents and we pick up the phone right away for them, even if there's a wait for others. We give them advance notice of sales; we give them triple points on their Travelocity MasterCard, and lots of other small perks. We're just really excited about this program. We're still tweaking it to refine it, because it's not comparable to a supplier program such as being platinum on American Airlines; we don't run the airplanes, we can't get you a special boarding line. But we find that there's a lot of value we can contribute. Most of all, when you come back to the site or you speak to one of our call center agents, you're going to be thanked for your business and recognized as a VIP. You're enrolled in the program based on how much you spend with Travelocity annually, but generally if you book five plane tickets or more, you are enrolled in the VIP program as a surprise and delight upgrade. So that's another way we're approaching earning loyalty.

The third pillar is our customer championship pledge. I think, in the end, loyalty is not about a loyalty program. People are really loyal to Google not to earn Google points, but because they love the site. They're loyal to Starbucks because they love the atmosphere and the coffee. If you buy a Starbucks card, you don't get any discounts, right?

I can vouch for that, unfortunately.

People are passionate about brands, not necessarily because they're getting some kind of buyoff. The best loyalty doesn't necessarily come from loyalty programs.

If you think where the values of Travelocity are based—around taking care of customers, helping them have great travel experiences, our customer championship culture, our customer bill of rights—these are the things that really differentiate us from competitors. They also help us drive a powerful point when winning new customers, too.

We've done a lot of research and the Travelocity Guarantee is particularly compelling to people who are buying more complex travel from us. So when we asked new customers who booked a vacation package (which is the most lucrative part of our business, and the fastest-growing), what was it that made you choose Travelocity?, over 60 percent of them said they're aware of the Travelocity guarantee and it influenced their decision to book with Travelocity.

The percentages are a little lower for other products, and it makes sense. With a package, you're trusting your whole vacation—your flight, your hotel, your car rental, your show tickets, and your tours—to one company. It becomes more important that [the company] is trustworthy and accountable across the whole trip experience.

You mentioned doing customer research. That must also be important in terms of determining what new features to add to the product, right?

Absolutely. We take research very seriously. We do all kinds of research, ranging from usability testing to usability labs, which are so important for any web site, to quantitative research, brand tracking, and specific benchmarking studies, you name it. We do focus groups when we're thinking about rolling out new features or promises for consumers, to help us decide what's relevant, and we follow that up with quantitative testing. So we're big believers in research.

> *"We were the first big online retailer to start advertising our 24/7 customer service."*

I think what Malcolm Gladwell has said about focus groups is also true, though, which is that focus groups require interpretation. They have their problems, and at some level they're not good at testing things that are wildly unfamiliar. There's an art to it.

Our biggest launch the last few years was the Travelocity guarantee. We came up with that idea after listening to a lot of consumers in listening labs. They were saying, over and over again, "I like Travelocity, I like Expedia, I like Orbitz, I shop them all. I look for the cheapest price." Which is the definition of no brand loyalty.

They were also saying, "I love these sites for research, but I call directly to the airline or the hotel or a travel agent to book. I worry that if something goes wrong, or if I hit the wrong key, I just don't trust it." They said in effect, "I wish there were people behind the web site." They thought there was nothing behind it but software. Of course, that's not true; we've always had several thousand trained professionals on the phone, helping our travelers. We just really weren't touting it, because customer service on the web was viewed as a cost. Amazon famously hid their phone number; you couldn't find it.

We were the first big online retailer to start advertising our 24/7 customer service, in 2004. Then in 2005, with the Guarantee, we actually pledged that we would be accountable for anything about your booking that wasn't described correctly. We pledged that the booking would be accurate, the reservation would be there when you got to the hotel. If we said there was a swimming pool and you get there and the swimming pool is under construction, we'll move you at our expense and find you a hotel that has a pool open; that's our fault, we should be accountable. That pledge was brand-new, and it grew out of that listening-lab culture.

You also have some strong thoughts about media planning and modeling. Could you talk about that for a minute?

I've done a lot of speaking about how people aren't measuring incrementality very seriously in online advertising, and they need to—particularly with search engines like Google and Yahoo! They're also not doing the right media mix modeling to be able to compare how their offline media— TV, radio, newspaper—are interacting with their search and online advertising. So people are often overbidding on the search engines, because they don't really understand incrementality online.

For instance, if you run a TV commercial and it causes someone to go to a search engine and type in your brand name into a blank box. If you're doing the modeling right, you should be attributing the lift to the TV commercial you ran, not to the blank box on the search engine (which might get credit thanks to the common use of "last click attribution" tracking).

How do they distinguish that, then?

If you're putting together a structural equation regression model, with all the internal and external factors and all the clicks and all of your spend and your competitors' spend, consumer confidence indicators, everything but the kitchen sink, you can start—over a period of years—to squeeze out the true drivers of incremental traffic or incremental bookings. That's how we've been able to detect that a quarter of search bookings come because of our offline advertising.

This helps us have other ROI data to use to complement online click tracking. Most marketers simply ascribe lift to the last click, what is known as "last-click measurement." If it was a newspaper ad that caused someone to type your brand name into a blank box, you really should be crediting that newspaper ad.

> "When you're doing search, you have to separate your brand name from other keywords."

More importantly, when you're doing search, you have to separate your brand name (say Travelocity and its various spellings) from other keywords, generic keywords such as "Hawaii hotel deals." We found, and many other large e-commerce players have found, when they deconstructed the data, that ¾ or more of their profit were coming from people typing the company's brand name into the search engine. The search engine doesn't cause people to type their name in. It's everything you do— your word of mouth, your reputation, your advertising offline, et cetera.

A lot of companies say to their marketing teams, "You're going to use this online channel or search engine until you hit zero-dollar breakeven on the incremental dollar." The problem is that they mix their brand profits with their non-brand returns, like from "top hotels in Chicago." When they mix the revenue streams into one, they're going to overpay for terms like "Hawaii vacation."

It's putting too much importance onto the search engines, is what you're saying?

I'm a big fan of search advertising, but you really have to separate out the incremental profit from a generic keyword on its own. You can't subsidize it with your own brand name. People are going to type your brand into the search engine regardless of whether you're buying generic terms like "tennis shoes" or "vacations in Hawaii."

It sounds like the quick and dirty way to approach it is to separate out your brand name from the generic terms.

That is the quick and dirty way to do it.

It's also important to subtract your variable expenses. If you think you earned $30 each booking, but really, once you subtract your credit cards and your call center average cost and your fraud cost and your order processing costs, you are only making $20 on a variable basis from every sale. So you should be bidding against that $20 variable margin, not against the $30 top line revenue.

That's a pretty common one—not recognizing all your variable expenses.

But I have talked to tons of companies that don't do these basic things!

So that's fueled a lot of overbidding. Until people start measuring right, they won't correctly bid and the market won't become more rational.

Sound Bites

You can learn a lot from a company that does $11 billion of business online every year. Here are some of the key points offered by Jeffrey Glueck of Travelocity:

- Offering superb customer service, and then marketing that service, will ease customer fear and make your brand more attractive.
- Marketable customer service often means some sort of customer guarantee and a very visible 800 number.
- Also important: customer communities and user reviews.
- A relevant offer is one that is both compelling and personalized.

Finally, heed Jeff's advice when it comes to planning your online advertising buys. Don't assume that every link you get from a search engine is attributable to the search engine itself; anyone typing in your brand name probably heard about you from a different medium, and the search engine shouldn't receive full credit.

Lauren Freedman:
the e-tailing group

6

"E-commerce is an evolution. You don't have to get every-thing right immediately; you can learn from it."

—Lauren Freedman

auren Freedman knows retail. She had worked with retailers and catalog merchants for 15 years before the web came along. Then, in 1994, she leveraged her knowledge and experience to found the e-tailing group, which provides strategic solutions to online merchants of all stripes.

> **FACT SHEET: LAUREN FREEDMAN**
>
> President, the e-tailing group
> (www.e-tailing.com)

Lauren's firm has worked on more than 500 e-commerce projects and her client list includes traditional retailers, catalogers and direct merchants, and online retailers—including Toys "R" Us, Bloomingdale's, The Vitamin Shoppe, J.Jill, Orbitz, and Kodak. She's also an in-demand speaker, has taught courses at Chicago's Roosevelt University, and is the author of the book *It's Just Shopping* (Direct Marketing Association, 2002).

Optimizing the Online Shopping Experience

If you're a web retailer, how do you maximize your online sales? By making sure your site provides an exceptional customer experience, of course. But how do you do that? Lauren has some advice.

Let's start by talking about your company, the e-tailing group. What is it you do, and what services do you offer to online retailers?

The e-tailing group is basically focused on two aspects of the business. The focus is half on the retail side, dealing with online retailers, really large retailers, and catalogers, shopping on the Internet as well as the cross-channel components of that. We've been involved in that for the past 14 years, so that's one piece of it.

> *"The focus is on strategy and merchandising and the customer experience."*

The second piece of the business is focused on dealing with technology companies who support those retailers, who try to sell those retailers services, and working with them from a customer research perspective and from a marketing perspective.

On the merchant side, the focus is on strategy and merchandising and the customer experience. We're pretty much known in the industry for a number of different research studies. We do an annual mystery-shopping study; this will be our eleventh year. We buy from 100 merchants, we return it all, we contact them, we check out their Internet email, their customer service, how they handle their online chats. So we have a lot of detail.

We kind of take the opposite approach from a lot of people. We're known for our practical solutions, we're the opposite of high-falutin'. We all have a retail background, so it's a little bit of a different approach into the business.

Then there are the other things. We have an annual merchant survey we do…this will be our sixth year…we have a couple hundred merchants respond to that. We have a lot of information that I think a lot of other people don't have. Since I've been involved in the industry so long, I look at that as a differentiator.

One of the services you offer is the site audit. Can you talk a little bit about that—what's involved?

The site audit has evolved over the years, needless to say. Basically, the site audit is intensively looking through your site, trying to find every possible thing you can do better.

Most jobs that we have, when it comes to the merchant side, are "I want to increase sales, I want to increase the average order, I want to decrease shopping abandonment, and I want the customers to buy more stuff." Our job is to do every single thing possible to help the merchant, so they can accomplish those objectives. The audit, for us, gives us a chance to not only shop a site, sort of in the same way we do our mystery shopping, but to take a look at the site in detail—look at all the key pages, look at the home page, the product page, the shopping cart—and look at all the places where we think there could be improvement.

What we typically also will do is benchmark that merchant against their category. So if we're currently working on a project for a sporting goods company, we might benchmark that against sporting goods; we might also benchmark that against apparel. We're able to leverage existing mystery-shopping data that might take us six months to compile, and benchmark any particular site against that.

Then we come up with a series of recommendations, and help the merchant to prioritize what should be done when.

In your experience in doing this, what are some of the most common mistakes you find retailers doing online?

One of the things that's really critical about retail is no two merchants are alike, so it depends. It really depends on who you are, who your customer is, and what your category is. Things have also improved over the years.

So it could be things like, how do they handle their navigation—is it clear? Not having their 800 number be visible. Not having customer-service links in the shopping cart. But a lot of it is really just little nitty-gritty things that are handled

> *"The number-one reason people shop online is convenience and time saving."*

on a merchant-by-merchant basis. Sure, it could be that not enough sites return the proper search results for misspelled words. And again, that's also improving. It could be visibility of the search box; it could be they don't have enough relevant merchandising tactics; it could be the product page is too cluttered or they don't have enough category-supporting content, if they're in a very information-intensive category. It just runs the gamut. They don't answer their email on time; they don't ship the goods in a timely fashion—for us, which would be no more than five days. (Three to five days is kind of standard.) They don't answer their emails within 48 hours. That type of thing.

We look at a series of 200 or so metrics and evaluate where that merchant is. It doesn't matter what the average does; it matters what they do—and that's how we approach it.

Let's go back to the beginning and talk about online shopping. From a customer's perspective, why do people shop online?

The number-one reason people shop online is convenience and time saving. Price is typically found to be a second dimension, but certainly it's a factor—and the comparison-shopping engines have made it easy for the consumer. But number one has always been the convenience component.

Is there a particular type of customer who shops online, versus someone who just shops in the brick-and-mortar world?

I think the online shopper is very much a directed shopper. They're very task oriented, in many instances. They have something in mind that they're looking to buy and they're going to find it online in the quickest way possible—they'll probably Google it—or they'll go directly to a merchant of choice and make their purchase.

You've got much less of a browser type of consumer online. Shopping on the Internet is a little bit browser-challenged; we still haven't made it very experiential. So it's still very much a focused customer.

Would it be fair to say that the old direct marketing/catalog customers have all migrated online?

That depends on how you define "migrated." The catalog customer from a catalog quick-shop perspective, who wants to just browse the catalog—which is a lot more convenient and a lot more engaging—and then basically enter the SKU number, I think a lot of them do it that way. But without the catalog, I don't think they would necessarily be leveraging the web to the same degree. The two kind of go hand in hand, and you haven't seen that much decline in how many catalogs are being sent out—at least in my mailbox!

I'll agree with you on that! But from the consumer's perspective, it seems that it was the catalogers and direct marketers who got online retailing better than anyone else did—at least in the early days.

The cataloger was early, but the cataloger also had all the systems in place. It's easier to get it early when you have the infrastructure.

I also think the cataloger had a profitable notion that had to be played within their company. Most of them are not that aggressive, in terms of risk taking. There were still business systems that they were currently doing; the dollars and cents had to make sense. They didn't have the luxury of the pure play money behind it. It was also a natural extension of their business.

The main thing was, their customer already transacted with them that way; the computer was just a different vehicle than the phone. They were used to making purchases without touching and feeling the product.

> *"Another thing the customer really wants to see is in-stock product."*

Every Christmas people are doing their shopping online, and you get the news stories of people disappointed that they can't order two days before Christmas and get it shipped out in time. It seems to me like unrealistic expectations from the customer's standpoint. What are customers' expectations when they're shopping online?

Customer expectations when they're shopping online are very high. You have a very sophisticated customer who's currently buying, but I also think the customers learn. They understand that a lot of changes have taken place over the last 14 years.

To the point that you can't get it delivered the day before, you can probably get it the day after—if you buy it from certain types of merchants who have that level of fulfillment. But if you need the immediacy piece, you probably ought to take advantage of merchants who offer buy online, pick up in store, or one of those other cross-channel capabilities.

I think some customers expect if they hit the buy button, the FedEx guy's at the door. There's a sense that it'll come, it'll come immediately, there's gonna be an order confirmation, they're gonna deliver the goods. If I send a merchant an email, they're gonna answer my question within 24 hours. That's a lot of pressure, from a merchant perspective.

Another thing the customer really wants to see is in-stock product. They expect when they go on your site, if you're selling it you're either going to have a thing that says this product's not available in this particular size, or you're only going to be selling them in-stock product.

The ability to track the order—that's something that was not necessarily a known piece. Before, they used to track a FedEx package or a UPS package, but now order tracking is a universal feature that the customer has come to expect.

It's a control thing. If a customer's online, he's pretty much a control freak. They want to buy what they want, where they want, find it immediately, and have it come immediately. Other than that, there's no issues.

The other thing is, they're becoming used to having a richer experience. The use of rich media, whether it's audio or video or multiple views, is helping to transition the customer who can't touch the product.

> *"It's easier for a small person to compete now than it was ten years ago."*

The tools that are becoming available to people, like customer reviews, they're participating in the experience. Where in the past, they really weren't a part of it. It was more like, here's what the merchant's going to sell you, now here's what you're gonna do. But now the customer's much more involved, and that, I think, will continue to grow. Because of broadband, the experience is richer—the product demos, the greater information that's available to the consumer—all throughout the industry, it makes it easier to buy with more confidence. Which is good, because that means there's less returns.

It seems to me that to meet these customer expectations requires some fairly sophisticated infrastructure and systems. How easy is it for a smaller merchant to compete in this fashion?

I'm not an operations person, so I'm not going to speak to all of that. But I think that, in a lot of ways, it's easier for a small person to compete now than it was ten years ago, because the cost of technology is a lot lower. Much of the features and functionality that was available at a million price tag is now available at a $100,000 price tag.

There are a lot of tools, like Yahoo! Stores and a lot of these on-demand capabilities from the e-commerce technology community that are leveling the playing field. There are companies that provide the backend systems, for a fairly inexpensive price point. They have a lot more available to them than was the case ten years ago.

As you mentioned previously, you've conducted a lot of research into online retailing. What is the state of e-commerce today?

Last year online revenues, without travel, exceeded about $100 billion. Right now, we have about a 20 percent growth rate for the first two quarters of 2007. Growth expectations for the fourth quarter are 15 percent to 18 percent. Online retail represents about 7 percent of total retail, so 93 percent of the business is still being done offline.

So 7% of retail business is online. Do you see that growing much in the future—or do you think it will stabilize close to that?

I think it's going to continue to grow. What's happening is, the more you do it as a consumer, the more you want it. I think it will continue to get to be a better experience. Will it get to 20 percent [of total retail]? I don't know.

I don't think so, but we also have to realize that there's an aging population. I'm turning 50, so for me this will be how I was engaged. But imagine my daughter; this will be all she knows. I think that's going to be a factor, and I would expect that to continue. I think you're going to get momentum as a result of that.

For me, I know the way I shop. I look for every reason to buy something online. I think that there's going to continue to be that factor. The population plays to our favor.

> *"It's about optimizing the real estate that they have on the site."*

There will also probably be more immediacy capabilities. There are more technologies that I'm being informed about that will play to the immediacy challenge. That's the number-one reason that people go to the stores—they need it now. The more you can counter the need-it-now factor, you're going to have additional growth.

There are still a lot of people who haven't shopped online. You have large categories, like apparel (which is now the number-one category online), that still have room for growth. I think there's a lot more to come.

As there's more competition online, what can a site do to retain its existing customers—and get more sales from them?

It's about optimizing the real estate that they have on the site. You have this sort of small, ugly box that you're trying to transmit a shopping experience with. So it's really critical how you lay that out, how you merchandise that, what your landing pages are, because that's the experience that your customer comes into your site with.

At the end of the day, retail comes down to product; it's the hot product that sells. So first you start out with the right product, then the right merchandising that goes with it, the right tools (whether that be from a social perspective or an informational perspective), providing the right content, and the look and feel connecting to the customer. It's a little bit challenging for people to establish an emotional connection with the customer, but it's doable.

Then it's going to be innovation, whether it's customization, tools, or the development of social shopping. All of those things are going to change the dynamics of this.

Let's talk for a minute about some of the new site features that you've mentioned previously, whether that's product reviews, "see how it looks on me" tools for apparel, or whatever. What new site features should we be looking forward to?

Site features are really category-specific. I think you're going to see a lot more videos—although we haven't really proven that videos are necessarily selling more product. So there'll be a lot of testing in that area. You'll see a lot more rich media with alternative views of the product, color change, view in the room, really being able to help guide the customer to make a better decision. In some categories, like in home, that will become a bigger issue. Apparel also has lots of room for those types of tools.

I think ratings and reviews will end up becoming standard. You're going to see them on every site, whether it's proprietary or non-proprietary, because the customers really embrace those. It bridges the information gap between what the customer's told by the merchant and what actually happens from the consumer perspective. It's sort of a reality check. I think you're going to continue to see more of those.

I think there will be more innovation in terms of the merchandise landing pages—how they look and feel, how they're integrated, and how much information they provide about a product. I think you're going to see more in-store pickup, eventually. More cross-channel efforts, more reasons to drive the customer into the store. Driving customers into the store will still be a big goal of the merchant community.

Another feature you're probably going to see more of is live chat, and the use of chat in different ways. That's kind of still in the early stages, especially from a customer service perspective.

Customization of product will continue to grow, because especially with the younger customer, everything is about the individual. All these capabilities play into that—hanging it on the model, manipulating the size.

Anything that really helps the customer to make the right choice, we'll continue to see more of those. And again, that's on a category-by-category basis.

You mentioned the concept of live chat in customer service. It seems to me that one of the frustrations that people have, when dealing online, is the customer service. Are companies improving the customer-service experience?

I wouldn't necessarily agree with the statement that you made. When you look at the satisfaction levels for online customers versus other channels, online seems to come out higher. In the hundred sites that we look at, the average time to get an email response was just over 24 hours. The average package delivery time was 4.26 days. Given the size of the industry now, we've moved on from a number of those issues.

The challenge is that there's still a small group of customers that doesn't want to buy online, because of the security aspect of it—or what they perceive it to be. We have to continue to address that issue, but I'm not sure they're going to be the people that make or break online shopping.

> *"At the end of the day, the best way to convince someone is a good experience."*

You're right; that's one of the first questions people ask me: Is it safe? I have to tell people that I've been shopping online for a decade and a half, but how do you convince people of that?

Certainly the use of the icons, the VeriSign logos, the kind of Good Housekeeping Seal of approval types of things, are effective. But I think that, at the end of the day, the best way to convince someone is a good experience. There's no substitute for that.

What advice would you give a retailer who's thinking about revamping his online operations?

Start with the customer. You should understand who your customer is and how they want to buy. If you have a survey done or talk to them, there's certainly an opportunity for you; there's a lot to be learned from that. There are a lot of cost-effective tools that you can use to talk to your customer, especially from an online perspective.

Then you have to know your category. You've got to benchmark against your own category. See where you stack up, see what you're missing, see what functionality you don't have that your competitors might have.

Additionally, shop your own site. The quickest way to learn something about your plant is to shop your own site and see where it performs and where it lapses. That's another important piece.

The other thing is to have an ongoing priority list. What are the innovations? What are the things that you're going to do this year that are going to drive your business up 10 percent or 20 percent? Depending on where you are in your own evolution, where are you going to push ahead? What's on that list, how you change that list, how you set up that list, how you keep it moving; if you don't make those changes, you won't be pushing ahead; you'll just continue to fall behind, incrementally.

You still have to go with what you think is right for your brand. Stick to your guns as to what your brand is and who your customer is. What may be right for the rest of the world is not necessarily going to be right for you.

Lastly, I think you have to deliver on the customer service, because people remember the customer service a lot longer than they remember the price. We did a survey last year, during the holiday time, where we asked what the best and worst gifting experience was, and most of the problems tend to stem from customer service. Answer your emails, ship your goods in a timely fashion, let people know if you're out of stock—then give them a chance to make another choice. They're not going to be mad at you; they'll be disappointed momentarily, but they're not going to be mad at you long-term. If you don't ship it to them until two days after Christmas, then you have an unhappy customer.

E-commerce is an evolution. You don't have to get everything right immediately; you can learn from it. In spite of the risks involved, you need to push ahead and be aware that you always advance.

Sound Bites

Want to make your e-commerce web site more effective? Then consider the following tips from online merchandising expert Lauren Freedman:

- Work to improve your shipping speed; customers want immediate satisfaction.
- Display only those products that are in stock—or let customers know that a particular item is currently out of stock.
- Set up a section for customer product ratings and reviews.
- Utilize rich media (video, interactive product displays, live chat, etc.) to enhance the shopping experience.
- If you also operate a retail store, integrate the operations to provide cross-channel merchandising opportunities.
- Benchmark your site's performance against other sites in the same category.

And don't forget to shop your own site—it's the best way to experience your company as your customers do!

Tamara Adlin: adlin, inc.

7

"If you consider a persona a character, then the experience you want to create is the story."

—*Tamara Adlin*

What a user sees and experiences when he visits your web site is part of the marketing of your site. If the user has a bad experience or receives an inconsistent brand message or just doesn't like what he sees, that negates all the other marketing you've done up to that point. That's why, as a marketer, you need to pay particular attention to the customer experience.

Tamara Adlin knows all about the importance of the customer experience. Her company, adlin, inc., specializes in customer experience consulting; before founding her own firm, she worked on the customer experience services team at Amazon.com. Tamara is an in-demand speaker in the field of customer experience and co-authored, with Microsoft's John Pruitt, a popular book on the topic, *The Persona Lifecycle: Keeping People in Mind Throughout Product Design* (Morgan Kaufmann, 2006).

> **FACT SHEET: TAMARA ADLIN**
>
> President, adlin, inc.
> (www.adlininc.com)
>
> Blogger, Corporate Underpants
> Blog (www.adlininc.com/
> corporate_underpants/)
>
> Interviewer, UX Pioneers
> (www.adlininc.com/uxpioneers/)

Creating a Customer-Centered Experience with Personas

As you can tell from the title of her book, Tamara likes to focus on what are called personas. A *persona* is a representation of your target customer, not a bulleted list of demographics and psychographics—a person with a name instead of a collection of data. By focusing on a persona instead of statistics,

Tamara helps companies fine-tune their efforts for real people. The result is true customer-centered design, which should be an extension of any firm's online marketing efforts.

You're running your own consulting firm now, but you used to work for Amazon—how did you get to where you are today?

Even back as far as when I was an undergrad, I was very interested in both art and how people perceive things. Over the years, that naturally somehow progressed into an interest in how people interact with systems. So I went from how people perceived art to how people perceived systems, and that evolved into an interest in human-computer interaction—and that's been the focus of my career.

I then went on to get a master's degree in technical communication, because that's all there was at that time for people interested in what I was interested in. Then I did a bunch of startups here in Seattle, and eventually ended up at Amazon, in their user-centered design group.

> *"Focus on who it is and what they're trying to do, and then you can focus on how you answer that need."*

At Amazon I had two different jobs. The first two years were consulting within the company to all the different teams who were designing different aspects of the Amazon.com web site. Then in the third year they asked me to start up a customer-centered design team for other retailers who were interested in using Amazon's technology. That's an initiative they had, so there's a white label version of the Amazon technology that would look like a particular brand's web site. For example, Diane von Furstenberg moved to the Amazon platform, and Target.com has used the Amazon platform for many years. I was a part of the team that would work with those online retailers, to help them figure out which aspects of the Amazon technology would work best for their customers and their brands.

Let's talk about what you're doing now. How can you help a site improve their customer experience?

I do a couple of things. I think what I'm best known for right now is helping clients really narrow in on exactly who they're trying to please, from a customer perspective, and exactly how they're trying to please them.

With a partner, John Pruitt from Microsoft, I worked for about five years to create a book called *The Persona Lifecycle*. It's all about how you create customer focus on an ongoing way in an organization. The customer focus should start with the executive team and be clear all the way through the organization and product-development process, and even transferred over to documentation, support, fulfillment, and all customer touch points.

The way I help primarily is way, way upstream, in trying to get the executive team and major stakeholders super-articulate about their customers. Usually that takes the shape of customer personas, which are based on customer goals. So instead of having a segment, like 35- to 45-year-old women who live in the suburbs, which is very hard to design a product for, you have Maryanne.

> *"I believe success comes from banning the words 'user' and 'customer' from your organization, because I don't believe they're specific enough."*

Maryanne is 37 and lives in Bellevue, which is an upscale suburb of Seattle, and she has two kids and very little time for shopping anymore, and so on and so forth. Her goal for this kind of purchase—which is, let's say, cleaning supplies—is she doesn't want to shop around a lot; she wants to get it done and get out. You really focus on who it is and what they're trying to do, and then you can focus on how you answer that need—and how do you answer things beyond that need that Maryanne might not even know she can ask for.

How do you go about defining a persona, based on a company's customers?

There are several different ways. One way is to do a bunch of research and talk to a bunch of customers, and then to create personas. Many consulting groups do that, and then present finished personas to the organization.

I have a different approach—in fact a very different approach. My belief is that the real magic of something like personas is in getting consistency of focus across an organization. To my mind, it's more important to make sure that the stakeholders and executives are involved in the persona-creation process than it is to collect a lot of extra data. So instead of starting with data collection, I start with what we call "ad hoc persona workshops." These require everyone who's anyone in the organization to get together in a room and get all their assumptions about customers out on the table, to get them super clear on what their business-, brand-, and customer-related objectives are, and go through some workshops where they move from these assumptions about who their customers are to very clear goal-oriented descriptions of ad hoc personas. Inevitably a lot of questions arise during these workshops; there's a lot of discussion about which persona should be prioritized based on market share, frequency, or even differentiation. And then you go out and find data to answer those questions.

That's the way I approach it. I believe success comes from banning the words "user" and "customer" from your organization, because I don't believe they're specific enough. I'd much rather see everyone in an organization going around and saying, "We want to create this feature for Maryanne, but we're spending a lot of time on this other feature for Bobby. Don't you think we should change our focus back to Maryanne, because we prioritized her?"

To me, that's success, because that laser focus on a very well-understood customer is absolutely magical in an organization.

Do you find, when you first start working with a company, that different people have different images of who the customer is?

Oh, a hundred percent—and they think they're all on the same page!

What often happens when I start working with a customer is they say, "We really do have a strong idea of who our customers are, so we may not need to go through this." And the truth is, even if they do have a shared concept of who their customer is, which they don't—they never do; they think they do, but they don't—the word "customer" can mean a different thing every day.

Alan Cooper was the one who originally came up with the idea of personas, and he calls that "the elastic user." If you ask me today who I think the suburban mom is and tomorrow who I think the suburban mom is, I might have very different answers, depending on the context.

To answer your question a little more clearly, if you send out an email asking everyone—stakeholders and executives and people throughout the organization—to describe three example people who embody their true customer base, you would be absolutely shocked at the variety that you get back. Almost never are those descriptions based on people's goals and objectives. Usually they're based on demographics or psychographics or behavior online. Goals are much more interesting and helpful when you're designing a customer experience online.

So how do you reconcile the differences?

You start out with how people in the organization are talking about users today. You have to get all of the assumptions out on the table if you want to change them. I always say that the only assumptions that can hurt your product are the ones you don't know about. Then, we use sticky notes—I would be out of business if I couldn't use sticky notes. Everybody in the room has to write lots of sticky notes, where each sticky note has one example person with a problem or in a situation that they think is important to their business—for example, a mom who doesn't want to spend a lot of time shopping for cleaning products, or a teenager who wants to get the latest ringtone.

Then we all get up and cluster the sticky notes. At first, they tend to cluster around the kinds of terms that have been floating around the company already, like "suburban moms" or "purchasers" or "SMB" or whatever. But then I force everyone to re-do the clusters and organize the stickies around "I want" and "I need" statements. Suddenly people in the company transition the way they're thinking about who their customers are. The exercise helps them transition from "old" ways of thinking about customers and users to thinking in terms of what their customers need and want, what their objectives are in their own terms. It really is a process of moving gently from one way of thinking about the customer to another way.

This is one of the reasons I think it's problematic to create these archetypal customers or personas externally from the company and then, for lack of a better way to put it, 'throw them over the wall'. If key stakeholders haven't been involved in that process and experienced the transition from the 'old' terminology to the 'new' goal-based personas, it's too easy to fall back into the old way of doing things. It really is a process, and that's why I'm a big believer in going in and working with the team, face-to-face.

Is a persona the existing customer or is it the customer that you want to have?

That's a great question. I think that it's a little bit of both.

When you create personas you create a set of them, and sometimes those sets of personas are a little bit of both. If an existing customer is one who's just looking to get a rate plan online for their phone, let's say, that might be the customer you have today. But maybe your future target is somebody who already has a service and wants lots of extra features. I say that you create personas for both of those—they may end up being the same person in different stages of their relationship with the company—and then you prioritize.

When you prioritize, you prioritize from a future-looking perspective. Who do we want to get? Because, when you're doing a redesign process, whether it's small or large, you're looking to change something to enable you to appeal to a different aspect of your customer base, a different set of needs of your customer base, or a completely different customer base.

Once a company has defined its multiple personas, how does that translate into what someone sees when they go to the company's web site?

You start with a persona that's driven by a goal—let's go back to Maryanne, who wants to buy cleaning products online because it's easier, and certainly doesn't want to spend a lot of time shopping for them. Then what I like to do is look first at the experience. If you consider a persona a character, then the experience you want to create is the story.

> *"Too many companies just look at it page by page by page, so the site ends up being not so pleasant to use."*

What I like to do is map out a story of her interaction with the site. So Maryanne shows up at the site, she's looking to just get the cleaners that she's used to getting and doing so quickly and making sure it's the best price, but she has a sort of "come-to-think-of-it" moment while she's at the site and she looks at other cleaners. Right here we may introduce her to the idea that there are organic alternatives to the cleaners that she wants.

So you map out that interaction path that you'd like to create. Once you do that, then you can go back and decide how you're going to design that interaction path into the site.

I think that far too many companies just look at it page by page by page, so the site ends up being not so pleasant to use. A different team has designed the search results than has designed the product page than has designed the cart. So there's a jarring experience going from one to another.

Whereas if you look at the end-to-end interaction you want to create—almost as if it's a story—that can influence your design decisions very strongly.

You can even look at your site today from Maryanne's perspective and say to yourself, what would Maryanne do first, second, and third? Is that really helping her do what we want her to do? Are we telling her the right things at the right time? Let's

> *"I like to treat competitive web sites as version 1.0 of our redesign."*

look at our competition's web site and see how well they're satisfying Maryanne, and whether there are things we can learn from them.

Then, like most customer-centered design people, I'm a big believer in starting with the blueprint of the site before going on to adding on branding elements or colors. I'm a believer in looking at the blueprint of the house and making sure that the kitchen isn't falling off the side before I go redecorate the living room.

It's about figuring out a way to go from a persona to the story you want to create to a way of creating a page flow or information flow that really supports that story.

You touched on something there. Most usability tends to be internally focused—what's happening on our site, what our users are doing. How do you bring what the competition is doing into the equation?

Usability is becoming an overloaded term. When you look at the field that I'm in, usability really refers to usability testing, which is one aspect of what customer-centered design folks really do. Usability specifically refers to putting prototypes or designs in front of people and seeing how well people can actually use them: whether they're tripping over aspects of the design. Hopefully we do that early enough so that we can fix things before we launch them.

What I'm really interested in is much, much earlier in the process—way, way earlier, back in the strategy and conceptual phase. If you really do understand "we're going after Maryanne and not Bobby" from very early in the strategy phase, and you can look at what the competition is doing from the perspective of the key customer that you want to go after, then you can learn from that.

I like to treat competitive web sites as version 1.0 of our redesign. What can we steal from them? What are they doing really well? What mistakes have they already made so we don't have to make them again? And this is before pencil hits paper on any kind of design decision.

If you create Maryanne and commit to her, you can get a lot of insight from looking at existing sites from her point of view. It will help you decide how you can be differentiated and what your value to Maryanne really is (compared to the other companies and services she can choose from). Once you clarify these things internally, you also have to find a way to express your value proposition and differentiators in a way that really does convey value and difference to Maryanne.

So it's way, way early in the process.

How do you measure success?

Measuring ROI is a topic that people in customer-centered design are discussing; there's a lot being written about it right now, and a lot being thought about it. What I like to do, very early, when I identify the business goals and the branding goals and the objectives in respect to customers, is to write down how things are today and how we'd like them to be tomorrow.

> *"I think customer experience should be a consistent focus in an organization."*

For example, there are process, product, and communication problems in any company. If you can write down the current problems related to each of these and how you'd like them to change, then you can measure success.

So in terms of the product, which could mean the web site, what are the problems we've identified with the web site today and are there symptoms we can point to that really display that problem? Are there metrics that are measuring that problem—and what do we want them to be? If you don't decide what you want to measure extremely early in the process, you can't measure it later.

That's my approach. I don't think it's just about moving the needle on conversion in the immediate release. I think it's also about being able to get better designs done more quickly, being able to get better communications between marketing and product development, being able to allow and help an executive team make a decision that they're not going to change halfway through the project. All of those things impact the bottom line and impact a company's ability to satisfy their customers, in my opinion.

How often should a company revisit their web site design, for usability?

It can and should be a continuous process. If you have a persona or personas, you can consistently review your site experience from their point of view. You can hire someone from outside your company to do expert reviews. Find someone who's immersed in, let's say, online commerce and best practices (which evolve over time), and have that person review your current site and recommend new approaches that might improve customer experience.

I think customer experience should be a consistent focus in an organization. There are ways to do usability testing and experience analysis that are ongoing. It doesn't have to be terribly expensive, it doesn't have to be terribly fancy. You can just bring in a couple of customers, sit them down, ask them to do something, and watch them do it. Ask them to talk aloud while they do their thing, and have a discussion about why they are making the choices they are making. Give them a nice gift certificate, and you're done.

I heard one company that brings in customers every Friday; they have "Persona Fridays." They bring in people who are similar to the personas they created, and they sit next to them and ask them to do something— hey, go buy one of our online games, here's $50, go buy one. And they just watch them; they just talk to them about what they're doing. In a way it doesn't even matter so much what thing you're asking them; it's sort of keeping in tune with what people think and how they behave around sites like yours.

What are some of the more common mistakes that you find when you're working with companies?

There's a big one that I love to talk about: Companies don't put their value proposition and their differentiator on their home page. They just don't!

For example, a company can assume, "Everybody knows my brand, so I don't have to put on my home page that I sell cleaning products online for a great price and deliver them free." They forget to do that; they think it's too basic and too silly.

The analogy I like to make is that even the most complicated technical book starts with a paragraph that everybody can understand. Reminding people of who it is you are and what it is you do is a very important basic thing that people forget.

The second thing that's a big problem, that I love to talk about, is something I call "corporate underpants." What corporate underpants means is that your org structure shows on your web site. If you can trace back each of your major navigation paths to a VP, you've got a problem. Just because you have these different P & L centers doesn't mean that it's going to make sense to Maryanne to go to a different place for each of them.

Corporate underpants can show up on a site in a lot of ways. It's making decisions about your site that are more about your internal organization and your internal goals than they are about the customer experience.

That's emblematic of companies that think internally rather than externally, right?

I think so. And even companies that think they're thinking externally often do it, as well.

> *"You have to have the executives watch customers actually use the site."*

One example of that is to think of the last home-page design meeting you were in. Everybody's clamoring to be on the home page, because they think that's the only way to get attention from customers. But it's not. It could be that the right time to tell Maryanne about the organic line of cleaners isn't on the home page; maybe it's after she's found the thing she thinks she wants.

How do you get stakeholders to stop begging for home-page placement? One way is to make them watch customers use the web site. See whether they get stuck. See if you've wrinkled up the carpet and people are tripping over it all over the place.

If an organization is not ready to think about a full redesign, you have to have the executives watch customers actually use the site. That is the quickest way to make people realize there's a problem. It's not about showing them slides full of metrics, it's not about bringing alternative designs, it's not screaming your head off about corporate underpants, it's having them sit there for an hour and watch Betty Lou try to buy a new pair of shoes.

If they agree and go, "Oh my God, we've got a problem," then you need to look in and see what exactly we want to solve here. Is this really a communication problem? Is this really a politics problem in our organization? It's usually not just a problem with the site; the site is showing symptoms of a bigger problem in your organization.

In my experience, I think it has to do with the strength of the senior management. A weak management kind of lets everybody have their say, whereas a stronger management will say, no, this is what the customer wants—forget the internal structure and politics.

I think you're right—and the word "customer" there is too vague. The other thing I like to go around saying is, "User is a four-letter word." You can argue for "the customer" all you want, but what does that mean? Scratch beneath the surface and ask anyone to describe who "the customer" is, and things start getting very, very wonky.

What I've found, over and over again, is that you somehow break companies out of that when they're able to talk about Maryanne and Bobby. When Executive X says, "We're doing this for the customer," you can say, "Which customer? Because it sounds like you're talking about something for Bobby, but we've prioritized Maryanne. Now,

> *"We're slowly getting to the point where people understand that customer-centered design isn't something you can put on at the end."*

you're an executive, you can change your mind about this, but here's the cost—it means we can't do X, Y, and Z for Maryanne. Your choice."

It gets it out of whoever is the loudest, whoever is the most persuasive speaker, whoever it is that everyone gets tired of hearing them talk so they just give in. And it somehow depersonalizes it, so it doesn't feel like you're losing; your feature actually isn't the best one for Maryanne. You can say, "Oh, that makes sense."

What trends do you see happening in usability?

I do think that people are starting to find less expensive ways to do "usability." More people are finding ways to bring in customers on a regular basis that are inexpensive and that involve more people. I think we still have a way to go in getting executives to realize that they have to be in on the sessions; it really can't be secondhand.

We're slowly getting to the point where people understand that customer-centered design isn't something you can put on at the end. I think it's the same thing that happened in marketing a while ago. I think many companies have realized that it's always better if marketing is involved early, so they can help you understand which products would be easier to sell. And why. I think that's starting to happen in customer-centered design.

I think people are starting to have more of a customer-centered design executive voice. Traditionally, customer-centered design has fit underneath marketing or fit underneath engineering. That's a big problem, especially if they're under engineering. It's a conflict of interest for a VP of engineering to be both managing the engineering/development process and to be managing the customer experience.

Also, it's starting to make more and more sense for people to outsource the technology of their sites—which also means they're outsourcing a certain portion of usability.

Do you often find usability in conflict with the technology?

It's not necessarily in conflict with the technology; it's in conflict with the decisions that are made about technology—what can you build and what can you prioritize. The things that are sexy and fun for engineers to build aren't always the things that are going to move the needle because they improve the customer experience.

Think about a few years ago, when everybody had Flash intros to their site. Well, they were very sexy, but they actually turned out to be annoying and useless.

It's still happening today. People are saying, "Wow, we need more of that Web 2.0 stuff. We need more AJAX on our site." That's silly. That's like saying, "We're building a building; we need more concrete in that." It's just part of the structure. It's not an end unto itself.

I dealt with a company a year or two ago, and one of the claims to fame on their résumé was that they had reengineered the Google interface for some ISP somewhere. So they'd taken the very clean, simple Google interface and made it all Flash-based for that ISP. It was totally unusable! But that was very symptomatic of what was wrong with everything that company designed. Did anybody even ask for that?

Exactly! But it was fun and interesting for the engineers, whereas maybe creating really great, clear text links wasn't as sexy.

The field of human-computer interaction started relatively recently. So people now are looking for great information architects or information designers or interactive designers. And it's tough to find one with a lot of really good experience. It's not the same thing as finding a great graphic designer. There's just starting to be enough people in the field that have that kind of experience. It's hard to find them; I can't tell you how many calls I get! "We're looking for a great interactive designer."

Is there any other advice you'd give to online marketers?

Marketing is a critical part of the stakeholder group that should be creating personas together, because marketers have so much great information about customers that they can bring to the table. Just like customer-centered design, the earlier marketing is involved, the better.

If your job was to market the Pinto, not so much fun, right? Wouldn't it have been great if you had been involved earlier and been able to say, "You know what? The market would really prefer a car that didn't explode." Of course that's a silly example, but I think the same thing happens over and over again.

One of the difficulties that marketers have that personas really help with, is unless your job's about data, it's very, very hard, if not impossible, to remember bullet points of data. For example, 35- to 45-year-old women in suburban areas who make a yearly income of $75,000 and are likely to be highly educated, blah, blah, blah. That's something that marketers and market researchers can hold onto in their heads. Other people can't, because it's not their job. What they can remember is Maryanne. In fact, if I ask you in three weeks who Maryanne was, you'd be pretty likely to remember it—whereas you probably wouldn't remember those bullet points.

I think a lot of companies and a lot of teams should think about how they make their own work product usable. How do they make the knowledge that they have easy to consume on a daily basis? We all have a tendency to whine about people not listening to us, but maybe that's because they don't speak our language. So the responsibility becomes ours to create something that's easy for them to consume. Sure you need details in a persona, sure it doesn't include everything that you've learned, but on a day-to-day basis, if Maryanne is the thing they're talking about and not "the customer," that's a huge win.

Sound Bites

The concept of personas may seem complex at first, but it's really quite simple. It's putting a human face on traditional marketing data; instead of describing your customer in terms of facts and figures, you create a character that represents all that information. Then, when you're designing your web site and defining the customer experience, all you have to do is focus on that character. What would our persona do? What does our persona want? Answer those questions and you'll create a great customer experience.

How do you go about defining your company's persona(s)? Here's what Tamara Adlin suggests:

- Don't let an outside agency define the persona alone; the creation has to involve internal stakeholders.
- The creation of a persona should involve all important executives, managers, and other stakeholders, in order to ensure their buy-in to the concept.
- To get the point across, bring in test customers who are similar to your company's persona, and watch them try to use your web site.
- Create your persona and work on your site's customer-centered design upfront, while the site is being designed (or before); if you wait until after the site is live, you're too late.

Again, the key is to put a very human face on all your marketing data, and let a persona represent your ideal customer. As Tamara noted, it's a lot easier to remember what a single person wants than it is to memorize a raft of marketing data!

Steve Rubel: Edelman

8

"The bigger story here is that the fabric of the Net has changed; it's a place for people to connect up around shared interests and then collaborate towards some sort of action."

—*Steve Rubel*

Steve Rubel is on the cutting edge. Always has been. And to Steve the cutting edge of online marketing isn't email or even blogs; it's social networking and whatever else captivates those known as Generation Y these days.

Steve has been on the cutting edge since the dawn of the computer era, and a fixture in the PR industry for almost as long. Today he works with Edelman, the largest world's largest independent PR firm, in their me2revolution practice. He also writes a regular column for *Advertising Age Digital* and has his own influential Micro Persuasion blog. Not surprisingly, he's a popular speaker on the tech and PR circuits and has been named to several prestigious "best of" lists, including *Media Magazine's* Media 100, the AlwaysOn/Technorati Open Media 100, and the CNET's News.com Blog 100.

> **FACT SHEET: STEVE RUBEL**
>
> Senior Vice President, Edelman
> (www.edelman.com)
>
> Blogger, Micro Persuasion Blog
> (www.micropersuasion.com)
>
> Columnist, *Advertising Age Digital*
> (http://adage.com/digital/)

Online Marketing on the Cutting Edge

Steve isn't wedded to the past; he's one of the most forward-thinking marketers I've met. It's not surprising, then, that my interview with him covered everything from PR research to blogging to next-generation social networks. Read on to see what's on Steve's mind today.

You've been in the PR industry your entire career. How did you get involved with technology?

I've been a technology enthusiast for almost exactly 25 years now; I got my first computer 25 years ago this month. I've just been hooked ever since. It's always been a huge interest to me, huge, because it's ever-changing and so dynamic. It's just continued to be, all these years.

What was your first computer?

I got an Atari 800 when I turned 13. Since then, I've had too many computers and devices to name.

I understand that.

Way too many!

When did you first get interested in and involved with the Internet?

Let me think. I was on CompuServe and GEnie in 1985. I ran a BBS in 1985. And then I was on AOL in 1992. I got a broadband connection in 1999. So I was an early adopter.

That's a good thing to do, to keep on top of trends.

Always. And that's virtually what led me to really be in the position that I am now. That background did not converge with marketing, in a powerful way, until about late '03.

Let's talk about that a little bit. When did you realize that marketing and technology could work together, and how they could do it?

> *"What's happened in the last few years is that technology has become more powerful and free."*

I've always been following the impact of technology on marketing, but it wasn't very applicable to me because it wasn't DIY [do-it-yourself]. It's when technology really became a DIY scenario, where you could really use the technology yourself in a very efficient way—to become more efficient and more effective at what you do—that was when it really began to catch my attention in a big way.

In '98 and '99 there was email marketing, and search marketing in the early part of this decade. I certainly watched that and I was intrigued by it, but it wasn't directly applicable to what I was doing as a PR professional.

I was using online databases and research tools, starting in the late '90s, for PR, but if the organization didn't buy it for you, you had to rely on what they gave you. I was fortunate to work in places where I had that, but still, it wasn't DIY.

It was in 2003 and 2004 when I saw that you could really do a lot of amazing things with free stuff, and what you could get out of that, that I became increasingly intrigued. Obviously, the advantages steamrolled, because of a number of different things that people are doing now. I really believe that a lot of the tools are free.

Early on, you were probably using LexisNexis, that sort of thing?

Yeah, and those tools are still widely used today by PR professionals, but you're right: it was Factiva and MediaMap and Bacon's. That was the lifeblood of the PR professional, and still is for many PR professionals. But what's happened in the last few years is that technology has become more powerful and free.

I think it's extremely disruptive on a number of fronts. One is that all these guys who sell high-end solutions are really going to have to worry about the lower-hanging fruit coming in and how that might impact them. And two is a lot of companies have big IT departments that spend a lot of money on initiatives and influencing information solutions, and Google can have something that's free—or Microsoft or Yahoo! or anybody.

Look at the content management systems that companies have implemented to put stuff on their web site. That was great, but it took many, many years to implement a lot of that stuff. Now, you know, if you have your own web site, you can do it with WordPress for noth-

> *"From an infrastructure perspective, the cost of doing business…is going down to zero."*

ing. The whole open source movement and also the big players have really pushed technology down into every person's hands. I don't think that people fully realize what you can do with free stuff.

On one hand, that enables a small company or an individual, even, to compete effectively with the big companies.

Absolutely—and it's global, too. I think that what you get from the big global companies, when they work well, is you get incredible smarts and brainpower together in networks. And expertise, specialized expertise, that allows them to maintain their business.

But you're right. My feeling is that, from an infrastructure perspective, the cost of doing business—the actual cost of it, not the people cost, but the cost of everything—is going down to zero.

So it's leveling the playing field for the little guy. What's the big guy doing?

The big guys, if they're smart, they have people who are on the cutting edge of all the new stuff, and are able to figure out how to apply it, ASAP. I think that's what our group does, in part.

How is a PR professional using technology today?

It really depends; it runs the gamut. I believe that people have to up their digital acumen in a hurry. The problem is, just when you learn something, the whole thing will change.

> *"Everyone is struggling with…how to work with Gen Y."*

Everyone is using Google, that's for sure. And I think a lot of people are using Google News. A lot of people are starting to use RSS, but it's not as much as I would like. I think wiki's used, but it really depends on the culture.

Email is still king, for everybody. Email is king for how we interact with everyone from the media to bloggers to social networks to each other, and so forth. This is just, the world is like this. I don't think everyone's moved off of email yet. I think email's still king and continues to be and might be for the foreseeable future—although there's obviously inherent problems with it.

Email now is, what, 15 years old or so? To many younger people, it's an old technology. The young people I know think of email as what the old people use—and they don't use it.

It's funny—they use it, but they don't call it email. To me, text messaging is a form of email. Facebook emails are emails.

But I think you're right. They certainly don't call it that, and they think it's old-school. They use IM a lot, also. For me personally, I used to love IM; I hate it now. I hate IM, because I like being able to control my time. When I use IM I'm instantaneously putting myself on somebody else's agenda.

I'm with you. I don't like other people to be controlling what I do. That's why I like email; I can do it on my own schedule.

Having office hours for IM is a good idea. An hour or two hours a day you put it up, so that people have instant access to you. But for the most part I try not to use it. On the one hand it's very efficient; on the other hand, it's very inefficient.

With the new generation being so instant message—and text message—addicted, is there a way to exploit that?

I think what everyone is struggling with is how to work with Gen Y. They have a certain level and kind of expectation that you and I just don't have. They expect to be able to come and go from work as they please, for example, as long as they get their job done. Companies that want to hang onto their talent, if that's where the talent's going to come from (and it is), they're going to have to figure out how to bend their culture accordingly. And I think people are doing that, but it's progressing slowly. *Fortune* did a whole cover story on that recently.

> *"It's not a matter of adapting your message; it's a matter of adapting your approach."*

The other thing that's happening with the high schoolers and college kids today is the whole social networking thing— Facebook, MySpace, and so on. How do you take advantage of that?

What you use it for is as a platform for collaborating towards some sort of shared outcome. You figure out where you and your community overlap, what you want and what they want, and how you use the social networks to make that happen.

Do the kids of this generation accept traditional marketing messages, or are they wary of that sort of thing?

> "*[Blogging] is a great consumer insights tool.*"

I think they accept it, but it's a matter of where you put it. If you were to put it in TV advertising, they accept it there. But if you start to put it into a social network, in a very intrusive way, they don't like it.

So how do you have to adapt your message for that type of media?

It's not a matter of adapting your message; it's a matter of adapting your approach. You need to figure out how you use these different channels and what some are good for and what others are not good for.

Speaking of channels, let's talk a little bit about blogs; that's a big part of what you're doing these days. How do blogs fit into a company's marketing mix?

Blogs are a great way to communicate very efficiently, to engage in conversation, and to work towards a shared outcome.

Do you recommend a company start their own blog?

It really depends. I think you have to find out where you community is and figure out what tools and channels are going to resonate with them, and use them accordingly. It's not right for every company.

Aside from starting up their own blog, how else can a company utilize the blogosphere?

It's a great consumer insights tool. It's a great way to research what's on the mind of the populace and figure out what the trendsetters are thinking.

So are you using blogs more for research or to put forth a marketing message?

We're using it for both. We're using it for research but also to build a closer relationship with consumers. Absolutely.

Let's say a company decides to put out their own blog. What sort of common mistakes do you see when that happens?

They're thinking about them and not thinking about the readers. They're not thinking about how to provide value, what people really want. They're using it as a place to just talk and less of a place for action.

> "The way you get smart about any community…is to spend time there and understand what the ethos is."

They're focusing on themselves instead of focusing on the customer?

It's not even a matter of focusing on the customer. It's what other bloggers are talking about, and how to build connections with them. They're not doing it that way; they're viewing it as a sort of push talk.

How does a company get smart about this?

Honestly, you should just spend time in the community. The way to get smart about any community, whether it's a social network, a blog community, a message board, whatever, is to spend time there and understand what the ethos is.

Your own blog is a very popular blog in the PR community. How did you get started with that?

I've always been curious about technology, and I started hearing blogs in '01. I found it interesting but really didn't pay a lot of attention to it. In 2002/2003 I really started to read blogs and play around with the platforms, and saw just how terrific they were and what you could do with them and how flexible they were and how free they were.

In my last job I worked with some clients to help them launch their own blogs. After that I said, look, if I'm reading blogs and I'm working with clients to help them launch their own blogs, then I really should have my own. One morning I just woke up and started Micro Persuasion.

How much time do you spend on the blog?

You know, it's changed a lot. For three years it was a lot—it was probably two to three hours a day, and I was blogging absolutely every single day, with a high volume of posts. But in the last six months or so I've changed, for a few reasons.

> *"I believe that community is going to be a river that runs through absolutely everything we do online."*

One is that I just had to cut back, because my workload became so high that I just couldn't do it all. Two is the nature of the blog changed after I joined Edelman. Edleman has 1,500 clients; everybody's either a client, a competitor of a client, or a prospect. It became very difficult for me to put up any kind of news about stuff because it was very possible I could run into trouble. So I had to find a way to blog about trends and be more substantive about it, and obviously that requires a lot more time and energy.

In addition, all these other places where you can spend time popped up. In particular, Twitter, and the whole mobile aspect of that and how it connects to your mobile device, really was appealing to me and I began to publish there a lot more.

Through that, now, I probably have it down to maybe two or three hours a week.

You brought up something interesting there, that a company with its employees blogging, not necessarily official blogs, there's certainly the potential for conflict. How much control does a company have over its employees and their personal blogs?

It's a matter of being upfront with them, giving them a blogging policy and helping them understand what the rules of the road are—the dos and don'ts, and how to think about it as it relates to the company. It's just being open about it.

The concept of video blogging—do you see that having much of an impact?

Less so, because video is very difficult to scan and it's very difficult to search. Nothing flies like text.

Blogging to me is a means to an end. It was the earliest thing, it was exciting, but the action's elsewhere now. It's still very powerful, but the action I think is in social networks and communities. I believe that community is going to be a river that runs through absolutely everything we do online—whether it be standalone communities or company web sites.

While there's a lot of hype and interest in blogging and video blogging and so forth, I'm more interested in the social change that it's creating, and that social change is the ability for like-minded people to connect around topics that they care about, no matter how they do it. Some people will connect over video, some people will connect through audio, some people will do it through social networks, some people will do it through blogs. But the bigger story here is that the fabric of the Net has changed; it's a place for people to connect up around shared interests and then collaborate towards some sort of action.

What advice would you have for a company that recognizes these trends and wants to take advantage of them?

You need to live it. You need to live in it, or you need to hire somebody who lives in it. It's like no other space and it changes every six to eight months.

The advice I give is to really live in it and understand it, and to know the motivations of the communities that you care about. You got to figure out where your audience is and where they hang out, which sites are important to them and what they do with those sites. Know what the ethos is and what they're trying to achieve. Only after you've done all that can you really begin to build programs that help engage them.

Sound Bites

So what's on the cutting edge of marketing today? As Steve notes, it's not the individual technology itself as much as it is how the technology is used—what people want to do online. And what Steve sees as the "killer app" is community, via whatever medium matters to the consumer—blogs, audio, video, social networks, you name it.

Some more points of note:

- Technology works best when it takes on a do-it-yourself character—and when it becomes free.

- Google's free search has replaced the PR professional's traditional paid research tools.
- Generation Y is abandoning earlier technology, such as email, in favor of text messaging, instant messaging, and social network communication.
- To take advantage of social networking, figure out where you and your community overlap and how they want to communicate.
- Going forward, the concept of community is the common element running through all online media and technologies.

If you learn only one thing from Steve Rubel, it should be this: Technology is constantly changing. What you might think is a new technology is already old-school for a younger generation. If you're just now getting involved with email marketing or blogging, somebody somewhere has leapfrogged you into social networking or whatever the next big thing may be. To stay in step with your customer base you need to be aware, be involved, and keep focusing on the cutting edge.

Greg Jarboe:
SEO-PR

9

"To the extent that you can get the PR people interacting with the search people, they will discover that there are lots of things they can do together."

—*Greg Jarboe*

Greg Jarboe has been around the public relations industry for about forever, and at the forefront of many trends and changes. That gives him insight matched by few others in the industry; fortunately for all of us, Greg is more than willing to share what he has learned.

FACT SHEET: GREG JARBOE

President and Co-Founder
SEO-PR (www.seo-pr.com)

Partner, Newsforce
(www.newsforce.com)

Greg started his career at Lotus Development Corporation, back in the days when 1-2-3 ruled the personal computer universe and Microsoft Excel also ran in the spreadsheet market. After working for Ziff-Davis and several other technology-related companies, Greg founded SEO-PR, a firm that specializes in public relations and search engine optimization—not as odd a mix as you'd think, once you start talking to him. He's a frequent speaker at all manner of tech- and PR-related conferences and seminars and writes for a number of online and offline publications. Jeffrey Tartar, editor of *Softletter*, says "Greg Jarboe always seems to be ahead of the curve whenever there's a major shift in technology marketing;" *Media Industry Newsletter* named Greg "one of the best PR people in magazineland."

I knew that Greg would have a lot to contribute to this book, but I wasn't prepared for the far-reaching conversation that was in store.

Moving Public Relations into the 21st Century

Greg's focus today is using the Web as a public relations tool. That means getting press releases directly into the hands of consumers via web-based distribution; it also means optimizing those press releases for Google and other search engines.

How did you go from working with Lotus and 1-2-3 in the 1980s to doing the web stuff that you're doing today?

It was a long, strange road. I was with Lotus from '86 to '88, back when DOS was the operating system of choice. Lotus was actually bigger than Microsoft back then. All ancient history.

From Lotus in '88, I joined *PC Computing* as the director of marketing, when it was being launched in August of '88, and was there for three years. *PC Computing* was published by Ziff-Davis, and in '91 the company decided to move the magazine from the East Coast, in Cambridge, to the West Coast, in Foster City. I figured it was time to update the résumé and find something else, because my wife didn't want to move to California.

And Bill Ziff called and said, "Why don't you start a PR agency? And I'll be your first client." Which had not been my plan but was certainly a lot better than some of the alternatives I had at the time. So in '91 I started Jarboe Communications.

> *"I found press releases in the [Google News] results along with news articles."*

After working for Ziff-Davis for a couple of months, Bill Ziff called back and said, I made a mistake, Greg, you shouldn't have started the PR agency, you should have started a PR department. Would you mind if I acquired your firm and bring you in-house, and you can be the first director of corporate communications for Ziff-Davis?

That was a really good deal, so in late '91 I went back inside Ziff-Davis as director of corporate communications, and was there until spring of '99. Then I went off to a dot-com startup called WebCT, which was funded by CMGI. I was the vice president of marketing there from '99 to 2001, when the dot-com bubble burst.

Having gone through the roller-coaster ride, I took a hard look at various marketing elements that I had used, and there was this one new thing that we had done which was absolutely surprising in its cost effectiveness; that was search engine optimization.

There we were in 2001, in what appeared to be a recession, what appeared to be a bad time for marketing. Although I had handled the entire marketing mix, if I was going to focus on something that might land me on my feet, I decided to focus on search.

At the end of that year I got hired as the chief marketing officer for a search firm called Backbone Media. I was there as the chief marketing officer until about October of 2002.

In September of 2002, Google launched Google News. I had been doing public relations since the 1980s, and I had been doing search for at least that year with Backbone Media, and it had been part of the marketing mix when I was at WebCT. When I did my first search in Google News, to figure out what it was all about, I found press releases in the results along with news articles. Google News did a lot of things that were radically different, but one of the radical things they had done was consider press releases as just another news source.

I understood the potential of that and took it to the president of Backbone Media and said this could be a really big opportunity. He looked at it and said, "No, actually we're thinking of going into web site design as an alternative for growing the business next year." At that point I mulled things over and decided to leave Backbone Media.

I called up a fellow I had worked with back at Lotus, Jamie O'Donnell, who was on the West Coast, and said, Jamie, there are press releases in the results here; I know how to optimize these things; this could be really big. He had gotten out of public relations—he went over to a

> *"If you aren't measuring success in concrete ways, things will change and you'll never see them."*

direct marketing firm; he was president and founder of IDM Partners, which did a variety of direct marketing, including email marketing. He said he'd learned how to track results really well; if we put all of that together, we might really have something. And SEO-PR was born.

We decided to be a little cautious, partly because of the dot-com bubble bursting. So we waited until after we'd had two clients before we actually launched the company, in March of 2003.

You've been doing PR with and for high-tech companies for decades now. Can you talk about how that's changed as the high-tech industry has evolved?

It's changed several times, and I think the PR industry has missed several of those changes, by and large, because they don't have the most important element in their arsenal. And that's measurement. If you aren't measuring success in concrete ways, things will change and you'll never see them.

For a hundred years, PR people have been measuring success by having press clippings. I remember the first time I went into Jim Manzi, who was the CEO of Lotus, in the fall of 1986, and I had a clip book with over 700 clippings in it, and I put it on his desk as a "not bad for a first month" kind of thing. And he took a look at it and said, "Jarboe, these are just little pieces of paper." He said, "If I could deposit them in a bank I'd know what they were worth. Until you can show me the relationship between these little pieces of paper and sales, don't waste my time."

So PR people have had that kind of challenge forever, and have never quite known what to do with it. We claim that we're increasing awareness, and the question is, terrific, how much awareness did you increase this month? And all you can fall back on is counting clippings again, and maybe estimating how many people read the clippings. But you don't really know.

> *"Sales is the thing that PR people don't think they're involved in—which is the biggest opportunity they're missing."*

Missing what we'll call real measurement, PR people missed a couple of things. One of the changes was the shift from print media to online, which happened gradually from about 1995 onward. But PR people could never quite figure out how much of what they were doing was resulting in good things happening because they were being picked up online, or because they were still getting picked up in print.

Another thing that they missed was the whole advent of news search engines. I saw press releases in news results and they were there, hidden in plain sight, for anybody to see. In other words, that's not proprietary information. But most PR people, not all but most, were not focused on that, didn't think about it, didn't recognize that that might be something that they ought to be optimizing for. They were perfectly comfortable pitching stories to reporters but they had no concept of pitching a story to a news search engine algorithm.

In my mind, because of lack of measurement, a lot of the serious changes that came about 1995 onward sort of slipped under the radar for most PR people.

> *"The return on investment was through the roof."*

When you're talking about being able to measure results, obviously clippings are not a way to measure them—if they ever were. What are you measuring today?

Different things for different marketers, but including sales. So let me start with sales and move backwards. Because sales is the thing that PR people don't think they're involved in—which is the biggest opportunity they're missing.

If you go to the Institute for Public Relations (www.instituteforpr.org), and you go to the Golden Ruler Award and look at the winner for 2005, you will see that SEO-PR and Southwest Airlines have a case study there that won us an award, against every other public relations agency in the United States. The title of that case study is, "You Are Now Free to Link PR and Sales"—sort of a takeoff on the Southwest Airlines slogan, "You are now free to move about the country." In it, we document the fact that we had optimized a series of press releases for Southwest Airlines, so that they got found in news search engine results.

Using some of the techniques that Jamie O'Donnell had used, with his direct marketing firm, we put unique tracking links in the press releases. If you clicked on the link and went to a unique landing page on the Southwest.com website, there's no other link like that in the world. So there's no confusion over where this person might have come from.

> *"The first time she went into a marketing meeting and said… 'We've…generated about $80,000 in revenue,' people fell out of their chairs."*

From that unique landing page, if people then went and bought tickets, there's no question about, did they wonder in here by accident from somewhere else?

What that enabled us to do was to track over $2.5 million in airline ticket sales from four, count 'em, four, optimized press releases. Trust me; Southwest Airlines did not pay $2.5 million to optimize the four press releases. So the return on investment was through the roof—the fact that people were actually reading the press releases, finding the news of interest, clicking on the unique link and going through and buying a ticket. In fact, we did some follow-up research and discovered that the average person was actually buying a ticket for two people, not one. And about two-thirds of them had never bought tickets from Southwest Airlines before, because they were announcing new service to Philadelphia. People who were interested said, wow, I can now get an introductory fare if I move quickly, and did so, based on that news. They bought their tickets.

People were reading press releases on news search engines, clicking on the links, and Southwest Airlines was measuring results—not in awareness, and not in some other kind of estimates of reach, but in cold, hard cash.

In the old days, a PR person was overjoyed if they got a story placed in a national publication. Now you're tracking actual results, actual sales. Does that make PR people nervous?

People are nervous for lots of reasons. I'm going to go back to the initial story that we optimized for new service to Philadelphia. We got news coverage in *The New York Times*. We got news coverage in *The Washington Post*. We got news coverage in about a dozen other media. So it wasn't that we didn't get press coverage; that's good, too. At the end of the day, that was normal.

When Linda Rutherford, who was then the director of of public relations [at Southwest Airlines], would go into a monthly marketing meeting and say, "Hi, we got some news coverage," everyone else around the table would have said, "Yeah, yeah, yeah, that's what PR is supposed to do." But the first time she went into a marketing meeting and said, "Oh, by the way, so far we've also generated about $80,000 in revenue," people fell out of their chairs—because PR people aren't supposed to do that. Linda Rutherford is now vice president of public relations, and she did a lot of things to earn that promotion, but I think learning how to optimize press releases and measure results in the same way that any other part of the marketing mix is measured certainly didn't hurt her career.

One change in strategy is you're not just writing a press release to be picked up by a reporter someplace; you're writing a release to be read by the consumer. How does that change the press releases you create?

In some respects it doesn't change things at all. Both the reporter and the consumer read a language called English, and the search terms that we were using in the press release were normal, vernacular words— not strange, occult phrases—like "Southwest Airlines" and "discount airfares."

> *"Keyword research is all about finding the phrases that people type into those search boxes when they're looking for something."*

I think this is one of the great myths; "My God, they're gonna make us optimize our press release!" Okay. Keyword research is all about finding the phrases that people type into those search boxes when they're looking for something. By and large, with a couple of small exceptions, what people are looking for are common English phrases. Making sure that those English phrases are included in your press release is not adding runes or some kind of fairy dust to the release; you're just making sure you've got the right words in the right places.

Let me give you an example, from this case study you can find at the Institute for Public Relations, to drive this one home.

Before we started optimizing press releases for Southwest Airlines, they would routinely put in their headlines, "Southwest Announces Red Hot Airfares." "Southwest" is a search term, but it's an ambiguous one that can mean New Mexico and Arizona, as well as the airline. We found that by putting the second word of their name in the headline, "Southwest Airlines Announces…," that you are now being found by people doing a search for the precise term. In the past, if all they did was put "Southwest" in [a head-line], someone searching for "Southwest Airlines" probably wouldn't find that press release.

Again, this is not learning to write backwards or in some kind of Esperanto. This is, "Oh, people are looking for us by name, and in this case our name is two words; let's use both words in the headline."

Now, in the second part of that headline, "Red Hot Airfares," in the past that would have been considered a clever headline, because it would have been about summer air specials and in the summer things are hot. But it turns out nobody searches for "red hot airfares;" that's just not a search term. It's a fun term to use, but it doesn't translate. People don't look for it.

What we came back with is that there are a couple of alternatives, and one of them is "discount airfares" and the other one is "cheap airfares." In one of our releases, we used the phrase "cheap airfares," and we thought, my, aren't we clever, because now we've used a very popular search term in our headline. The press release had to go all the way up to the founder and still executive chairman of the board, Herb Kelleher, to get approved before the release went out the door. Herb saw the word "cheap" in one of *his* press releases and he went nuts. He said, "For over 30 years I've been fighting this stigma—we're not a cheap airline; we're a low-fare airline."

Fortunately, the PR people had done their keyword research; they had their data with them. They said, "Before we go back and make these changes, can we show you how popular this term is? If we don't want to be found for 'cheap airfare' then somebody else will be happy to, and we'll probably be leaving millions of dollars on the table for one of our competitors to scoop up." And he said, "Gee, it's that popular, huh?" And they said, "Well, yeah, it's not 'cheap airfare,' it's also 'cheap airline,' and it's 'cheap flights.'" When you add up all the searches that are conducted in a given month, with all the variations of "cheap" and something that we do, that's an incredibly popular term. If we can't use it, people who are looking for that will find something else.

> ## "What are people looking for?"

So after 30-plus years of fighting "cheap," Herb modified his policy. It was okay, from that point forward, to use "cheap" in a "marketing press release." (We had never heard the term "marketing press release" before, but that was okay; whatever.) He said, "Just don't put it in one of the quarterly earnings announcements; I don't want my investors to think I'm cheap." That's only four releases a year, so that was no problem; we could make that compromise. Four releases a year we don't use the word "cheap." All the rest of them, we could use it if it's appropriate. Again, we don't use it in every release, but we do use it, especially when we're announcing fare sales.

That brings up an interesting issue. On one hand you have the marketing guys who create the slogans, like "Red Hot" this and that, and on the other hand you have what people actually want to hear, which is "cheap airfares." It seems to me that there could be a potential conflict in a lot of companies.

It can be. If often is. What it really is, is a conflict that I'll call old-school branding and search engine branding.

What the search engine branding starts with is, "What are people looking for? If they're looking for that, which one of those terms is actually relevant for me?" As opposed to the old-school branding, which is, "If I repeat this often enough, long enough, sooner or later it will actually get associated with me."

Let me give you a real-life anecdote to tell you how these conflicts can actually get perplexing. We did some work for *Consumer Reports* magazine. We were to optimize a press release announcing their December cover story one year; this would have been around 2005. The cover story that December was their annual Holiday Gift Buying Guide.

Well, guess what? The term "holiday gift" is not a search term. You don't look for "holiday gift," I don't look for "holiday gift;" it's not clear anybody in North America looks for "holiday gift." There are some searches for "holiday gift" in the U.K., but that's because they use the word "holiday" the way we use the word "vacation." And those searches tend to spike around June, where if you're going to go and use somebody's house, you might bring them a holiday gift to thank them for using their house. But that's a different meaning than what was on the cover of *Consumer Reports* magazine.

When we said that the right search terms were either "Christmas gift" or "Hanukkah gift," the *Consumer Reports* editor, to his credit, said, "Yeah, but that's not politically correct. 'Holiday gift' is the politically correct term."

And I said, "Well, I'm sure it is, and I'm sure if I saw it on the cover of a magazine on the newsstand I would say, 'Oh, yeah, that's politically correct, I know what this story is about.'" But if you want to get found in a search engine, people don't think that way. They don't pause and say, "Wait, wait, I don't really want to search for "Christmas gifts" because that's not politically correct." They just do. So you either want your news to be found, and you need to use that term somewhere in your press release, or you don't get found.

In that case we had to make a compromise, because "holiday gift" was already on the cover [of the magazine], and that's what it was called. We couldn't rewrite the cover. So we used "holiday gift" in the headline [of the press release], but we added a subhead underneath it that explained that in the holiday gifts article you'd find lots of good ideas for Christmas gifts and Hanukkah gifts and other things for New Years and the rest of the holidays. We were able to get our search terms in the subhead as a compromise.

What we're talking about here is search engine optimization for press releases, just as firms have been using SEO for their web sites. Is the process any different when you're doing it for online articles?

When we got done optimizing one press release for an article for *Consumer Reports*, in September of 2005, we came back to show that the release had been well optimized, because it was ranked number one for the target term, which was "air cleaners." And there, in the number-four position, was the actual cover story from *Consumer Reports*, about the air cleaners review. The editors said, there's something wrong here; why is your press release ranked higher than our story? And we said, because ours was optimized.

To their credit, the editors at *Consumer Reports* said, "Fine; is this something you can teach us?" And we did. We held a workshop.

One of the things you learn quickly is that a news search engine is going to treat press releases just like they're articles; it's the same algorithm. So if you want to optimize your article, you do it the same way that you would optimize a press release. You focus on the headline, you focus on the subhead, you focus on the lead paragraph, et cetera.

> *"Clarity is the new cleverness."*

It turns out a number of other media companies have since gone through search engine optimization training—not all of them by us, by the way—because search engines are contributing somewhere in the vicinity of about 20 to 30 percent of the traffic to many news sites. If you aren't optimizing your articles, you're walking away from a lot of potential visitors.

There's a wonderful, very funny article in *The New York Times*, in about April of 2006. The headline is, "This Boring Headline is Written for Google." In it, Steve Lohr, tongue in cheek, talks about going through search engine optimization training. One of the things that the journalists at the *Times* were learning, to their shock and dismay, was that when you're writing a headline for an optimized article, cleverness isn't as effective as clarity. In fact, one can say clarity is the new cleverness. So writing a headline, using a term people are looking for, gets you farther than writing a clever headline that nobody can quite figure out what it is you're alluding to.

Sometimes you wonder whether journalists are all repressed novelists. They love writing clever headlines. For years, normal readers of normal newspapers sometimes had to puzzle through what the headline was actually about. Well, on the Internet, you don't even get found; nobody puzzles through what it was you were writing about. You just aren't found.

So one of the laments is, "Oh my God; now I've got to write for my readers! And my readers are all busy people, and they want to get the gist of the story by reading the headline and maybe the first paragraph and saying, 'Oh, maybe this is a subject I'm interested in'—as opposed to me teasing them into a long feature story, about a subject they weren't quite sure what it was about."

Are there any new developments in this type of optimization that companies should know about?

There's been one new thing that's come along this year [2007] that has taken what we were doing, which was interesting and nice and useful and measurable, and just suddenly poured gasoline all over it. And that's what Google calls *universal search*.

If you're in front of a browser, go to Google, not Google News, and do a search for "Hillary Clinton." If you scan down the results, you see a little photo somewhere around the fourth listing, in the section labeled News Results. If you click on that News Results link, you'll find that all those results are coming from Google News. They're being imported and integrated into the regular Google web results.

What we've been doing from early 2003 until May of 2007 was optimizing content for Google News. People had to go to Google News to find it. Now you're beginning to find news results in Google. All of a sudden that's a big boost in circulation.

> "Universal search is the biggest thing to happen since the advent of Google News."

Which gives you more presence for everything you do.

Let's just throw some numbers around. There were about 5.5 billion searches on Google last month [August 2007]. So, yeah!

That suddenly means Google has more readers than the front page of every newspaper and magazine in America. If you added [their web sites] all together, they wouldn't get close to the kind of numbers that Google can put up.

I would say that the advent of universal search is the biggest thing to happen since the advent of Google News in September of 2002.

Everybody's focused on how universal search can benefit the consumer, but there really hasn't been the focus of how it benefits the news organizations.

Well, it hasn't impacted the news organizations [yet] because this is new and the organizations are working in the middle of their fiscal year. Maybe this fall they'll do some planning on what they should possibly do about it next year.

That's one of the traps that people fall into, is that they plan for a calendar year as opposed to when major events happen, maybe it's time to rethink things. That's just a classic marketing challenge.

How else do these universal search results change things?

One of the things that make news search results in the web page different is, more often than not, they come associated with a photo. You're looking down these blue links of results—blue link, blue link, blue link, *photo*, blue link. Gord Hotchkiss, who's the CEO at Enquiro, has done research that when that photo appears in the results, that's where the eye goes.

> *"TreeHugger generated more traffic to the* Consumer Reports *site than* CBS News *did."*

You could be listed number four in the old days (and by the old days, we're talking April of 2007), people would scan down the first three results and they might or might not get to link number four. Now, if you've got an image at link number four, associated with a news story, that's where the eye *starts*.

This is why it's particularly radical and very dramatic. It's like Google just rejuggled all of its results. When people see that first it can have a very, very dramatic effect on click-through rates, traffic generation, lead generation, sales, you name it.

The world continues to change.

The world continues to change.

One of the other folks that I interviewed for this book was Brian Lusk, who does Southwest's blog. It seems that you have new venues for PR these days, in blogs and podcasting; how important is it to take them into account?

Huge, huge. And again, if you're not measuring, this can slide under the radar.

The first time we learned this was in 2005 when we were doing work with *Consumer Reports*. We were tracking where the traffic was coming from, because that's a key part, not just to generate traffic, but to actually watch where it comes from. If it comes from an article that's been written about your announcement, that's just as valid as if it came from your press release. Don't focus narrowly on how much traffic does my press release generate; focus on how much traffic did the news coverage generate, or the blog coverage generate—and from where.

One of the things that we saw, for an announcement that had to do with EPA ratings—the miles per gallon that you'll get from buying a new car are probably inflated, because all the formulas were created back in the '70s when traffic patterns were very different—that announcement generated a very positive story on CBS News.com. It also generated a very positive news story on TreeHugger, a blog.

Okay, cool. What's the big deal? Well, TreeHugger generated more traffic to the *Consumer Reports* site than CBS News did. It was like, time out, wait a second, what's going on here?

What we recognized is that this whole idea of there is "The Press" and then there are "blogs" does a disservice to some bloggers. Not all bloggers, but some bloggers have built up significant audiences, and they have significant impact on those audiences. If they write about you, they literally can send more traffic your way than some mainstream media.

> *"Blogs are the new trade press."*

So that was the first time that had happened. It happened again a couple of times in 2006. In one case it was in a very narrow B2B case, work that we were doing with MarketingSherpa, a marketing research firm. In another case it was work we were doing with *The Christian Science Monitor*. In the *Monitor* case, we discovered that The Huffington Post and Boing Boing were sending more visitors to the CSMonitor.com site than ABC News, which was featuring the story on its home page. They'd also put it on their evening television broadcast, and had repeated it on their *Good Morning America* broadcast. Nevertheless, a couple of blogs were sending more visitors to the *Monitor* site than ABC News.

That's an eye-opener.

So we sort of got our arms around that in 2005 and 2006, and have since taken that insight and worked with a variety of other clients since then, some in specialist categories, like the Windows Secrets Newsletter, some in higher education, like the Wharton School, we've worked with Harlequin Romance, et cetera. In all of those cases, we found that blogs—and focusing particularly on the most influential blogs—can send more traffic to a site than chasing after the trade press. The little slogan we've come up with is, blogs are the new trade press.

Is there anything special you have to do when targeting bloggers?

Oh, absolutely. Among other things, you've got to treat them like people. Nobody likes what I would call a drive-by meeting. You need a relationship. You know what? In some respects, that's just like traditional media relations. No reporter likes getting a cold call, where the first time you talk to them is when you're pitching the story. What journalists tend to like is knowing who you are, knowing they can trust you, et cetera. So in that sense, blogger relations is a lot like media relations.

> *"You've got to get the PR people out of the silo."*

But there are differences. Among the differences is the time of day where you may want to reach a blogger. For journalists it's generally 9:00 A.M. to 5:00 P.M.—and you know you don't want to be up against their deadline in the afternoon, because we've learned over a hundred years that's a bad time to call. With bloggers, it depends on the blogger. Are they blogging more heavily on weekends? Are they blogging before they go to work or after they come home? It's getting to know who it is you're pitching, building a personal relationship with them, and understanding what works for them.

What advice would you give a company today, looking at PR as part of their online marketing mix?

You've got to get the PR people out of the silo.

For a good part of the 20th century, every part of the marketing mix was in a different silo. Advertising had its lingo and its metrics, and PR had its lingo and its metrics, and if you had a group that was focused on trade shows and events, they had their lingo and their metrics, et cetera. One of the things that is sort of a byproduct of keeping people in their silos is that things that the email marketing people learned ten years ago, or the search engine marketing people earned five years ago, the PR people in the same organization haven't learned yet. As a result, they keep doing what used to work but stopped working a long time ago, only nobody noticed.

To the extent that you can get the PR people interacting with the search people, they will discover that there are lots of things they can do together.

Sound Bites

Radical thinking—based on years of experience and solid research. That's what Greg Jarboe preaches: Stop relying (solely) on the old model and start learning how new technology can benefit your business.

In particular, pay attention to these important issues:

- Pitch your press releases directly to consumers, via web search engines.
- Optimize your press releases and online articles for best placement on Google News and other news search engines
- Think about what people are searching for, and write simple, easy-to-understand headlines accordingly.
- Measure your PR results in terms of actual sales, not press clippings.
- Recognize that blogs can drive more traffic to your site than traditional media—and treat bloggers as you would members of the mainstream press.
- Get your PR people out of their own little silo and get them interacting with other members of your marketing and technology teams.

Eric Ward: Link Marketing Consultant

10

"No matter how much you spent on it, a web site is invisible until somebody links to it."

—Eric Ward

One important part of online marketing is link building—that is, building a series of links from related sites to your site. Links are important not only because they drive traffic, but also because they help your site's ranking on Google and other search engines.

FACT SHEET: ERIC WARD

CEO, EricWard.com
(www.ericward.com)

Owner, URLwire
(www.urlwire.com)

When it comes to link building, you can't do any better than engage Eric Ward. Eric founded the web's first link-building service way back in 1994, when the web was still wet behind the ears. One of his first link-building campaigns was for Amazon.com, which itself was wet behind the ears back then. Since then, Eric has helped to build links for a large number of websites, from PBS.org to Medical.com. He has written a number of columns about the topic, and continues to be an in-demand consultant.

Building Links to Your Site

Eric was involved with the Internet before the Web exploded, back when information was accessible by Gopher and Archie and other services that only we oldsters still remember. Here, Eric shares his history with the Web and his strategy for building strong links to a web site.

Let's talk about your history. How did you get into online marketing?

I would love to make it sound as if I was prescient and realized that the Internet was going to explode, so I sold the farm and hung out my shingle. The truth of the matter is I was a victim of good luck and bad luck at the same time.

I was working in the field of advertising for a company that had really clever vertical advertising properties, but who weren't the smartest money managers. That company ended up going out of business, and I was without a job. I was in my late 20s and I knew I didn't want to work in traditional advertising, so I decided to take what little severance and savings I had and go back to grad school at night—without really knowing exactly what I wanted to do.

In visiting various departments and programs, I kept coming back to meet again and again with a woman who was, at the time, the dean of the college of library and information science, of all things. I ended up getting accepted into the grad program for library and information science.

It just so happened I was in night school at the time that the first graphical web browser, Mosaic, was released. Up until then, my fascination with the Internet was limited to Gopher, WAIS, USENET, Archie, Veronica, FTP, and Lynx, because that's all we had. All the information sites at the university level were Gopher; instead of `http://www.harvard.edu`, it was `gopher://harvard.edu`. I was at the University of Tennessee here in Knoxville, and few if any companies had web sites yet.

As I was taking those courses and learning more and more about the Internet, the dean of the college of library science ended up offering me a position. She was invited to become the vice chancellor for computing and telecommunications, on an interim basis—which was what we call now a CIO [chief information officer]. She took that position and asked me to come to work on her personal staff, as her research associate. My unstated goal was to help the university understand that it was time to migrate from Gopher to the Web. She figured I with my background probably would be pretty good for that, with sales and marketing. My passion for the Web was pretty obvious, even to her.

Anyway, I took that position and continued to go to night school, and was taking a night-school class called "Entrepreneurship in the Information

Profession." The grade in that course was based upon creating a fictitious business. You were to spend the semester researching, putting together a business plan, and then at the end of the semester you would present your idea. It was all supposed to be made up, kind of like a business-school project.

So I was riding around town, researching Internet service providers, looking for anything I could find out about online marketing. I kept noticing new web sites would

> *"Who can help them become known to the world?"*

launch and I'd think to myself, "Who knows they launched?" They're nothing but a bunch of files on a computer, no different from a Microsoft Word file; it just so happens these are HTML files on a computer that's connected to the Internet, therefore anybody can get to them. But ultimately, they can only get to them if they know they exist and somebody links to them or somebody gives you the URL. Otherwise they're invisible.

That made me wonder if there was a role for communications, public relations, publicity for these web sites. Who can help them become known to the world? In discussing this with a local Internet service provider, I asked him, "Does this sound like an idea that has any kind of merit?" This idea is like a web-based public relations service or publicist.

And they were like, "Yeah, we have to do that now for the clients that we're putting on the web. It's part of the package we sell them, but it's not one of those things that we're really organized in. If you'll do that for us, that would be great. We'll just pay you to do that." That made me realize that, gosh, my idea's not bad.

So the semester went on and I worked on my business plan and I realized, man, this idea can work. I was doing that more and more for local companies here in Knoxville, smaller sites, very first launches, everybody getting their feet wet on the Web, 1993, 1994, in that time period. Making a couple hundred bucks for doing a miniature promotional campaign for these web sites.

One of the other things I had done during that semester was I had joined one of the very first, if not the first, Internet marketing discussion lists, run by a fellow named Glenn Fleishman, who is one of my Internet marketing heroes. What I didn't know when I joined that discussion list was that lurking on that list as a member was a fellow by the name of Jeff Bezos, who was getting ready to make some noise on the web, as well.

One day, on the discussion list, I put a post out there saying, "I wanted to let the group know that I really appreciate all the information you're sharing. I work at the University of Tennessee in graduate school and I also offer a service to do publicity for web sites. There's nobody out there doing this yet, and there's no reason I couldn't offer this to you guys on the list, rather than just offering it locally."

I'll be darned if I didn't get an email back from Jeff Bezos, asking if we could talk on the phone. I distinctly remember covering the receiver with my hand to tell my girlfriend at the time, now my wife, "This guy says he's gonna sell books on the Internet. I don't think that'll work. Do you think that would ever work?" I thought he was crazy. Who knew?

To make a long story short, he hired me as the very first publicist and link builder for Amazon.com's web site. Now, he would have been successful no matter who he hired, but I'm sure glad that he hired me!

> *"Link building is the fundamental essence of the web."*

As I announced to that Internet discussion list the services I offered, and as I helped people like Jeff Bezos and some other now very famous sites, I got a reputation for being very meticulous about what I do, very white hat, not a spammer, understanding the rules of the game, doing it politely and properly and doing it well—succeeding for my clients. As the Internet frenzied and really took off in earnest in the mid- to late-'90s, people would hire me because they had heard good things about me. Within a couple of years, by 1995 or so, I was doing this full-time.

Let's talk about link building, which is what you do. What is link building, and why is it important?

Link building is the fundamental essence of the web. If you go back to Tim Berners-Lee, who wrote the hypertext [transfer] protocol (HTTP), his goal was for documents to be able to link to other documents, so that researchers, academics, and scientists could find documents more easily. So the basic essence of the World Wide Web is that it is a web of links, where anybody can link to anything. For any web page, any web site, all these years later, that fundamental essence of the web is still there. You can ask the question, "Does a web site exist if nobody links to it?"

Link building is that process of looking at any given piece of web content—an entire website, an individual web page, an image file, a podcast. Ultimately, all these things are files, whether it's HTML, PDF, Flash, GIF, or JPG, or even an MS Word document. Ultimately they're files that are on computers that are connected to the web, and links can be pointed at those files. My job is, for my clients, to help them recognize—based on whatever their content is about—what its linking potential truly is.

There's a hundred different ways to build links. There's what some people call the white hat approach, where you have a web site devoted to a particular topic, so you reach out to people who care about that topic to let them know about that site, in hopes that they'll link to it or write about it on a blog or whatever. Then there's black hat, which is trying to fool the search engines or sending out a million emails with links in them, saying "Buy Viagra today, click the below link." That's the junk stuff that's made the Internet an ugly place. But ultimately they're trying to accomplish the same thing, which is get a link in front of a mouse—meaning, get the link in front of somebody who can click it.

What are the strategies that you recommend for a site building links?

My nickname in the industry is Link Moses, for two reasons. One, I've been around longer than anybody. And two, I'm pretty vocal about staying white hat and making the Internet a more useful place, not less useful. The approaches that I recommend are always centered upon the content itself that the client has created.

On the high-end content side you have somebody like PBS.org, who is launching new web content every week. One week they may be launching web content for their PBS Kids site, for Arthur the aardvark reading content for kids, then the next week they might launch content for the science of a tsunami. Whatever content they're creating will appeal to a certain audience on the web. If PBS is launching content about volcanoes, I can go onto the web and do a search to see what are the web sites out there now that point to other volcano-related content. What people out there are blogging about volcanoes? Or teaching volcano-related subject matter in a classroom? Who are the key online influencers about topics related to geography or volcanoes? There will be an audience of writers, reporters, teachers, bloggers, librarians, even discussion lists that focuses on that topic.

What I'll do is politely engage with these influencers to let them know that PBS has launched new content that may be of interest to them. I'll try to build links from the audience that make the most sense from a subject's standpoint for any given piece of content.

Is this a hands-on thing, or is it somehow automated?

For me, every bit of it is hands-on. There are parts of the process that you can use tools to help. Google, for example; if I'm doing a project for the Discovery site devoted to asthma, for example, I can do a Google search for asthma web sites, asthma content, asthma links, asthma resources on the web. Google is a tool that helps me get closer to that potential target site.

> *"I personally do not believe in automated link requests."*

But at that point, then, it's still me and my web browser, looking at those sites, making that qualitative decision. Do I feel that this is a site that is good quality? Could I reach somebody that could make a decision about editing a link on their site to my client's site? Then I reach out to them. Sometimes I'll pick up the phone; I won't even use email. But for the most part I use email.

I personally do not believe in automated link requests. The thing I say at the conferences, when I talk about them, is any link that you can get because you have sent it to "Dear webmaster, please link to our site," is not worth it; it does not have any value. Any link you can get that way is useless, and anybody that would give you a link upon receiving an email addressed to them in that way obviously doesn't understand what they're doing and must not have content that would be useful.

I hate to say it, but it's the truth. I get them every day, "Dear webmaster, please link to us." And I delete 'em.

Obviously, some links are more valuable than others.

Absolutely—depending on how you define value.

For example, some people are interested in building links because they feel it could help their search engine rankings. And to some extent, that is absolutely true. Each of the four largest and most popular search engines all do some sort of linking analytics or assessment or analysis to determine when I do a search or you do a search on any given phrase, the sites that they rank highest will have something about their links pointing to them that the engines feel they can trust. So yes, you can try to improve your rankings via link building.

But there are also other types of valuable links that the search engines could never have found. Those are the more ephemeral or current events type of links. Maybe they're a link that can't be crawled because there's something about the URL that makes them impossible for the engines to even get to.

A link that is sent via email in the form of a newsletter, say a Yahoo! Picks of the Week, let's say that ends up in 500,000 people's inboxes. Well, that's a pretty useful link. If one out of every five people click that, you're looking at 100,000 visitors to your site the day that hits their inboxes. But that's also a link that the search engines don't even know exists. They can't crawl my personal inbox.

So when you're out trying to get links, how aggressive should you be?

I wish I could give you a statement that would be a perfect fit for all web sites. But the reality is, every web site needs a specific approach or tactic.

A great example would be if you have an e-commerce site that's purely product, and it's a generic type of product that doesn't really have a lot of loyalty to the seller—for example, tennis rackets or golf clubs. I know that I want a specific brand of racket or golf club; I don't know

> *"Every site has its own linking potential, depending on its focus and its subject matter."*

that I care where I buy it. I just want to know that I can trust the merchant, then I'm looking for a good price. Why would anybody link to that kind of content? There's 500 stores out there where I could buy the same exact tennis racket. So why is anybody going to link to one of those stores over any other store? You're going to have to be extremely aggressive and probably pay for those links.

That's a much different style and approach than when Paramount launched the web site for *Indiana Jones 4*. They really don't have to do a lot of aggressive link building. First of all, you've got built-in fan loyalty to Harrison Ford and to the movie franchise of Indiana Jones. With nothing more than a minimal link-building campaign—that will go viral almost on its own— you will have reached the majority of the most influential venues that will provide links that you were probably going to get anyway.

> *"For a majority of sites, [link building] is an ongoing process."*

Every site has its own linking potential, depending on its focus and its subject matter. Some sites need a heck of a lot more than others. I have clients to whom I've said, "You don't need to build links; don't spend money with me—you don't need it."

I was in a consult with a *Sports Illustrated* site. I said, "Guys, you have content here that every teenaged kid in America is gonna love. All you've got to do is put an announcement out there to a few strategically influential places, and watch this catch fire on its own." That's hard, sometimes, to tell them, but it's the truth.

You mentioned something earlier about paying for links. Is that a big factor?

There's any number of ways to build links to your site. Paid links just means money has changed hands. It could be as simple as I write a check to somebody or PayPal them some money and he puts a link to my site on his site, because he's selling them. I might do that for any one of a number of reasons—some of which are considered to be spam and black hat, others of which are considered to be perfectly acceptable.

If I'm a plumber and I am looking for some used tools that typically are very expensive, I do a search on Google for used plumbing tools and I land on a web site that's called UsedPlumbingTools.com (if such a site exists). If anybody sells used plumbing tools, wouldn't it make sense for them to buy a link on UsedPlumbingTools.com so they could reach me, the plumber, looking for that tool? Sure; it's a perfect match. It's not about search rank, it's not about algorithms, it's about the demographics of the audience that's at that web site. Who goes to UsedPlumbingTools.com? I dunno, how about plumbers looking for used tools. That's a natural, logical place to buy a link.

If UsedPlumbingTools.com, the web site, decided that they were going to buy links from ESPN.com or CNN.com, because they thought that was a high-value site and maybe that'll help their search rank, that's where you're starting to venture into the more gray and black hat areas. How many people that visit CNN.com every day are looking for used plumbing tools? You haven't bought the link because you're interested in finding that perfect match demographically. Now you're just after traffic and/or search rank.

And the engines, specifically Google, do not like that. They don't like it when you try to manipulate their rankings algorithm.

Is link building something that just happens when the site is new, or is it an ongoing process?

It depends on the site, but for a majority of sites, it is an ongoing process.

Now, there will be some types of content that are such high quality, so good within their niche compared to the others, that they will attract links and continue to attract links; there is a snowball effect for some content. Once you get out there with a new site and people are learning about it, finding out about it for the first time, linking to it, telling other people about it, sharing it, bookmarking it, it takes on a life of its own and it will start to attract links. Some people call it trickle-down linking; there's ways that links beget more links. Then you'll hit that point where the majority of people who ever were going to know about it and link to it will have done so.

Or you launch a web site and maybe there are only 50 people out there who care and will link to it, and as they learn about it, they'll do so. Well now what do you do? Really all you can do is try to stay up with your niche online; continually look for new resources, web sites, blogs, RSS feeds, newsletters, whatever's devoted to it, so that you can continually make sure that your site remains in the online public eye. Even though, in many cases, it will, it won't for every type of content—depending, again, on how competitive your niche is.

What are some of the common mistakes that you find companies making when they're trying to put together links?

First and foremost is the belief that there is some strategy or tactic or approach that you can use, that anybody else could use, in any sort of cookie-cutter manner. You'll see web sites selling link-building services and packaging them together, like "We'll build 300 links for $3,000." It's comical to me to think that any web site, without even knowing who the potential client is, can say that this 300-link package has any use.

What if my web site is about a narrow topic; what if it's about the mating habits of the brown bat? How many web sites are there out there devoted to that? There might not even be 300 *potential* links for that content. Likewise if your web site is devoted to the latest Britney Spears problems dot com, you might need 5,000 links to make any impact there, because that's a very popular topic.

The idea that there's a link-building package that is just perfect for you and for everybody else is crazy. Yet it's out there and being sold every day, by people who often don't realize what they're selling isn't effective. They make the mistake of thinking that, "people are buying it, it must be a great service. Let's keep selling it."

> *"Ultimately, it's a very human process to build links."*

I have so many clients who come to me and have told me, over and over, they've tried this, they've tried that, they tried this and it didn't work, what did they do wrong? It's not that they've done anything really wrong—it's just that they forgot that their content is designed to reach a very specific audience—and therefore they need a very specific link-building campaign.

So mistake number one is you cannot cookie-cutter-approach link building.

Mistake two is automating parts of the process that you really should not. Ultimately, it's a very human process to build links. At the end of the day, you're trying to get a person to do something that will help you. Why would you try to automate that? In some ways this is public relations—it's human relations. Don't automate that. Don't say "To whom it may concern" or "Dear Webmaster." Take the time to find out the name of the person who runs the web site and address them as such—"Dear Mike," not "Dear Webmaster."

When I see "Dear Webmaster, I was just looking at your web site and I thought it was great," I know that the very first thing this person did was to lie to me. My web site is EricWard.com, my logo says Eric Ward, and there's a picture of me there. If you really were visiting my web site, your email would say "Dear Eric." There's no way you could miss that. So to say

"Dear Webmaster, I was just looking at your site" is a lie. And the worst thing you can do, in my opinion, is to start a relationship out with a lie.

That makes sense. Now, what kind of advice would you give to a company that's trying to build links to their web site?

Piece of advice number one: There is absolutely no relationship between the money you spend to build links and the quality of the service you're going to get—whether you hire a consultant, hire a link builder, or buy links. Just because somebody is willing to sell you link-building services for $25,000 that somebody else will sell for $1,000 does not mean the $25,000 services are any better. Absolutely not.

I've got an inbox filled with horror stories from people who have spent a fortune for nothing. Sadly, a lot of these services play upon people's ignorance. A lot of times it's big companies and older marketing folks who didn't grow up on the web, who suddenly are in charge of web marketing, who have been told that links matter, and who trust other people to not take them. It's sad, but it happens.

So price is not indicative of quality. You have to ask questions and dig deeper.

I don't want it to sound self-serving, but sometimes the best thing you can do is spend a very little amount

> *"Take more time to do your link building than you took to build your site."*

of money to have somebody who knows what they're doing look at your site and give you some advice on what a link-building program for your site really ought to look like. And I don't mean just me. There are other people who can do that. Don't be too eager.

Take more time to do your link building than you took to build your site. People spend six months launching a web site and want links for it in a month. There's no reason to shortcut the most important process of all. No matter how much you spent on it, a web site is invisible until somebody links to it. So don't shortcut that most important process.

So what's the future—where are we going to be five or ten years from now, regarding link building?

Nobody can know for sure, but based on what I've seen over the past 15 years, links are too useful and valuable to analyze for the engines to ever give up—to say, "There's just too much spam in links now, the golden goose has been killed, we're not going to do link analysis." I think the engines will always be able to glean something from the worldwide collection of billions of links.

But what will happen is, the overwhelming majority of the links on the web will not be trustworthy, because there are just so many spammers. For every Library of Congress web site, there's gonna be a thousand sites devoted to make money fast, porn, pills, and casinos. Every day on the web there's millions more crappy links, useless links. The engines will have to continually get better and trust an ever-shrinking percentage of those links for their analysis.

The joke in the librarian world, where I came from, was librarians were asleep when the web happened; two grad students created the web's first library, Yahoo! But in some ways it's like "Revenge of the Librarians," 15 years later, because thousands of librarians have been slowly, methodically vetting and cataloging the web in every imaginable topic. And you can't buy links from them, and you can't steal links from them, and you can't scam links from them; you'll get a link because you have good content and they recognize that and it's a fit to their site devoted to your topic. I think it's wonderful that the engines can come back and forever know they can trust those links.

So where will we be in another 10 years? Probably analyzing a smaller collection of completely trustworthy links—and ignoring the vast bunch of junk that's out there.

Sound Bites

It may not be as sexy as social networking or mobile marketing, but link building is at the core of any successful web site. If you want to build high-quality links to your site, follow this advice from link builder extraordinaire Eric Ward:

- Link building should be personal—you can't automate the process.
- Search for sites that contain content relevant to your site; links from general-interest sites are worth less.
- Contact a site's webmaster directly, by name, to ask for his link.
- Don't forget non-website links—such as links in email newsletters and blogs.
- In some instances, you may have to pay for a link.

Jordan Gold: Freedom

11

"I think people are more informed because of the Internet than they were before."

—*Jordan Gold*

A confession: I've known Jordan Gold for more than a dozen years. I used to play with his son Adam, when Jordan brought the toddler into the office on weekends; I attended Jordan's wedding to his

> **FACT SHEET: JORDAN GOLD**
>
> Vice President Product Marketing, Freedom, Inc. (www.freedom.com)

wife, Karen. He's one of the good guys, and I know that from working with him firsthand.

Jordan started out as a technology journalist and then moved into the book-publishing side of the business. Early on, he became involved with the Internet—in particular, moving print media online. It wasn't an easy task then, and it's no easier today.

Books, magazines, newspapers; Jordan has worked with them all. He's helped market books online, developed magazine content into compelling web communities, and converted print newspapers into local web sites. In the process, he's helped develop online strategies and award-winning web sites for Biotrainer, Dog Fancy, Dummies.com, Databreaker, and many other old-media companies.

Marketing Print Media Online

Today, Jordan is the vice president of product marketing at Freedom Interactive, the interactive division of Freedom Communications. Freedom is one of the largest media companies in the United States, with 33 daily newspapers, 77 weeklies, and 8 TV stations in its portfolio. Jordan's current challenge is no different from what he's faced in the book and magazine businesses: turn an old media company into a new media powerhouse.

What is it that you do at Freedom?

I'm responsible for all products and content for our new interactive division. It entails working with the newspaper properties to implement technologies like Monster.com or Zvents or Brightcove, implementing best practices for content to drive user engagement, identifying products and services that will help us in terms of increasing traffic to our web site, that kind of stuff.

When you're working with your newspapers, you obviously have ideas in terms of new products and services. Who ultimately makes the decision to whether it gets done or not—the corporate office or the individual newspaper properties?

It's not that we just tell them we're going to do it; we work with them. We identify what we think we need the most and we work with the properties to implement those. It's kind of a joint thing; it's not a dictatorship.

Do you get ideas flowing up from them, also?

Absolutely. We just did a site about the Carolina Panthers that was driven entirely by one of our properties in North Carolina. There've been several other very local kinds of products that we've had driven at the property level.

Who does what when you put together a site?

> *"Just taking a newspaper and putting it online is not interesting, in the Internet sense. You have to do more."*

I don't think there are any set rules. We tend to take the development tasks on, working with our IT department, but sometimes the local properties do more of the work in that realm. Then we'll work with the properties to drive traffic, and we'll give them tips about usability, templates, things like that. So we're driving traffic in lots of different ways.

Working with the newspaper folks and trying to put content online, what challenges do you face in adapting the newspaper content for online consumption?

It's actually not any different than any other old media moving to a new media. Some of my favorite analogies are the early days of movies, where they just basically recorded plays and called them movies; the early days of television were essentially radio shows with a camera in the studio. It took awhile, in those cases, for different kinds of thinking to come about. And in the newspaper industry it's no different.

Just taking a newspaper and putting it online is not interesting, in the Internet sense. You have to do more. There's gotta be video, there's gotta be audio, there's gotta be web-friendly headlines; the length of the article is different, the tone of the article's different. Because it can be done immediately, it changes the way the

> *"That's the challenge: making sure you're customer-focused and getting your people to be customer-focused, also."*

newspaper's written. And this isn't any different from any other old media/ new media kind of transition.

When you're working with a newspaper reporter, somebody who's been doing this for years or decades, all of a sudden you want audio content and video content and all this other stuff. Do they have the skillset for all these new tasks?

We provide them with the equipment. We do training to help them. Obviously, some people are adaptable and some people aren't.

Any time that you move to a new technology, and not just in newspapers but pretty much anywhere, you're going to have people who look at this and say, I just want to do things the old way. Why can't I just keep doing things the old way? Frankly, in a customer-oriented business, you just do things the way the customer wants.

It's really not any different in any other printed medium; I've done this with books and magazines as well. You're giving customers content how they want it, when they want it, and where they want it. That's the challenge: making sure you're customer-focused and getting your people to be customer-focused, also.

Most people are adaptable, but it's always a difficult road. Any time a new media comes along, the old media people are at a bit of a disadvantage. A good example there is when books started being sold online. The old traditional bookstores were at a major disadvantage. Barnes & Noble and Borders had their physical bookstores to protect; Amazon didn't have any physical bookstores, so they created an online product that was something that customers wanted. In the case of Barnes & Noble, it took them awhile to create something that was interesting to consumers, and they really have never caught up to Amazon online. In the case of Borders, they had so many false starts that they finally just gave up—and now, if you go to Borders.com, it's actually [run by] Amazon.

[Note: Since this interview, Borders has announced that it will be discontinuing its relationship with Amazon and launching its own online bookstore.]

Your working with Freedom isn't the first time you've worked with an old media company online; you have a long history of bringing print and other old media to the new media. How did you get started working online?

I started on the Internet in 1994. I was at Macmillan Publishing and we started launching web sites for Macmillan's imprints. That included, for their computer books, Que, Sams, New Riders, and Hayden. Also, for their reference division, which included Frommers and Betty Crocker and other brands like that. We worked with Simon & Schuster and their properties to help them get online, as well.

It was truly the "bleeding edge." We didn't even have a T1 line in the building; it was kind of the early days of the Internet. Our server was in the system administrator's office with an umbrella over it in case the fire alarm/sprinkler system was activated. Just putting book content online, we learned in a hurry that we needed to do something more interesting than that.

So we put audio on the web site, and lots of graphics. This was obviously before video, but we were able to build a web site that was interesting enough to consumers that in a hurry the Macmillan web site got a lot of traffic. We were successful, to a degree, as much as you could be back then.

> "Making sure there was mention of the web site in the books…drove traffic to the web site."

At the end of the day, we still ran into issues. When we started the web site, essentially the goal was to sell more books directly to customers. We realized that, in the long run, that's probably not a good strategy, because all that does is make your [existing] channels upset.

So the web site kind of changed tack and became more informational and more oriented towards getting customers to go to their local bookstore or to Amazon or places like that. The only problem with that, of course, is that you drive people to an offline location and you have a hard time tracking the effect of your activities.

It's hard to believe that was 13, 14 years ago. What did you do back then to draw attention to this relatively new thing?

We had a strategy that really isn't unlike what you do now. Which is, we got as many people as possible to link to us—and quickly became one of the most linked-to sites on the Internet. Now, it wasn't a huge community, but we worked with different vendors and other companies and we linked to them, they linked to us. It really did help drive traffic to the site.

The other thing was, we were aggressive in making sure that our books had mention of the web site. In fact, we worked out an agreement with our production department that every book had a house ad for the web site, and every book, before it was considered 100 percent into production, had a sample chapter and a table of contents that was web-ready. Every time we published it a book, it was there.

Publishing all those books, making sure there was mention of the web site in the books—in lots of places, on the front cover, the back cover, the title page, other places in the book—drove traffic to the web site.

Think about it; between Frommers and the computer books and everything else, you're talking millions of individual advertisements every year. Using the old media to promote the new media—is that something that you still do?

Oh, yes, cross-promotion is a big deal. You have to do cross-promotion; it doesn't work otherwise.

What about moving print content online?

Before I was at Freedom, between Macmillan and Freedom, I had an Internet consulting business. One of my clients was Bowtie, Inc., which publishes *Cat Fancy* and *Dog Fancy* magazines and several other magazines and books. We launched a couple of web sites called Dog Channel (www.dogchannel.com) and Cat Channel (www.catchannel.com), which essentially took content from all their magazines that were pet-related. Bowtie has several dog magazines— *Dog World*, *Dogs for Kids*, a magazine for show dogs, they've got just a ton of different dog magazines, plus some interesting dog books. The same thing with *Cat Fancy*, *Cats for Kids*, and several other cat magazines and books.

They had had individual web sites for each of their magazines, and they were not interesting. They just put the table of contents of the magazine online, the typical moving from offline to online. They were afraid to put too much article content online.

> *"You put the same headline that you use in a newspaper article online, and it's not interesting."*

What we did is say, why don't we create just one web site for each animal that takes some of the content from each magazine, accumulate it [in] one place, make it web-friendly and interesting, and create a community of interest around that content? So that's what we did. We launched those two sites in late 2005 and immediately increased traffic. From all the dog sites combined going to the single Dog Channel, we increased traffic by 500 percent.

How do you draw people into the content you put online?

It's one thing to drive traffic to a site; it's another thing to keep people there. That's actually my main focus with Freedom—user engagement, keeping people there. What we did with Dog Channel and Cat Channel, I hired someone from an Internet company, iVillage, who had run the pet section there. We enlisted her expertise to create web-friendly headlines, plus quizzes, contests, web-only content, and a look and feel that engaged users.

That's something we're still working on with the newspaper companies. You put the same headline that you use in a newspaper article online, and it's not interesting. You take a headline that's intended to get someone to click, that becomes more interesting. Typical web-friendly headlines often have numbers in them or are somewhat mysterious. AOL and MSN do a very good job of this. Things like, "The 10 Things You Should Never Do at Work." You're gonna click on that; you just want to find out what it is. Last week there was a headline on one of the sites that said "Eagles Release ProBowl Linebacker." I had to click. Who the heck did they release?

It's things like that. It's things that are interesting, topics that are interesting, but headlines that are web-oriented. If you just put the same headlines that you would put in a traditional medium, nobody's going to be interested.

In print journalism, you go to journalism school to learn how to write headlines and leads for newspaper and magazine articles. Where does somebody go to learn the web version of this?

There's a lot of places online that teach this kind of thing. The Poynter Institute offers a course on writing web-friendly headlines and content. Actually, a lot of journalism schools, with their curriculums, are now starting to add writing for the web as a part of it. You can get a print journalism degree, but now you can get a web journalism degree.

> *"You look at the web and everything's free. How are you going to make money from that?"*

It sounds to me that it's applying a marketing focus to journalism. You're not just telling what's in the article; you're really marketing the article.

You know, it's not any different than you did before, because you always wanted to write good leads, you always wanted to write good headlines. It's really not that different.

In the past, you wrote a good lead to draw the person into the article. You wrote a good headline to draw the person into the article. They didn't have to click. You didn't need an action on their part; they already had opened the magazine or newspaper. People writing magazine covers, however— that's actually somewhat related.

Working with the magazine company and the book company, what challenges did you face in moving these guys online?

Probably the biggest thing is fear—because you look at the web and everything's free. How are you going to make money from that?

For a magazine company, it's somewhat easier, because they're already losing money on circulation. In a lot of ways, if you get rid of the circulation part and create communities of interest around content, you can make more money online than you can in print. You don't have to pay for printing, you don't have to pay for distribution, and you don't have to pay as much for acquiring readers.

But there's still fear associated with that, and there's fear associated with selling advertising, because the CPMs tend to be lower online than they are in magazines. So you probably will get less money from an advertiser than you would if you sold them a print ad, at least in the beginning.

It's difficult. It's difficult to get salespeople to sell online—they don't understand it; it's different. It's difficult to get editorial people to embrace online, because they're afraid if people are reading their articles online, then they're not reading the magazine, and eventually they're going to lose their job.

On the book-publishing side, there's still that fear that the whole book's gonna be online. But I saw that the more of the book that you put online, the more copies that you sold anyway. I think that's because the more someone can see it, the more likely they are to buy it. They're not necessarily just going to pick what they want to read, and then that's it.

So being online serves as advertising for the book?

Exactly. And that's not any different than if you go into Barnes & Noble and they have couches and chairs where you can sit and read a book as long as you want. They haven't found that that negatively affects sales, because they're building, essentially, a community of interest from people coming in, and they tend to buy books. Same thing online, if you can build that community of interest.

We tried, when we first launched the Macmillan web site, to take the whole book superstore approach and put in a [virtual] coffee shop. We tried to do a deal with Starbucks, who wasn't online at the time.

It was like selling coffee beans and such.

> *"What we're looking for is reach. The more people in the market that we get, the better."*

Yeah, exactly. But they weren't that interested, and it was just kind of cute; it really wasn't the same kind of experience.

But now, with user-generated content and the ability to do comments and things like that, you do have a much more interesting opportunity.

Do you find, with the magazines and now with the newspapers, that if you have a good web site, that it favorably affects circulation of the periodicals?

What we're looking for is reach. The more people in the market that we get, the better. Typically, newspapers have several times more people looking at the web site than actually subscribing to the newspaper. Which is interesting.

On the magazine side, I think it does help. One of my pet peeves is I'll read an article in a magazine, it will link to something else and say "For more information, go to our web site and we've got all this stuff," and you go to the web site and they really don't. You either can't find it or it's not that interesting.

> *"In general, newspapers are the number-one local web site in every market."*

One example of that: I was reading an article last week in *The Sporting News*, and they said "Go to SportingNews.com, there's an additional article about this subject." I went there and couldn't find it. I thought, wow, that's just a bad user experience. You should never do that.

Some newspapers across the country do a good job online. On the other hand, I've run into newspapers across the United States that at best are just articles put online—and sometimes they're not even that. Which ones get it and which ones don't? What are the factors?

The newspaper companies with a large preponderance of metros, large circulation in large cities, they have to get it. They've been affected by the Internet more than newspaper companies with a large preponderance of smaller community newspapers. But, in general, newspapers are the number-one local web site in every market.

So visitors go to the newspaper site, as opposed to a radio site or a television news site.

Right. But that's getting more competitive, so newspapers have to react.

This is an evolving process. Most newspaper companies are getting it; it's just taking some more time than others.

Obviously, you have to promote your companies online, other than just in the newspapers. What are the best media that you have to draw traffic to your sites?

It's search engine marketing. It's doing pay-per-click. That's the best way to drive traffic.

Who do you use?

We use everybody. Google, Yahoo!, MSN—we use all three. Some people go to Google, some people go to Yahoo!, some people go to MSN. Google's got the lion's share, but those three combined are right around 90 percent of all search-engine traffic.

There are other ones that are interesting, but the problem is, you get to the second or the third tier of search engines, you start to run into more dubious type of traffic, such as click fraud. You get people from other countries who are just clicking. It's just not a good idea to go to some of these second- and third-tier search engines.

I have friends who say they just don't have time to read the daily newspaper any more. Do you think that the move online will change that, that we'll get more people being more informed?

I think people are more informed because of the Internet than they were before. They used to have to run home and watch the national news, and of course nobody does that anymore. I think they are more informed.

If you can fast-forward five years, what are the newspaper and magazine web properties going to look like?

They are going to be very local, more local than the newspapers are now. They're going to be personalized, so that you get what you want, when you want it. Major multimedia—everything in every format. Communities of interest, so that you can comment on articles, you've got friends that you are communicating with online. Maybe even your own home page online, as well. And they will be compelling and interesting.

Sound Bites

Few people have Jordan Gold's experience marketing old media properties in the online world. But it's been good experience; he knows the challenges faced by print media companies, and by their employees. And he knows how to work around those challenges and take advantage of the marketing synergies between the old and new media properties.

What can you learn from Jordan's experience? Here are some of the most salient points:

- You have to get past the fear of obsolescence and show print management and staff the opportunities that exist online.
- Work with existing print employees to help them develop the new skills they need for the online world.
- Don't expect existing print content to translate as is to the web; you need web-friendly headlines and articles to attract web visitors.
- Take advantage of marketing synergies by promoting the website in the print publications, and vice versa.

Heather Lloyd-Martin: SuccessWorks

12

"Do you ever want to sacrifice tone and feel for what you know the search engines are looking for on a page? That answer is no."

—Heather Lloyd-Martin

In the previous chapter we touched on the topic of online copywriting, in particular how writing for a web site is different from writing for traditional print media. No one knows that better than Heather Lloyd-Martin, who makes her living writing copy for web sites large and small.

FACT SHEET: HEATHER LLOYD-MARTIN

Chief Executive Officer, SuccessWorks
(www.searchenginewriting.com)

Heather is the CEO of SuccessWorks, a firm that offers web copywriting and consulting services. She's recognized as the pioneer of what is known as SEO copywriting, and her e-book *Successful Search Engine Copywriting* is considered a best-practices guide in the field. Heather is also a member of the Internet Marketing Advisory Board and is chair of the Direct Marketing Association's Search Engine Marketing Council. She speaks at various industry conferences and has written articles for Inc.com, ClickZ, and other online and offline publications.

Copywriting for the Web

A lot of web sites feature really lousy copy. You can't just transfer copy from a print ad or direct mail piece to the web and expect it to be effective. The web requires a different style of writing, and it also requires you to optimize your copy for search engines. That's right; when you're writing for the web you're writing for the site's visitors *and* for the Google and Yahoo! search bots. Sound complicated? Then read on to learn some valuable tips from copywriter extra-ordinaire Heather Lloyd-Martin.

Can you talk a little about your background and what it is that you do?

I have always been in writing, in one form or another, especially copywriting. I started back in the print world. I would do a lot of display ad copywriting, some advertorials for clients, a lot of press releases. Back in the early days of the Internet—we're talking '96 to '97—I would create introductory Internet marketing strategies. But I hadn't got into search yet.

It was about 1998, 1999 that search was just starting to be considered as a more mainstream Internet marketing strategy—although most people didn't know how it worked. Back then it was considered just a bunch of back-end code tweaks. Nobody talked about the marketing aspect of search engine optimization.

> *"Reading online is harder than reading something in print."*

A woman from a business discussion list emailed me and said, "I do search engine optimization for clients, and I know that the writing is important. I want to have good writing on their web site and I also want keywords on the pages. Can you help me do that?"

At the time, I was writing for *Entrepreneur Magazine's Business Start-Ups* and writing a lot of "how to start a business" articles, as well as doing some print and online copywriting, so that seemed like a very interesting place to go. Again, search engine optimization was considered very new and technical back then.

So we started working together; her name is Jill Whalen and she still works in search today. We started a newsletter, which we discontinued, called the Rank Write newsletter, that talked about search engine optimization and how content played a part.

[Note: Jill is currently the CEO of High Rankings, and the subject of our interview in Chapter 17.]

That's really how it started. When everyone was trying to find their space in the search world, we started a newsletter where I would talk about how writing content really goes back to direct marketing principles; you're just doing this with the search engines as another target group. Jill focused more on the actual optimization side and how to work with a site. The rest is history. From there, we did speaking engagements as a team and also, since then, individually.

In 2000 or so, when I would talk about how important content was to search engine optimization, people would get up and leave. They said search engine optimization has nothing to do with content, it has to do with making the technical tweaks. Now, I'm speaking all over the world to people who are heavily engaged in learning about SEO copywriting. For many folks SEO content writing is their full-time job—either in-house for a corporation or on their own as a freelancer. SEO copywriting started from nothing, less than 10 years ago, to something now considered another niche of online copywriting and a respected part of the optimization process. It's been fun!

I know it's hard to generalize, but who is writing the copy on web sites today? Is it marketing people, is it copywriters, or is it technical people or designers?

It's across the board right now.

Many times the designers are writing the copy because they consider that part of "building the site." They might not know anything about how to write for engines, but they feel like any type of copy creation should come from them.

Within larger corporations, the marketing department typically writes the content. A lot of times that marketing department might not know how to write for search. But they are good writers who can be trained.

Smaller businesses have it rough. It's typically the owner who is writing the content—with no idea how to write for engines and no idea, in a lot of cases, how to write good compelling content. It's all do-it-yourself.

And every once in a while—and I see this less than I used to—it is the technical team that writes the pages. Although these folks are typically great at technical tweaks, they are not often the best copywriters. Sales and conversion often suffer when IT writes the copy.

Before we get into the whole search engine optimization part of copywriting, can you talk a little bit about how copywriting for the web might be different from writing for other media?

Writing for the web is a different kind of medium for several reasons.

Reading online is harder than reading something in print. The joke is, if you've been working online long enough, you're probably needing glasses, because all you're doing is squinting at a computer screen. You lose a lot of your readability online. That's where a good, web-friendly layout and tight writing come into play.

For example, take a direct mail type of layout, where it's typically two pages double-spaced. Sure, that's easy to read if you have the letter in front of you. However, if you translate that same layout into an online environment, people will not necessarily scroll through two pages of copy to take action.

> *"You want to have your main benefit statements above the fold."*

From an online-copywriting perspective, we know how people look at a web page to find the information they want. The calls to action need to be placed in strategic areas of the screen real estate that are easy to spot. The copy blocks need to be a lot shorter because long copy blocks can seem overwhelming to a reader. And keyphrases should be strategically placed within the copy—which is something you don't need to worry about when you're writing for print.

Writing for the web is a faster direct-response medium, in that every hyperlink is like a little conversion. So, that means learning to write for that faster conversion medium. That doesn't mean that people make the macro conversion right there and automatically buy from you; but every time people click deeper into your site, it engages them more. It helps encourage that eventual purchase, however that sales cycle works for a particular company—which could be months with a B2B (business-to-business) or moments with a B2C (business-to-consumer).

Is there a general rule in terms of how much scrolling you should do or not do, versus clicking to additional pages?

It depends on the industry.

When it comes to prime copy placement, writing for online is similar to writing for print because you want to have your main benefit statements above the fold. People will scroll down and read additional copy below the fold. But the above-the-fold copy is what engages them and keeps them reading.

People in technical fields are often happy to download an entire white paper and read it off the monitor. Some research supports that longer copy is better for that kind of industry. So people will scroll. They just have to be engaged with what they're reading—and the layout has to be clean and easy to navigate.

> *"The search engines need to see the keywords on the page."*

Now let's get into the SEO aspect of copywriting. What do you need to do?

A lot of the principles are exactly the same as direct response. The only difference is, you always have to keep another target audience in mind—the search engines.

Do you ever want to sacrifice tone and feel for what you know the search engines are looking for on a page? That answer is no. You're always going to be writing that copy for your main target audience.

At the same time, the search engines need to see the keywords on the page for them to consider that page relevant for keyword queries. Thousands of different things make up the algorithm of why a page will position number 1 versus 1001, but we know one of the main parts of the algorithm is the content and how the content is presented.

For example, if you're writing a direct-response sales piece, then we know that things like headlines and subheadlines are critical. They allow readers a very quick-glance way for folks to review your benefit statements and learn what you offer. If they like what they read, then they can go back and read more detailed information.

> *"Keyphrase research is incredibly important."*

In the search engine world, subheadlines and headlines are important. They're emphasized text, and the search engines consider words that appear in emphasized text more relevant. So keyphrases within that text can have a bit of a relevancy boost that helps the overall page position.

Keyphrase research is incredibly important. Keyphrase research tools, like KeywordDiscovery.com and Wordtracker.com, allow us to type in, say,

"Portland Oregon travel" and find related keyphrases that people are searching when their intent is to find out about Portland, Oregon travel.

Another different aspect is including keyphrases in hyperlinks. From a search engine perspective, hyperlinks are incredibly important, because hyperlinks are how the search engines find new pages and find new sites. To have a keyphrase within the hyperlink, for example, "Portland Oregon travel," instead of "Click here," helps build the relevancy of that particular keyphrase, thus increasing the possibility that that page is going to position better in the engine. In other words, instead of "Click here for Portland Oregon travel information," where "Click here" is the hyperlink to another page, "Portland Oregon travel" would be the main keyphrase and would also be the hyperlink.

A copywriter who wants to learn more about SEO copywriting needs to know how the search engines work—how the search engines think and how they parse a page and how they look at that data. But once you understand how the search engines work—which, again, is like a different type of audience—then it's easy to fold in the additional steps to write for the engines. It's easy to create content that has the corporate flavor a business wants—but at the same time will also position in the top 10 or top 20 results for a particular keyword query.

It seems like if someone focuses too much on the SEO you might get a lot of keywords in the copy, but not compelling copy.

That happens all the time. I call it the "Easy-Bake Oven" approach to SEO copywriting. There's a myth that if writers just shove as many of the keyphrases as they can into a 250-word text block, they've done their job. I've even reviewed copywriting courses where the examples they use are what's called "keyphrase stuffed," where it sounds like: "Our cashmere sweaters are the best cashmere sweaters. This is a cashmere sweater store for cashmere sweater prices."

That is a bastardized version of SEO copywriting. What it does is ignore direct marketing principles. It ignores the primary target audience—your customers. The search engines are not paying your bills; they are not going to buy from your site. Your customers do. Even if you (temporarily, until the search engines penalize the page) position at number one because you've stuffed your pages with keyphrases, you're not necessarily going to benefit. Customers will come in, read that content, not feel comfortable about making a purchase, then back away to find a competitor that has balanced writing so the customers are first, rather than the search engines.

What might be some of the other common mistakes that you find in online copywriting today?

Keyphrase stuffing is a big one. The opposite is when no keyphrases appear on the page—or the keyphrases might appear in a graphic. So you might have a pretty catalog site with text inside the pretty pictures, but the search engines can't read the text inside the graphics.

The page title is something that marketers should control as much as possible. The title is the blue bar above every web page, which also appears as the clickable link on the search engine results page. Many times, people consider titles as just code with no marketing benefit. But titles are actually like headlines, compelling the reader to click through to the landing page.

Yes, titles should have keyphrases in them because the title is such an important code element. But what's also important is what Yahoo! talks about, the clickability of the title. Think of titles like a headline. You want someone to see that result on

> *"The search results page is your first opportunity for conversion."*

the search results page and think, "Okay, this company has exactly what I want, so I'm going to click on their link versus the nine others that are vying for my attention on the page." The search results page is your first opportunity for conversion; it's not when they hit your site.

Really short copy can be another SEO copywriting mistake. Short copy typically does not position as well. From the search engine perspective, if you're trying to work keyphrases into your content and you're only working with, let's say, 75 words, it's difficult to make those keyphrases flow within your content without making it sound keyphrase stuffed. If it's keyphrase stuffed, you lose any type of tone and feel, and conversions suffer.

Around 250 words is what I say is a good fuzzy rule of thumb per page. Some pages can definitely be less, because you might not have as much to write about. Some pages might be more; for example, the technical folks, as we talked about earlier, might enjoy and benefit from longer copy. But if you write 25 words on a product, you're not controlling what you can control with Google—and the odds of positioning are not as great. Can you write more than one page around a product or service? Yes! That's not a problem. Prospects love sites with lots of good information. They just don't need to see all your information packed on one page.

What advice would you give to a traditional copywriter moving online, trying to get his feet wet in this?

My advice is to learn about how the search engines work. The more you know about the search engines and how they work, the more you can get paid as an SEO copywriter, because you can start doing some really advanced strategy of how content can work with a dynamically driven site.

If you're just getting your feet wet, you can learn how the search engines work by reading. Wiley has *Search Engine Optimization for Dummies* (Peter Kent, Wiley Publishing, 2nd Edition, 2006). And possibly attending a conference, maybe a local conference, or a national conference. That will help you understand the "why" behind the "how to."

As far as SEO copywriting training and how you would learn more about it, some resources online are helpful. One resource is my online book *Successful Search Engine Copywriting*. Resource sites such as SEOCopywriting.com and SearchEngineLand.com have information about what SEO copywriting is and how to integrate best practices into your writing. Training is available; some of it is locally based, where someone conducts a half-day seminar in SEO 101 and the basics of SEO copywriting. Classes at major conferences discuss what SEO copywriting is and how to set up your own site or clients' sites. Sometimes the best way to learn is to contact an SEO copywriter and say, "I want to learn all about that you do. I'm willing to work for a discounted rate because I know that you're training me. But my eventual goal is to become a member of your team."

I've worked with a number of copywriters who have used that technique, because they're motivated, they have good skills, and they want to learn how to do everything right from the ground up. Once they have the training, the career possibilities for a SEO copywriter are truly endless.

Sound Bites

Even if you're an experienced copywriter, you need to fine-tune your craft to write effective web copy. As noted by Heather-Lloyd Martin, that means doing the following:

- Get your main message "above the fold" on the first screen of your page.
- Include relevant keyphrases in your copy, including your page's title, so search engines can find and rank your site.
- Don't hide keyphrases in graphics; they have to be in bot-readable copy.
- Don't stuff keyphrases into your copy; remember your primary audience consists of your site's users, not the search engines.
- When you're including keyphrases in copy, slightly longer copy is better than shorter copy.

And remember: You're the marketing person. Don't let the tech people or designers write your site's copy; the best content is derived from a marketing perspective.

Chris Baggott: Compendium Blogware

13

"It used to be that if you wanted sophisticated marketing tools, you had to be rich. That's not the case on the Internet. Anyone can compete, just at different levels."

—*Chris Baggott*

Chris Baggott is one of those guys who can't keep still. He started out in the corporate world, got bored there, and decided to become an independent business-man instead. That kept his attention for a while, and then he got inter-ested in the Internet and Internet marketing. That led to his co-found-ing ExactTarget, a firm that provides email marketing services to other companies large and small. While he was helping ExactTarget grow into the largest email marketing firm on the web, Chris got interested in blogging, through his own Email Marketing Best Practices blog. Now

> **FACT SHEET: CHRIS BAGGOTT**
>
> Co-Founder and CEO, Compendium Blogware (www.compendiumblogware.com)
>
> Co-Founder and Former Chief Marketing Officer, ExactTarget (www.exacttarget.com)
>
> Blogger, Email Marketing Best Practices Blog (exacttarget.typepad.com) and Blogging Best Practices Blog (blogging.compendiumblog.com/blog/blogging-best-practices/)

blogging was his passion, which inspired Chris to launch his latest company, Compendium Blogware. Compendium offers software and services to help companies launch and manage their own corporate blogs, and to use those blogs to market themselves. Naturally, Chris has a new blog to support this new effort, the Blogging Best Practices blog.

Somewhere in there Chris found time to write a book about email market-ing, *Email Marketing by the Numbers* (2007, Wiley). He also travels to 50-some

conferences a year, speaking on both email marketing and blog marketing—
and how the two work together.

Blog Marketing and Email Marketing: Attracting and Maintaining Customers

In moving from email marketing to blog marketing, Chris has created solutions to both sides of the customer equation. Blog marketing is a powerful
tool for attracting new customers, while email marketing is equally powerful
in maintaining the customer relationship. And, as Chris explains in this interview, these are tools that businesses of any size can utilize; in fact, a savvy
small business can use blogs and email to more than effectively compete
against the big guys.

**Let's start with a little background. Can you tell us where you
started out from, and how you got to where you are today?**

My basic background, career-wise, is in database marketing, specifically in
catalog marketing. I spent a number of years with the R.R. Donnelly organization, in both Chicago and New York, primarily focused on letting catalogers use their data to send better catalogs with better timing.

It was always very frustrating, though, because I could only know so much
about you and I still had to send this hundred-page book. And I've got to
send it February 2nd, which may or may not be spring for you, right? You
may live in Atlanta and spring may be February 2nd, or you may live in
Minnesota, where it's not going to be spring until May 2nd. So that was
always been a nagging problem of mine.

I was married in Chicago and my wife is from Indiana and we decided that
we did not want to grow old in New York. So we packed up and moved to
Indiana and I started a dry cleaning business.

The real idea behind the dry cleaners was their database. I was looking
around at different kinds of businesses to get into and dry cleaning seemed
very mom and pop-ish; it hadn't been consolidated, and it had a great database. The customer comes in, says, "Hi, I'm Chris, I live on Maple Street.
I'll be back on Tuesday."

Tell me all my new customers? Well, I know that. Tell me people who've
spent $100 a month that I haven't seen for 10 days. Tell me people who
bring me shirts but never bring me pants.

So the database possibilities were really huge, compared to clients I'd worked with at Donnelly in the retail space, like a MacDonald's or something. They have no clue who their customers are. So I thought, here's an advantage.

So we went out and built a database. And, after we spent a ton of time building this database, we realized that, holy smokes, we have absolutely no way to really leverage this data. I can't talk to people in the micro-segments that I want to talk to them.

This gets us toward 1997, 1998. I started playing around with my AOL and email, and said, "Wow, I wonder if my customers have email?" That's kind of how it all evolved.

We started pulling lists from our database and sending AOL emails. That gradually evolved into FrontPage and Outlook pastes, and then doing this as a service for other

> *"In the future, almost all acquisition will be through search."*

dry cleaners. We quickly decided, hey man, there's something here. It became a better business than the dry cleaning. And we started building software to perform what we were doing manually.

That's sort of the evolution. ExactTarget is now the largest company in the industry, based in Indianapolis with almost 300 employees. Every kind of business from the smallest dry cleaners to the largest Internet companies in the world is now on the ExactTarget platform.

Our new business is Compendium Blogware, which focuses on the front end of the relationship. How do I win a search organically, and then how do I convert people? Whereas email is a great tool for conversion and retention, it's not a good tool for acquisition. Search is a great way to acquire new customers. In the future, almost all acquisition will be through search, we believe.

Let's focus first on the email marketing. What exactly is it that ExactTarget does for a company?

ExactTarget is an email service provider. At the low end of the spectrum, we help small businesses and businesses of any size, really, create, send, and then track their emails. So we have a nice user interface that allows anybody with very, very few web skills and no technical skills to use a sophisticated tool to create good-looking HTML emails without having to know anything about HTML. Then we deploy those emails, we send them and we get them into the inboxes, and then we report back what happened to those.

You're also managing the database of names?

In the small businesses, yes. The real revolution, and we hit it with ExactTarget, was focusing on the data. When email evolved, and it's still a lot this way, most marketers were focused on the reach and frequency model: I buy a big list of catalog prospects and I dump a ton of catalogs out there, and I hope enough of them hit and those people buy that I cover my costs. The more names I can buy, the more catalogs I can send, the more money I'll make. It was very much this pound, pound, pound, carpet-bomb universe. That's your mass-marketing tactics.

When email came along, it kind of first fell into the hands of mass marketers. What happened was, they were using mass-marketing tactics with the new medium. So now they're saying, holy smokes, I can reach more people because it's so cheap, right? So it became this cheap paper that they're just going to distribute more and more of it. It was never about putting any additional value to the database.

The way ExactTarget approached this problem was that we've always been about the database. We don't really have lists, so much. It's more integration to other databases, or what is the right message to the right person at the right time.

> *"[It adds] a whole layer of what I call 'marketing democracy' to the system."*

It's just like the catalog problem. I want to talk to new customers this week. So at the end of the week, every Friday, I send an email. If I'm a small business, I'm going to send an email to all my new customers that week. "Dear Mary, thanks for coming into our store on Maple Street. We really appreciate your business, and here's a coupon for your second visit." Because my database tells me if I can get people to come in three times, I'll have them for a year. If I can only get them to come in once, well, 80 percent of the people who come in once disappear forever. So I need to get that second visit.

There's intelligence that starts working into this, versus just, "This is my sweater sale," and I send it out to 10,000 people.

ExactTarget really, really focuses on the database. So for smaller businesses, we'll host their database. For larger businesses, we integrate. We have what's called an application programming interface, or an API, that integrates with any other data sources and makes all this data talk together.

This is the common theme, all of these tools working together to give me this central view of the customer. Omniture can be my web analytics vendor, ExactTarget can be my email vendor, Compendium can be my blogging vendor, CrownPeak is my content management vendor, Salesforce is my database, and all those tools work within that. And you know what? Some day, if I don't like Omniture any more, I can unplug it and plug in WebTrends or WebSideStory or something else.

That's the great model. It's very, very flexible, but what it also does is add a whole layer of what I call "marketing democracy" to the system. Because now these tools are so inexpensive that really what you pay for is consumption. Small companies

> *"Marketing now is about the person, about the relationship, about the individual."*

can buy a little bit, big companies can buy a lot, but they're all using the same tools. It used to be that if you wanted sophisticated marketing tools, you had to be rich. That's not the case on the Internet. Anyone can compete; just at different levels.

Given that you can really fine-tune the marketing promotions, campaigns, and mailings via email, as opposed to the way it used to be in print, what kind of return rates do you look at? A typical print campaign, you're talking the low single digits in terms of returns. What do you look at via email?

You have to think of email as a component now. Seth Godin's got this great analogy about getting married. A typical marketing guy is like a guy going into a bar to get married. He walks up to every woman he sees, maybe not even that discriminate, "Will you marry me? Will you marry me? Will you marry me? Will you marry me? Will you marry me?" in the hopes that one person or two people might say yes.

The model of marketing in 2007 and beyond is much more about the relationship. So now we have all these tools, we can manage long-term relationships. It's not about campaigns. A campaign is a dirty word to Internet marketers.

I've got these flowers to sell today. I've got to come up with a campaign to sell these flowers. I don't care who I sell them to, where I sell them, as long as I sell them for this price by this date. That's a campaign.

Marketing now is about the person, about the relationship, about the individual. Now the goal is I want Chris Baggott as a customer because I want Chris Baggott to buy $10,000 worth of flowers over the next five years. How do I get that relationship going? Well, slowly. Baby steps. Is this seat taken? May I sit down? My name's Chris. Can I buy you a drink? Where are you from? That's how we build relationships.

> *"It's return on customer, not return on campaign."*

To say I can do an email campaign and get this kind of return, compared to a direct mail campaign, is really asking the wrong question, if you will. Because it's all about lifetime value and the return on the customer.

Some people may take two emails a year. Some people may take 200 emails a year. But the fact is, the medium is so inexpensive, it's all about measuring what you actually wind up with from that customer over the lifetime of that customer.

So what type of mailings would a typical firm send out, and how frequently?

It depends. Let's take an example of American Airlines. I'm a platinum flyer on American Airlines. They love me, I mostly love them. Every Wednesday I get this email called "Chris Baggott, here are your weekend escapes." These are options for me to take this weekend. Except I live in Indianapolis, and if you've ever seen one of these emails, it has about a hundred different city combinations on it, none of which are Indianapolis.

I get that same email every Wednesday. I know what you're talking about.

So that is a campaign. That is a waste of time that trains me to delete, delete, delete, and demeans the brand.

Now, as a campaign, it might be, for all I know, very successful. They seem to have a lot of L.A. trips on there, so maybe they get a very high response rate from people in L.A. They look at the cost, and they say, well geez, that cost me $5,000 to send 5 million emails, and I made $25,000 in ticket sales; this is a good deal," except they didn't make anything off Chris Baggott.

In fact, they may have annoyed Chris Baggott by sending that out.

Right. Now if you say, my goal is Chris Baggott, times five million, maybe the people in L.A. do get an email every single week, because they have a lot of trips coming from L.A. or Dallas, where their hubs are. Maybe Chris only gets five emails a year, because I only have five trips from Indiana that I can give away on my weekend escapes a year. So I'm never going to see them, mixed in with these other 52 emails times a hundred different pieces of content. I'm only going to see it if they say, "Chris, by the way, welcome back from Seattle. Glad your plane was on time. I know it's probably too soon for a weekend escape, but I can get you to San Francisco this weekend and back Sunday night for X amount of dollars."

Well, you know what? I'd probably respond very highly to that.

You know what I'm saying? You can't look at the mesh; you've got to look at the individual. Every single email now is an individual communication. It's return on customer, not return on campaign. You can't say, I sent out 2 million emails and then made 500 bucks. Is that good or bad? I don't know. But chances are, if you did something like that you've probably annoyed 3 million people. Most customers send less email when they come to a company like ExactTarget.

How does a company keep from annoying their customers? There's a fine line between a useful email and spam, in the customer's eyes.

Exactly. Gartner calls it "permission spam." I signed up. I wanted to hear weekend escapes from American Airlines. I like American Airlines. But they're just spamming me. They're not holding up to their promise.

The way that you can do this in email or in all Internet media is, just listen. You pay attention. If you're not opening my emails, if you're not engaging in them, I better slow down the frequency and think why that is. I better do some testing and variables and things like that to keep you engaged.

Maybe ask me, "Geez, Chris, you signed up for these weekend escapes and in two years you've never taken a weekend escape. What's the story?" Because it's a human-to-human interaction. It's not institutions-to-many, which is what mass marketing is. It really gets us to that one-to-one.

I've got a database. Chris Baggott opted into weekend escapes. Over a period of time I realize he's not even opening the emails, he's never taken a weekend escape. Why not? You know what I'll tell you: Because they don't originate in Indiana. Why don't you just tell me all the Indiana trips? A light bulb goes off in their heads and they send me Indiana.

It's a dialog. That's what's great about all these metrics. Any kind of database marketing is all driven by customers' behavior. They're telling you; all you have to do is listen, and then respond appropriately.

I have this joke I use in presentations, where I talk about what goes wrong with relationships. When your wife is angry with you, what's the problem? Well, the problem is, you're not listening! And then the problem is, you're not responding appropriately. "Uh huh, that *does* make your butt look fat." Obviously, you weren't listening. And even if you were listening, you didn't respond appropriately.

What's wonderful about the universe we live in is that was never possible before. When Sam the butcher from *The Brady Bunch* had his little shop and knew all of his customers by name and face, he could obviously listen and respond appropriately, treat each customer a little bit differently. Everyone felt special, everyone enjoyed the relationship, and Sam made a lot of money in the butcher business.

> *"In email, even a negative reaction is still a reaction that you can listen to and adjust your tactics accordingly."*

As that scales beyond the ability for any one person to manage, that's when it falls apart, because there's no other way to have a relationship with people. You can meet them face-to-face. You can talk to them on the phone. Beyond that there's nothing—except for email. Everything else is a one-way, pound-on-you medium. Television, radio, billboards, newspapers, magazine ads, direct mail flyers, brochures, everything else is one-way. You have no idea how the customer's reacting to that. In email, even a negative reaction is still a reaction that you can listen to and adjust your tactics accordingly.

This new type of marketing seems like it takes more work and intelligence to do. How big a company do you have to take advantage of this?

Well, it takes more intelligence. It doesn't take more work. It actually takes less work, because the systems are all in place.

Think about if I want to do a direct mail flyer, what I actually have to do to execute on that. I've got to think about what I want, I've got to write copy, I've go to design it, I've got to run it around my office, I've got to send it to a printer, then I have to send it to a mail house. Then it has to be distributed, then I have to sit back there with my phone staff hoping the right thing will happen. That's a lot of work.

Execution, you know. Forrester has a study that talks about the pain of marketing, 83 percent of which is in execution, not actual marketing; not thinking up the ideas, but actually doing them.

On the Internet, execution is simple. That's where you get into this whole concept of democracy.

I have a friend who owns a liquor store. She's running Compendium software to run her blog, she's running ExactTarget to run her emails. That's basically her business. She does a little bit of advertising to build a brand, gets people to the site, they sign up, opt in, she listens. She has a frequent-buyer club, so she keeps

> *"Before, great marketing ideas never saw the light of day because the pain of executing them was too hard."*

track in her database. Chris Baggott seems to go through a fifth of Jim Beam every week and likes merlots. Well, that's what she should be talking to me about. And if a week goes by that I don't buy my fifth of Jim Beam, maybe she triggers an email saying, "Hey, Chris, we've got a special on Jim Beam next week, two bottles for the price of one," to get me reactivated.

The database is telling her what to do and everything triggers from the database, so all she's doing is contemplating different great marketing ideas. Before, great marketing ideas never saw the light of day because the pain of executing them was too hard.

So the small business and the large business can all use these tools, because they're cheap. You pay for them by usage.

There's this conception that small businesses aren't smart. We know that's not the truth. They are smart; they're just resource-constrained. What's great about Internet marketing tools is that they don't cost anything.

So you're saying that these new tools, the new way of doing things, can actually make a small business appear to be a large business, in terms of how they do things?

Or at least be successful in what they do. There's nothing about appearances necessarily; it's just presence.

Home Depot is a client of mine, and True Value Hardware Store in Greenfield, Indiana is a client of mine. True Value is run by one guy and Home Depot is run by mega staff. Think about their marketing. Home Depot will destroy this little local True Value in every marketing metric known to man. Home Depot is going to beat him on TV, direct mail, newspaper ads—except online. Because True Value can be online, he can have a web site, he can have as deep an inventory (through distributors) to be the fulfillment and back end. He can do email just as well; he can obviously do the web just as well. He can blog.

> "A blogging platform enables you to allow lots of people within your organization to talk about your business."

Then you get down into the intangibles of what can the True Value guy do better than Home Depot. Well, the True Value guy can localize. The True Value guy, he goes to my church. The True Value guy's kids play on my kids' soccer teams and football teams. The True Value guy supports Little League in my community. The True Value guy helped build a house for Habitat for Humanity, with his own hands. He's actually got an advantage now, because of Internet marketing. Now he has the ability to actually put a human face on his business.

So now I've got this faceless Home Depot and I've got equal product, relatively equally priced, and a guy I really like. You know who's going to get my business at the end of the day? The guy who I really like.

Zig Ziegler said this, a hundred years ago: People buy from people. That's what's really great as we flip over to the blogging side and social networking side. What's great about all that is that human beings are now getting involved in Internet marketing. It's not institutions-to-many; it now gets much, much closer to one-to-one, as Peppers and Rogers tried to teach us in 1992, the one-to-one future. The fact is, back then, it was the future, because there was no way to do this. But now, with Internet marketing technologies, it's in fact easy.

Explain, then, how a company can incorporate blogging as part of the marketing mix.

A blogging platform enables you to allow lots of people within your organization to talk about your business, to talk about what they do and their role in it, and how they help customers. It depends on the scenario.

I have a friend who owns a camera shop, a retailer. He's got four or five people blogging all about photography and cameras. One guy's a video expert; another guy's a digital 35mm expert. And they just blog. They just fill that space with content about what they love and what they're passionate about.

What happens is—and part of this is what Compendium does— the search engines love that. So companies are beating their heads against the wall with paid search, when blogging will get them ranked for free in the organic [search]. And 90 percent of the clicks on a Google page happen on the organic results. It's really, really important to score well on that. So again, that's another place where blogging helps you with [customer] acquisition, because it helps you win the search.

Blogging also helps you with the conversion. Because if I'm shopping for a camera and I see Wal-Mart has it at this price, I've got to go someplace else to get a review. And all these other vendors, who I've never heard of, are trying to sell me this camera. Meanwhile, there's Frank,

> *"Blogs, by definition, are much better for search engine optimization than a traditional web page."*

and Frank works at this camera shop, and Frank loves this camera and Frank has examples of the beautiful pictures he takes and here's this seminar Frank runs every Tuesday night. And, you know, Frank is going to get my business.

Price and brand are no longer differentiators. Anyone can sell any brand for almost any price. So now it comes down to the intangibles. It comes down to who do I like, who do I trust, who's going to take care of me, who do I want to have a relationship with. And that's where things like blogging and other social networking technologies are really shaking up the Internet acquisition world.

What does a company have to do to turn their blog viewers into paying customers?

The obvious answer is to convert them, right?

Yeah, but how?

Just like on any other web page. You have to suspend what you know about blogging and what a blog might look like. A blog can look almost like a web page. There's no reason why you can't have a bar running down the side with your specials of the week, or a call to action to register to download this whitepaper on best practices for Canon photography, or any other kind of conversion mechanism. It can happen on a blog just like on a web site.

> *"The biggest mistake companies make in blogging is trying to appoint a senior executive as sort of the voice of the company."*

The whole idea is first you've got to get people to the page, any page you put up there. Blogs, by definition, are much better for search engine optimization than a traditional web page. They're better titled, there's more frequency, there's more recency, there's more keyword density, and they're written by a human being. Well, Google likes all of that stuff. So they deliver blogs before web pages. Then, when people get there, they see this person.

But there still has to be a call to action. What do you want people to do with this information? If you're shopping for where to buy a Canon SLR 50 and land on a blog that's talking about the Canon SLR 50, the blog should also have a call to action that says, here's how you can buy it from me. I work at Roberts Camera. You can come into our store or click here and immediately go to place an order.

What does a business have to do to create an effective blog? What makes for a good blog and what makes for a bad blog, in terms of attracting customers?

The biggest mistake companies make in blogging is trying to appoint a senior executive as sort of the voice of the company. So General Motors has the chairman blogging—but, of course, he doesn't blog. We all accept that the blog was written by somebody in PR.

He doesn't even answer his own email.

Exactly. What we say, and what our tool does, is to enable you to free up everyone in the organization to blog. So essentially, you give blogging tools to everyone. In fact, lots of people in your company are already blogging—and you're not getting any benefit from that. In fact, you may be hurt by that.

> *"Blogging and search is the acquisition mechanism, and email is what you do to maintain the relationship."*

So how do you channel all these people and all this passion into blogging? Well, you make sure that everybody has the ability to do it. And then you just collect all that content and then you organize that content. This is what our system all does automatically, so that it's all organized, or what we call compended, into categories. So everyone in the company may be talking about anything to do with photography, but when someone talks about digital video photography with a Sony camcorder, I may have a blog called `digitalsonycamcorders.robertscamera.com`, and anytime anyone mentions a Sony digital camcorder, that content goes into that compended blog. It's great; that's how you leverage content to win at search.

So basically, you might have 20 people blogging—presumably on separate blogs—and then the content all goes into a central repository, but then gets parceled out by content into more separate blogs.

We call them compended blogs. If I'm Roberts Camera, all of my compended blogs are going to be a compendium of things that people search on that I want to win.

It would seem to me that a larger company might have a benefit there, if they have more employees blogging. Is that necessarily so?

It may be, but a lot of search is local. According to a Piper and Jeffries Internet study last year, 50 percent of all searches have what's called "local intent." So even if I want something from Home Depot, I may type in "lumber Greenfield." That's my search term. So my True Value Hardware guy has just as much shot as Home Depot in winning that search. In fact, if Home Depot's not localized enough, they're not going to win that search.

Then, of course, once you capture the customer, either via sale or request, you tie right back into the email marketing.

That's where it all fits together. We look at it and say, blogging and search is the acquisition mechanism, and email is what you do to maintain the relationship.

So, really, a company that isn't blogging is going to be at a disadvantage going forward.

Absolutely. Think of any industry and look at the top five competitors, and look at their web sites. What's the differentiator there? "Our customer service is the best customer service in the world. We're open 24 hours a day, and our prices are the best." Let me see; I can go to Target and I can go to Wal-Mart and I can go to Kmart and I can go to I can go to Kohl's, and every web site is going to be identical. How do I actually differentiate that?

Well, boom. "Hi, I'm Mary. I just started at Kohl's this week. I'm a new buyer, and I'm really excited because, boy, we take such good care about how we look at our sweaters. A lot of stores will sell a sweater that has a blah blah blah, blah blah blah, but our sweaters have…"

Right? I land on Mary, and Mary loves her job and is passionate about what she's doing. You know what? All things being equal, what's going to convert me to something? Well, people I like! And the more people you have blogging and participating, the more opportunity I'm going to find somebody I like.

The great thing about keywords is I type in the problem as I see it. If you're doing traditional search engine optimization, you've kind of got to pick. How do I want to discuss this problem? When I'm blogging and I've got lots of people blogging, I can discuss this problem a lot of different ways. So when someone types in a search term, it may not be my search term or what I thought they were going to type in, but that doesn't mean I don't want to win that search. But if they land on the person's blog post that speaks to that problem exactly as they spoke to it, then they're going to convert at a much higher rate.

I know a lot of people are blogging now, but not everybody has the writing skills to do blogs. How do you get the people in your organization up to speed on how to do it?

One of the things that we do with our tool is a keyword suggestion tool that's integrated into it. As we work with clients, we figure out what the keywords are and what they want to talk about, and then we put that right in the user interface. This way the blogger employee gets some direction.

We also have a hierarchy, a workflow if you will, so that every blog post created by an employee or constituent needs to be approved by someone. You get someone that approves it, or if they disapprove it, they have the opportunity to make comments and suggestions so people get better over time.

> *"The great thing about a blog is [that] it's supposed to be imperfect."*

The great thing about a blog is [that] it's supposed to be imperfect. It's a human voice. It's about passion. You want somebody controlling it just to make sure that people are saying kind of the right things and that there's no profanity, but it's not like a web site. Because I write something today and I'm going to write something else tomorrow and the next day, that stuff is going to get pushed down.

So people can get better over time. Things start shaky and then get stronger, versus a web site or any other kind of marketing collateral, where it's got to be perfect from day one. A blog doesn't have to be perfect ever, and it certainly doesn't have to be perfect from day one.

How important is video blogging going to be?

I think video blogging is going to be interesting. There's still pain of execution with video blogging, but the whole world is excited about it.

My personal opinion is, big brands are moving into Google. They're moving into the web, and pushing out small guys—because they're raising the cost of keywords and they're raising the cost of banner ads. But they're reach and frequency marketers. They want to do things the way they've always done them. You know, Google is buying DoubleClick to get into old-fashioned marketing, because that's what the customer wants.

> *"Usually the best way to do these things is to start small."*

So video blogging, for me, is still kind of mass marketing, impersonal, and hard to execute. I think that it's cool and there's a role. We looked at YouTube for our own business, and said, okay, maybe we'll just set up a camera here and talk to the camera every once in awhile or interview a customer every once in awhile. But it's not going to be our full-time thing.

Google still needs to search keywords. It needs words. That's what makes it work. So words are still going to be more important than video.

To wrap up here, what advice would you give to an existing company who wants to move into email marketing and blog marketing and customer acquisition? What advice would you give that company on how to do it, and what to do?

I think the biggest piece of advice that I give, especially to large companies, is find a little corner of low-hanging fruit, and start working and experimenting there. These guys are so used to working in such big numbers that oftentimes they get wrapped around the actual trying to get a program off the ground, because they're trying to boil the ocean, if you will.

Usually the best way to do these things is to start small. Pick a little corner and say, okay, I'm going to talk about red daisies. Even though I sell every kind of flower in the world, let's start working on some specific tactics. Or let's pick a specific geography to work on this tactic. Once stuff starts working, it gets funded; resources get applied to it.

The biggest challenge to most marketers that I meet is they're these middle-level guys who are afraid to stick their heads out and make a mistake, because it's going to be so noticed. The key is, because these tools are small and scalable, you can start small.

So I'm Home Depot or I'm a sports team or something like that—pick something that nobody's really going to notice but that you can get some real tangible results without having to spend a lot of money. Let's see if we can get more season ticket holders out of nursing home patients. Or let's just work on Greenfield. Let's pick a store and let's start collecting a database of names and let's do searches that are strictly blogging specifically about, maybe not Greenfield, but maybe Atlanta or Chicago or something like that, where you can just run tests. Because it's cheap; it doesn't cost a lot of money. And the smaller you are, the less expensive it is.

And it's so testable. You know immediately what's going to work and what's not going to work, or what is working and what isn't working. It's not like spending $200,000 on a catalog and hoping for the best, or a brochure that happens to be green because my boss likes green. The customer's going to tell you right away. And the tools are quick and easy enough to change on the fly. It's constantly evolving. It never stops. It just grows.

So you think a company gets better results by setting up a small little shop within the marketing department?

Not necessarily that. I'm just saying that they should not say, okay we're going to start emailing. But email marketing isn't going to make sense to a $7 billion company until we have 200 million email addresses. Well, that's just silly because now you've got to execute on this gigantic strategy that takes years to execute and millions of dollars.

The real way this works is that you pick off something small. Say, okay, what is my goal here? I want 20 people to come to my birdhouse-building clinic in Greenfield. Great; let's focus on the birdhouse-building clinic in Greenfield. You don't have to set up a separate group of people to do it; you just have to set up smaller projects. If those small projects work, then you say, great. I got birdhouse builders in Greenfield, now let's get birdhouse builders nationwide. Or let's expand our Saturday morning programs to whatever. There's so many ways it can grow.

Often, people are afraid to take the first step, because traditionally, especially in large companies, the first step is such a doozy. That's why Internet marketing works. You see the innovation never happens at big companies; it happens at the small

> *"Now the big guys really need to feel threatened by the small guys."*

and medium-sized companies. Because they're the ones who don't have a budget, they're the ones that have to be more innovative and more nimble.

I have this analogy I use about sports marketing. You get out of college and you want to get into sports marketing, your first job out of college is with a minor-league, single-A baseball team. If you do a good job, you might get into hockey, and then you get into basketball, and then you get into major-league baseball, and then finally, at the peak of your career, you get to the NFL. Well, all you care about when you get to the NFL is, I don't want to mess this up! I'm at the top of the food chain.

All the innovation in sports marketing happens where? There have been books written about this. It all happens in minor-league baseball and hockey. That's where mascots come from and fireworks nights and concerts and bat giveaways and all that stuff. It all starts in minor-league baseball, because those guys have to be innovative. When it's proven, that's when you start seeing it in the National Football League. You think Frisbee dogs started at the NFL? Huh uh.

Anyway, that's the nature of it, and the same thing happens in business. You're a small retailer; you just have to be more nimble and more clever. The problem is, you've never had the resources. You've never had the tools that you can use. And now you do.

Now the big guys really need to feel threatened by the small guys. Because it's not the same theme that Wal-Mart can come in and just stomp the small retailer. The small retailer now has tools at his disposal that compete online as equally as any other business. And business-to-business is the same way. It's all about desire and intelligence.

Sound Bites

I think Chris Baggot has a good handle on how Internet marketing changes the relationship with the customer. As Chris likes to say, Internet marketing isn't about campaigns; it's about relationships. You don't get ahead by trying to sell a single product to five million individuals; you make your mark by focusing on what you can do for a single individual, and then repeat that times five million.

And, of course, you can do this with a combination of blog marketing and email marketing:

- Blog marketing taps the information potential inside your organization and uses that information to attract new customers (by placing unique information high in organic search).
- Email marketing maintains the customer relationship, feeding each customer information and promotions that are specifically useful to him.

It's one-on-one marketing from start (blogger-to-reader) to finish (company-to-customer)—and it's a cost-effective way for small companies to compete with large ones online.

Ed Shull: NetResults

14

> *"[It's] a way to build up buzz in blogs, for people who want to get information out there to the blogosphere."*
>
> —*Ed Shull*

If you thought product placement was only for movies and television shows, your thinking is so 20th century. In the 21st century, product placement is everywhere—including your favorite blog.

Blogitive is a service that pays bloggers for mentioning products from the company's clients. It's kind of viral; instead of placing advertisements on web sites, Blogitive seeds blog posts. Client companies get mentioned in posts across the blogosphere in an organic fashion, without the taint of traditional advertising.

The guy who thought up Blogitive and is spearheading this social media marketing movement is Ed Shull. Ed used to be the CEO of USWeb, one of the largest strategic Internet consulting firms, but he left the big company to form his own smaller one. His new company, NetResults, focuses on social media marketing; Blogitive is one of NetResults' first initiatives.

> **FACT SHEET: ED SHULL**
>
> Founder, NetResults
> (www.netresults.com)
>
> Founder, Blogitive
> (www.blogitive.com)
>
> Blogger: One Blog Too Many
> (www.oneblogtoomany.com)

Marketing to the Blogosphere via the Blogosphere

So what is this social media thing all about—and how can you use it to market your business? Ed knows, because he's using it himself. Read on to learn more.

You were with USWeb for a half dozen years; now you're with your new company, NetResults. Can you talk a little about your new company, and what it does?

NetResults is primarily my own kind of Internet marketing consultancy, whereas USWeb was a firm of a lot more people. It consists of a couple of small divisions.

We have Blogitive, which we started when I was at USWeb, which is a network of bloggers that will actually take a press release and write about it, for money. We give them a press release, they log into a system, and they're able to write up on that press release, similar to the same way that a writer would get a press release at a newspaper or whatever and write up on it. The difference is we're actually paying them to write something. So it's kind of a way to build up buzz in blogs, for people who want to get information out there to the blogosphere. That's one division. I have one and a half people who run that.

Then I have the consultancy, which is just me and one other person, as an assistant. I actually get hired by companies to help their search rankings or help them figure out ways to market their sites more effectively, tackle new markets, launch new products, whatever they want.

Then I also own a couple of small e-commerce sites that sell flowers and candy and stuff like that, mostly just to kind of keep up with what's going on in the marketplace.

Why did you leave USWeb? Why go out on your own like that?

> "The primary benefit of [social media marketing] is that it builds up some buzz."

I think I was just getting a little restless, to be honest. The bigger the company gets, the more solidified they get in their ways. It's more difficult to change things, and you're less able to move things around. USWeb definitely hit a point where it was difficult for me to do new things. Having my own company, where it's just basically me, allows me to try out some new things. The social marketing space really interested me and USWeb is more about search engine marketing, and it was difficult to change that.

Let's talk about the use of social media in marketing. Specifically, let's start with the concept of paying for placement or for notice in blogs. Can you talk a little about how that works, and why that's valuable?

The way a client handles it is they write up a press release. So if they're going to be launching a new product and they want to get some exposure, they write a press release about that the same way they would normally. The difference is, they submit it to our system. They pay on average $20 to get it out there. They put it into the system, the blogger then logs into our system, then they see there's an offer there to write up about this press release. If the blogger finds that release to be interesting for them, they can write about it and they make on average $5 per posting. They go through it, they write up something unique about that press release. They then submit the URL for what they wrote to us, and we review it. If it meets the requirements that the client set forward, we release payment to them.

The primary benefit of it is that it builds up some buzz. It gets on a lot of blogs, and someone that reads that blog will now know about this sort of content. All of our blogs in the system are syndicated through RSS feeds, through Feedburner and stuff like that, so the content is syndicated out and has a bigger reader base than just people that are on the blog.

Then, also, a big benefit is search engines. Trying to get a search engine ranking, a lot of times, is trying to get people to link to you. And all these press releases are linking back to the client, to the relevant page of content about what they do.

For example, I have an e-commerce site DotFlowers.com. We send out press releases about things that we do at DotFlowers, and we have a lot of people who link back to us, from pages about flowers. And that puts us on the first page of Google for the term "flowers," which is very valuable. It has an ancillary benefit of making your search rankings very high.

It's got a few benefits. And from the blogger's perspective, they don't have to write about anything they don't want to write about. They can write whatever they want about that, so

> *"Last year we had a blogger make over $17,000 in one year."*

just because we put out a press release that says something great, the blogger can actually take any stance they want on that. They can decide that they don't think it's great, they can write their opinion. And as long as they write up something and meet the requirements, then they're still paid. They're not being paid to sway their opinion; they're just being paid to have one.

So who are these bloggers, and how do you get hooked up with them?

All the blogs in the system have been around for at least six months; that's the minimum time they're required to be up. They're all indexed on the search engines—Google, Yahoo, MSN, and Ask. They have to keep an active blog, at least three times a week. And that's at least two non-sponsored postings between each sponsored posting, so they can't just write up a bunch of sponsored posts. We're looking for active bloggers who actively blog.

As to the bloggers, we have everything from stay-at-home moms to students. Really not industry-specific, just general blogs, and they make a little extra money. Last year we had a blogger make over $17,000 in one year, just by doing this. They can take it really seriously, but most of them are just recreational. And it does have a pretty nice impact on the search rankings for our clients.

Not only is this good for your clients; it also sounds like a good way to make money for the bloggers. How would a blogger join your network if they wanted to participate?

They just go to Blogitive.com and apply. And then after they apply we review the application, make sure their blog meets the criteria. The only thing they need to get in is they need to be over 18, they need to have a blog that matches the criteria, and they need to be able to accept PayPal payments. That's how we pay them, and we pay them weekly.

> *"The first way to start building up search visibility is to keep building content."*

There's a new thing coming out from Blogitive called the Blogitive Directory, and that works even more [simply] for the blogger. They install a directory onto their WordPress or any other blog they have. The clients can then submit to their directory, so they get exposure on that blog. They also get those links that the search engines are looking for. All the blogger has to do is when someone submits it to them, they just take a look, make sure they want to have that site in their directory, and if they think it's a good site they click "approve," and they make money that way. That's an even faster way to earn money as a blogger. It's easier, it's faster, and it requires less writing. It's a way of taking advertisements on your blog but placing them off to the side, so you don't have a lot of banner ads on your blog.

This is one way for a company to exploit the blogosphere. How else can companies use blogs in their online marketing?

Maintaining a blog is important. Obviously, the first way to start building up search visibility is to keep building content, and blogs are an easy way to do that. Especially with syndication, it gets that content exposed to more eyeballs than just people who are on your web site. So having your own blog and contributing to it constantly is a big way of doing it.

Other things are starting to make that syndication a little nicer. Sphere (www.sphere.com), for example, is actually a great little tool to use. We had one client who was contributing pretty consistently to their blog. One of *The Wall Street Journal* sites used Sphere, which is a system that shows related blog postings to articles they put up. Our client's blog postings were getting found in Sphere on the *The Wall Street Journal*, and that ended up driving thousands of hits to their site. It was just great traffic, driven from the *The Wall Street Journal*. That was incredibly valuable.

Running a blog, you really never know which content is going to bring it in, necessarily. But you can certainly target keywords. If you want to rank for a very specific term, we write a blog post about it, just about that very specific term. So blogs are an incredibly effective way of adding content to your site and also adding some links automatically because of syndication.

I think everyone's familiar with the concept of search engine optimization. What is social media optimization, and how does that work?

There are two kinds of services we offer: social media optimization and social media marketing. Social media optimization is the process of going through the web site and tweaking it the same way you might with SEO, but tweaking it for social media systems. For example, the "add this" button, one button that people can click on to add it to Digg or del.icio.us, reddit, StumbleUpon, all those sorts of things, so they can easily add it as a social bookmark. Or an "add this" button for subscribing through My Yahoo or iGoogle or any other ways of syndication, to subscribe to the content. Those types of things are part of social media optimization, kind of tweaking the site to use the new technology of social media.

Social media marketing is about taking advantage of those things to bring more visibility to your website. Obviously, Technorati tags are part of the optimization for social media marketing. It's something you should be doing on blog posts on your site. But also, those bring in traffic. If you put those Technorati tags into your postings, theoretically you're going to make it on Technorati for certain terms—people search there, they're going to find you and come to your site.

How does video play into that?

Having a plan for YouTube, making some videos and tagging them correctly for correct terms, to intercept traffic there, is important. More and more people are putting their videos on YouTube every day, so it's becoming important for companies to go in and register their name on YouTube, start making videos. Or at least start converting old content to that format. Basically, YouTube's nothing but a big video search engine. So if someone has a term that's important to them, just like in Google, they want to make sure they rank for that on YouTube.

> *"The thing with big companies is that very few of them truly want to be innovators."*

There's ways that they can take advantage of that. For example, take a car wax company, looking to get branded as a high-end car wax. People go to YouTube and they search for "Ferrari" or "Lamborghini" or "Tesla" or something like that. To have a video where they're waxing one of those cars with their car wax and showing off how much it shines, that's going to be a great branding experience for the wax. It's something someone looked for, nothing to do with car wax, but now they've had a nice branding exposure. So there's a lot of opportunities in social media marketing, to bring branding and traffic to your web site, just by adding the right content.

It's taken awhile, but a lot of companies are just now getting used to the concept of online marketing and search engine marketing. How quickly is social media being adopted by the business community?

Right now I feel that they have a lot of interest but not a lot of understanding. The thing with big companies is that very few of them truly want to be innovators. They're very much into the "what did they do?" model. Unfortunately, a lot of companies treat it like the advertising model.

I had one client that I pitched the idea of YouTube to and they thought it was silly, because they were already on YouTube with banner ads. They were missing the point that YouTube is a way to get the right visibility, and a banner ad isn't the same thing. It doesn't matter which technology the banner ad is sitting on—it's still a banner ad. People are still going to be banner-blind to it the same way they are on Yahoo's home page [and] as they are on YouTube. It doesn't matter.

Social media is something that requires a little more thought. Some of the big interactive agencies, they claim to be innovative, but really they're just trying to find innovative ways to sell you CPM some more. They really hold people back from it. What might the branding appeal be to a half a million people that search for different car types and find someone waxing the cars with your brand of car wax? That could be an incredibly valuable thing. They may not rush out and buy your car wax, but now they kind of have it in their heads that your car wax is what you use to wax a Ferrari. So when you buy your Volkswagen or Acura, maybe you're going to buy that car wax.

The problem is, that has a difficult time being justified into a CPM that's reasonable. You have costs of creative, stuff like that, that don't really back into something that interactive agencies are used to dealing with. The same thing happened in search in the beginning, the interactive agencies didn't know how to handle search. So they kind of missed the boat. And then there was a huge rush of acquisitions in the search space by agencies—like Isobar buying iProspect because iProspect was the absolute expert in natural search and paid search. So Isobar wanted to acquire them, so they could acquire that talent.

It seems that many people tend to consider content more "real" on a blog post or in a YouTube video than in a traditional advertisement.

When Blogitive first came out there was some backlash among bloggers who were concerned that it was going to be stealing the opinion of people. I think it's really up to the content producers to decide where their loyalty's going to be. I can remember reading in Mike Lewis' book, *Next*, the kid with the web site about penny stocks and how he was arrested for the boosting of stocks, and all he did was post up press releases of companies whose stock he thought was good. He really wasn't making anything up, either. He was just posting what they said. He was just talking about them and how they were a good buy. And somehow that was manipulating things.

So I think it's up to people to know that a blog is written by a normal person. There's no journalistic integrity at stake there. It's a blog. You see bloggers sometimes who want to be treated as journalists, but they're unwilling to take the accountability that a journalist would take. They don't cite sources, they don't keep it free of biased opinions. Some of the biggest opponents of Blogitive, you look at their sites and they have almost zero journalistic integrity. They just want to go out there and state their opinion. Because they think their opinion's better, that they shouldn't have the same rules to follow, but they should get the same access and respect.

There probably is a need out there for some sort of organization that sets forth journalistic-type rules for bloggers. If they follow those rules, they get some sort of bumper sticker on their web site or something that lets people know that. I think that would be great.

> *"A lot of content out there is self-serving."*

I think that blogs often contain information that is self-serving. Obviously, some companies put up corporate blogs. When a blog talks all about how important it is to invest in gold and they happen to be a gold investing company, then obviously it's a bit self-serving and the content is a bit skewed. It doesn't mean it's inaccurate; it's just that it's presented in a certain way.

How different is it than when you see analysts for big firms go up on CNBC and talk about stocks they've invested in? Clearly, as they talk about them, you see the stock price go up and they make more money. A lot of content out there is self-serving, and hopefully you can separate the noise from the national news.

Have you had some bloggers oppose your efforts to put placement on their blogs?

Oh, definitely. It's an important part of Blogitive—you can decide which posts to write about. We have some bloggers disclose right up front that this is a paid posting. We have some that just work it into their content.

On my personal blog, I'll mention that this is a press release; I have an actual press release section. I'll put my opinion on a press release in there, but for the most part, I'm making it very clear that this company put out a press release and this is it. I think from that standpoint I'm being ethical by informing my readers that, hey, this is a press release. I'm not necessarily saying that for this post I'm being paid, but I do have a disclosure on the site to let people know that I do accept offers from Blogitive for paid submissions. I'm not a journalist; my blog is relatively boring, and there are very few people who go to my blog that don't know me personally. I think by putting this in the way I'm putting it, it's pretty clear of any ethical issues.

Obviously, if you're blogging for a major news site, you probably don't want to be taking part in Blogitive at all, because even the appearance of impropriety could be damaging. Most of our bloggers are people who blog about whatever's going on in their life. When they get a Blogitive offer they talk about that offer in general. They don't usually have a strong opinion of it either way, which is the way we prefer it.

What can a company do, in their press release or in the information they put out, to improve their chances of being picked up in the blog space?

The traditional press release doesn't seem to fly as well in the blogosphere: Making the content complete and easy to follow; using bullet points; referencing web sites; knowing the person you're sending this to is on the Internet; not having to deal with one piece of paper; that they can go to more places—that's all important.

They should put as many links to the information as possible, as well as their contact information. The better bloggers might actually want to email and ask you some questions, so their content's more unique.

> *"Give them all the information they need…to put an interesting post up."*

One of the rules of thumb we give to our clients for SEO when they're doing a press release campaign is to have a page on their site dedicated to press and the media. To have pictures—a lot of times, bloggers like to put the logo of the company they're talking about in the thread—having that logo available, in a nice format, is important. Pictures of screenshots, photographs of your products, whatever, is great to put on there, having links to those.

So give them all the information they need, all the detail they need, to put an interesting post up. The easier you make it for them, obviously the more likely they are to do it. If you send a blogger everything—images, history of the company, bullet points of what the product does, links to more information, client quotes, stuff like that—all that information in one little email, that's going to be helpful to them.

People focus on those A-list bloggers. Everyone wants to be on TechCrunch, everyone wants to be on the big blogs. They kind of ignore those small ones that, in aggregate, get an awful lot of traffic. Sometimes the traffic numbers can be skewed. People look at how popular a site is, with Google PageRank or Alexa, and try to figure out if that's who they should submit to. It's possible that people don't visit this website but subscribe to the RSS. So they really should be focusing on blogs that are specific to them, even if it's a smaller target audience, because it's going to be the same people, the lay people.

There's more to submitting to blogs than just TechCrunch. That's one area that people seem to ignore.

What advice would you give to a business today, who wants to take advantage of the blogosphere and the social media out there, in promoting their business?

I think that the best way to approach that is to get rid of some of the preconceived notions of things. Businesses tend to be very used to trying to determine ROI [return on investment]. It's hard to throw ROI out the window, because there definitely is a return on investment in going after the social media space. It's just to do something that's really going to catch on, they're going to have to be innovative. And with innovative, there's no past history to go off of.

I get clients all the time who hire me for social media marketing and they want something really innovative. When I bring things to them, they say, great, who else has done that, so we can see how they did? Or, why can't we do the same thing these guys did? And they want to kind of replicate.

For a while it was viral video. Everyone wanted a viral video. It was really difficult to make them understand that viral videos just kind of happen. We were talking to one client at the time, who was saying, hey, we need to get as many views as these videos here, the most popular videos on YouTube. We tried to explain that that was a video of someone that put butter on the floor so his roommate would fall. I doubt you're going to do anything that crazy. It was a 30-second video that got popular because of that fool falling down.

Most viral videos are not going to be anything that's incredibly beneficial to your brand. Some companies pull it off with a little bit of luck, but for the most part viral videos are from people. Try to remember that there is no past history of success in innovation. Try it out, and hopefully it won't backfire.

I'm thinking of GM with their trucks. They released to the creative community to make your own commercials. And, sure enough, people made very funny videos about what gas guzzlers these trucks were, and how bad they were for the environment. So that backfired. Now you find more videos that are hurting the brand than enhancing it. They took a chance, but they probably should have foreseen the type of people that were going to be taking advantage of that.

That's another big part of this, knowing that the blogosphere is made up of people who have a certain type of opinion. They're not the corporate drones who work for you. They're going to have opinions on how they use your material. So keep that in mind as you release it.

Sound Bites

Want to use the blogosphere to market your company or products? Then you have to give the bloggers what they want and need to create an interesting post. Here are some of the things that Ed Shull recommends:

- Sell a unique story or message—not just a blatant advertisement.
- Include plenty of links to your web site and product pages.
- Embed or attach pictures, logos, and other images.
- Include contact information for further details.

Brian Lusk: Southwest Airlines

15

> " [The blog has] become a real conversation tool and forum to have a conversation with our customers."
>
> —Brian Lusk

We've talked a lot about blog marketing and corporate blogging so far in this book, so it's about time we talked to somebody who is actually doing it for real out there on the Web. Hence our introduction to Brian Lusk, who runs the Nuts About Southwest blog, the corporate blog of Southwest Airlines.

Nuts About Southwest is a very popular blog, and a great testament to the importance of blogging in a company's marketing mix. Brian manages about 30 different internal bloggers (and a few external ones) who contribute to the blog. As Brian relates, the blog helps the company establish a communication with its customers.

> **FACT SHEET: BRIAN LUSK**
>
> Manager of Customer Communication, Southwest Airlines (www.southwest.com)
>
> Corporate Editor, Nuts About Southwest Blog (www.blogsouthwest.com)

And it's not just a one-way communication, either. Brian's blog has provided valuable customer feedback about various company policies, even inspiring change in some key company operations. That makes the blog important for both outbound marketing and for market research.

The Power of a Well-Run Corporate Blog

A quick read of the Nuts About Southwest blog reveals why it's such a valuable tool to the company. The blog is well-written from a variety of different internal bloggers; it covers topics both mundane and vitally important to both the company and its customers. And, most important, it doesn't shirk its responsibility when big issues arise. I talked to Brian about the blog, and about his role in making it what it is today.

The Nuts About Southwest blog has gotten a lot of attention across the industry. How did the blog get started?

I got involved in discussions in late '05. The thinking was that these discussions are going on online about us, without us being involved. So we wanted to join the conversation and have our own voice. That was the primary initial impetus to start a blog.

So how did you get the project off the ground?

Angela Vargo, who was in our public relations department at the time, and Linda Rutherford, who is our vice president of public relations, they're kind of the mother of the blog. Angela invited people from a lot of the customer contact departments across the company to come in and discuss our feelings about the blog, the pros and cons.

She got Andy Lark as a consultant, to help guide us on the approach that we wanted to take with the blog. Whether we wanted it to be a one-person blog, or the way it wound up, being kind of a consortium of people. Whether we were going to moderate some of the technical details about that. The kind of tone and what's involved in the blogosphere, courtesy and some of the ground rules. So we relied on him a lot for that.

The gestation period probably took about five to six months. We came up with a plan for the blog—how we were going to approach it, who was going to manage it, who was going to participate in it. We came up with the user guide that's on the blog now, with the ground rules for participating for the public. We really tied everything together into one proposal. Then a local company, RD2, did the design, the layout of the blog.

So we met with our executive planning committee, which is Gary Kelly, our CEO; Colleen Barrett, our president; and our executive vice presidents and our senior vice presidents. We made a presentation before them—the layout of the blog, explained what we were doing with the blog. Once we got their final sign-off on the blog, then we went live.

That obviously sounds like a lot different process from the typical individual starting up their own blog! This is typical in a corporation, of course; you have to have those people involved.

Did that present many problems in getting the thing launched, and then running it?

No, actually, the biggest fear that was raised was that we might be revealing proprietary information, because some of the people that we had signed up to blog have some inside information. That hasn't been an issue at all. But that's one reason we have a fairly stringent proofing process before any of the blog posts go out on the blog—just to make sure we aren't revealing stuff like that. I don't think we've ever had to remove anything like that before we've actually published one of the posts.

The other thing was to get the support of our senior management. I think we're really lucky that we have it. As we've gone through the year and half now with the blog, and they've seen some of the things that it can do for us, that support's even grown stronger.

> *"We wanted it to be a place where we could have a conversation with our customers."*

Before it got started, what kind of expectations did the company have for the blog?

I don't know that we had any preconceived expectations. We wanted it to be a place where we could have a conversation with our customers, where it would be informal and fun, kind of like our general culture. We wanted it to be widely read, but we didn't know what kind of readership we would have. We were kind of going into it as a big experiment, I think, more than anything, just to see what would happen, what kind of response we would have.

Let's talk about that response, both from the customer and inside the company. Start with the customer base—how have customers responded to it?

I think it's been real great. Our readership continues to increase, and people are starting to turn to the blog when there's a big issue involving Southwest. We've had a couple here in the last two or three weeks that have really driven the comments. We've had the instance, some people are calling it " Skirtgate," with the customer that was asked to cover up her short skirt on a flight; between two different posts, that generated about 1,100 comments within four or five days. Then Gary Kelly, our CEO, a couple of days ago put one up about the announcement of our new boarding process.

And there are some other examples we've had where what's been on the blog has changed or guided our policy, based on customer comments.

We have a real loyal, kind of a core base of people that we've become friends with, really developed the relationship even beyond the online world into the real-world, face-to-face contact with some of our more prolific readers. And we get a lot of people who read but don't comment unless there's a big issue involved. What's probably been for me the most gratifying thing about the blog is that it's become a real conversation tool and forum to have a conversation with our customers.

What about the response inside the company—has the company embraced it?

Yeah, they really have. As the blog has progressed, people—both leaders and employees—have really embraced it. There are a lot of employees who participate in comments on the blog and read it daily. We encourage folks to go there when there's some breaking news. I know Gary includes it as part of his communications strategy, about when he's going to blog and what issues he's going to blog about. So I think the overall support has really been gratifying, internally.

Let's get into some of the mechanics of the thing. Who, exactly, posts on the blog?

> *"We try to have a big variety of bloggers, so we can always have a supply of new content."*

We have a core team of about 30 employees; it's kind of expanding as we get farther along. We've got mechanics, pilots, flight attendants, station employees, we've got reservation employees, and then here at headquarters we have support employees, we have people from schedule planning, we have the executive office, marketing, a lot of groups there. And we have one officer from our people department, Jeff Lamb, who's on the blog team, and then some of the other officers will post from time to time, like Gary and Colleen Barrett, our president.

So we have about 30 and are still looking to grow that. We ask that they submit two or three posts a month. Because they have day jobs, sometimes they may not be able to meet that quota. That's why we try to have a big variety of bloggers, so we can always have a supply of new content.

So you're getting, what, at least a post a day?

Yeah, on average. Monday through Friday we try to post at least one post every day.

Do you ever have any customers post?

We have, and that's been really successful. Right now we have a really good customer, Francisco Delgado, who's a sailor on the *Nimitz*; he's a big Southwest supporter and a frequent customer. The *Nimitz* is on its way back from a six- or eight-month deployment to the Persian Gulf, and from the ship he's been submitting his deployment diary posts. We've been running those about every three weeks or so.

We have another customer, Kim Seale, who has done a couple of guest posts. One of them was about what Southwest means to him as a customer. Both with Kim and Francisco, we've really developed offline real-world friendships with those guys, and with some of our other regular readers, too.

That's pretty cool. Now, you mentioned earlier about a proofing process; could you talk about that a little bit?

We use WordPress, so the bloggers will put their posts up on Word-Press, and when I see a new post up there, I will look at it and edit it. Most edits are really minor; we don't want to take anything away from the blogger's voice. Once I'm finished with it I'll run it by Linda

> *"What the blog showed was that a huge, overwhelming number of customers wanted to keep open seating."*

Ruthorford, who's our VP of public relations, and then also by Ginger Hardage, who's our senior VP of corporate communications. They'll both look at it and then they'll give it back to me, and I'll make any final changes that they have.

What about customer comments? Obviously you allow comments on your blog. Are those moderated? How do you protect against people who just want to complain about the last bad flight they had?

They are moderated, but we won't go into a post and edit it unless it's missing a "b" or something and it needs it just to be literate; we won't edit the post for content.

We put up some negative ones. With the skirt issue we put up some pretty negative comments. I don't think a lot of companies would have posted that kind of negative response on a corporate blog.

We do ask folks, and we put it in our user guide, that we don't accept specific customer issues, like what you were talking about—my last flight was bad, or you lost my luggage, what are you going to do about that? We won't post those on the blog. What we usually do is email that customer back and explain why we didn't post it, and give them the correct venues to address their concern.

You just want to make sure the comments are appropriate to the blog post.

Sometimes we will post off-topic comments. I mean, we aren't 100 percent faithful to staying on topic. We want the comments to be general—that would apply to anyone reading it, not specifically about one person.

Has the blog affected the way Southwest does things? Have there been things that come up on the blog that have changed your operations?

Oh yeah. There are two big issues that I can think of, and one of them is going on right now [September 2007].

We just announced that we're going to keep our open seating process, but we are streamlining the way we board with open seating. That really has a long history with the blog. Last year we started doing some testing of assigned seating in San Diego. Late last summer in '06, Gary Kelly did a post explaining what was going on, and he also did one short follow-up post. Those two posts generated, to date, about 700 comments. And those comments, I think we were kind of taken aback by them, because up until we'd announced that we were going to be testing assigned seating, our number-one requested customer service amenity was to start assigning seats. What the blog showed was that a huge, overwhelming number of our customers wanted to keep open seating.

I think the passion and the number of those folks didn't really surprise us, but it made us stop and think. A lot of those folks would submit suggestions about how to improve the boarding process but keep open seating. So we went back to San Diego a few months later and tested some of those suggestions. What we're going through now, dividing people into groups of five, came directly from customer suggestions on the blog. So that's one big issue.

Another issue was that we have a relatively shorter booking window than a lot of airlines do. For example, we'll only open our schedules up 180 to 220 days ahead of time, instead of being able to book 11 months ahead. We did a post about a redesign of our main web page, Southwest.com, and we started getting a lot of comments on there like: " I like your new web page, but why can't I book my flights for summer?" This post came out around the first of the year, so people were anxious to book their summer travel and we hadn't released the schedules yet.

So we asked Bill Owen, who's a lead schedule planner, to do a post explaining what our scheduling process is and why we have a shorter window. He did that post and we started getting bombarded by people wanting to know why can't I book my summer travel? So our schedule-planning folks and some of our other folks took a long, hard look at the issue and decided we're going to start publicizing the dates that the schedules open. We'd been hesitant to do that because sometimes the schedule opening dates change and we didn't want people to expect it. But we found out that, yeah, people want to know ahead of time, and even our own employees did— with the understanding that it's possible that it might change. The blog really played a definite role in that, and Bill wrote a follow-up post that was titled, "I Blogged, You Flamed, We Changed."

So those are two really big issues.

Any other important issues that you've had to deal with?

We had another instance where we used the blog to deflate a possible issue. On another blog out there, this woman had done a post saying that we essentially tried to kill her ill father by denying him boarding in Phoenix on a flight. He was a larger customer, one we call a "customer of size," which requires the purchase of two tickets, because they take up two seats. Then, if the flight doesn't oversell, we'll refund the ticket after travel.

Anytime your company's out there and somebody's saying that you're trying to kill somebody, it's pretty inflammatory. And we had several issues. We couldn't really talk about his medical condition, because of privacy rules, but we did put a post up explaining our policy, explaining that we had contacted the customer with an apology. Then we went out to some other sites, asking them to link back to our site. It pretty much quieted the issue down.

That brings to mind another question: What do you do to promote your blog?

One thing we've done is we try to develop some relationships with other blogs. Here locally, both *The Dallas Morning News* and the *Fort Worth Star-Telegram* have aviation blogs; we have their blogs on Link Luv, which is our blog roll. And they have us linked on theirs. I will correspond with them and let them know that we're putting up a post that they might be interested in. We've done that with several other blogs.

> *"Your blog has to reflect your culture and who and what your company is."*

We've also mentioned it several times in pieces in *Spirit Magazine*, talking about the blog. This was probably several months after it went live, explaining the blog and giving the link. And then Colleen Barrett just recently did her page about the blog. We've put it in the emails we send out to our Rapid Rewards members. (That's our frequent-flyer program.) Several times we've put mention of the blog in there. That's generated a lot of traffic, also. I think there's an awareness now among a lot of the media that cover Southwest about the blog, and then with our customer base. It's been kind of an evolutionary thing.

What advice would you give to other corporate bloggers?

There are a couple of things that we always tell them.

One is that it's going to take more time than you probably expect. So be sure that you can devote the time to it, to keep it fresh. Once it's out there, it's a living thing and it devours material. So you've got to be prepared to keep it fresh and keep it functioning.

Then, two, and this is kind of a catchword all across the blogosphere, but it's important to be transparent. If you're blogging to try and change somebody's opinion or to make your company seem what it isn't, you're gonna fail. Your blog has to reflect your culture and who and what your company is.

Sound Bites

Brian Lusk's Nuts About Southwest blog is a real online marketing success story. The blog promotes Southwest Airlines, of course, but it also establishes a direct relationship between the company and its core customers—which is essential in 21st-century marketing.

What does Brian do to keep the blog successful? Here's a short list:

- Get buy-in from across the company—from the lowest levels to the highest management.
- Recruit a team of bloggers from all areas of the company.
- Keep the blog fresh, with at least one post every weekday.
- Don't overly moderate the comments; keep it honest by letting customers speak their minds.
- Maintain transparency; the blog has to reflect your company and its culture.

Lee Odden: TopRank Online Marketing

16

"That's where a lot of the benefit of social networks comes from; the ability to promote information to communities of like-minded individuals."

—*Lee Odden*

TopRank Online Marketing is a leading search engine optimization and marketing firm, located in the Minneapolis area. TopRank's founder is Lee Odden, a recognized expert on both search engine and blog marketing. Lee is an in-demand speaker and interview subject, and

> **FACT SHEET: LEE ODDEN**
>
> CEO, TopRank Online Marketing
> (www.toprankresults.com)
>
> Blogger, Online Marketing Blog
> (www.toprankblog.com)

is also a board member of the DMA Search Engine Marketing Council.

Lee's Online Marketing Blog is well-read and well-respected in the industry. It's been recognized as one of the top marketing blogs on the Web, due to both its depth and breadth of content. Lee supplements his own observations with guest posts written by a variety of industry professionals; the result is a treasure trove of content for any serious online marketer.

Promoting Your Business with Blogs and Social Networking

If you're not sure just how to promote your business online, Lee has some suggestions. Our discussion covered a range of topics, from search engines to blogs to social networking. It's all interesting and useful stuff, as you'll soon read for yourself.

There are all these new aspects to the Internet—blogs and videos and social networks and such. How are all these things changing online marketing?

In the past, the method of searching these different data types has been tasked to the user to go and find a unique search engine—an image search engine, a video search engine, a standard text-based search engine, or one for blog or news, what have you. Just recently, in the past couple of months, one of the biggest changes is that Google and Ask.com followed by Yahoo! and Microsoft Live have incorporated something called unified search; in Google's case, they branded it Google Universal Search. What they're doing is they're bringing disparate data sources into the standard search results. So rather than having to go to Google Images or Google Video or Google Book Search or whatever to look for those kinds of resources, what Google is doing (and the other engines too, but in a slightly different way) is to bring in the results from various different databases of different media types, find out which of those are the best answers for that query, and then bring them into the standard search results.

Overall, you can go way back and say it used to just all be text that you could find on the web. Of course, with more bandwidth, images, video, and interactive started to come on the scene. What's great, in my optimistic view of things, is that the search engines are doing a really great job at rounding up all these different types of information and media types and bringing them all into one place, if possible.

The idea is, I might be looking for a ping-pong ball or something, and the search engines are deciding that users might be best served being presented with, here's an article, here's a blog post, here's a news item from main-stream media, here's a video, here's some images, here's some product results. You decide, the user that is, which is the best—but here we're giv-ing you a smorgasbord to pick from.

I can see where it definitely benefits the user, getting more results from all around the web in the search results, but how can a business take advantage of that?

Universal search creates both challenges and opportunities, just like any-thing new. For those types of marketers, whether they're in-house at a com-pany or they're at an agency, that have been actively optimizing different media types for as long as those types have been around, they have a huge advantage right now—because they're already optimizing images for search. The fact that search engines like Google and Yahoo! and Ask are bringing video into search results, well, how do they decide which videos to rank highly? It's by using the same criteria they make web pages rank highly.

Some marketers publish videos and forget about them. Others will use a variety of short-term methods to drive traffic to those videos, like paid advertising, banners, interactive or offline advertising. But for those marketers that are actually optimizing these different media types, or at least that are scrambling and starting to learn how to optimize different media types, it's actually creating an advantage.

Let's say a small business has a small e-commerce web site selling baby clothes, and this site has product images. Those images could be submitted to the image-sharing sites, along with a description, and there's a link in the description back to the page that sells that product. Because search engines are now picking up on images as they find them on image-sharing sites, this e-commerce site could have a ranking for the web page that sells the product and they could also have a ranking right below it, from an image-sharing site. If someone clicks on that, they'll arrive on the image page, and then they can drill down into the product page on the e-commerce site.

> *"It's a way of occupying multiple search results on the same query."*

In other words, it's a way of occupying multiple search results on the same query. Normally when you go to Google and you search for something, at best one domain name will occupy two positions. That's the maximum. This e-commerce web site we're talking about could improve their footprint within the search results by optimizing and promoting their digital assets on other search and content-sharing sites. For example, they could put up videos on YouTube, such as customer testimonials, or a new-product product announcement, tips and how to's, or maybe they've got a blog and in that blog there's an RSS feed that can be promoted. These different media types or data types can all be brought into the standard search results and they could rank well in each scenario. In some cases you may find that three, four, five, six, or even more of the top ten search results are all information about the same company—just existing in different formats, from different places.

So you're saying that one of the secrets here is not just to keep all the media on your own site, but to post images to Flickr, videos to YouTube, and that sort of thing?

Exactly. You hear about content optimization and link building as the foundations of SEO, search engine optimization. What it's about now, even more so because of unified search, is ongoing promotion.

Companies like ours treat a web site just like a business. Okay, great, we've got our storefront up, now let's go market this thing. We've got to go out and promote it. In order to promote it effectively, there's got to be promotable content. Therefore, if we have images, great, we've got something to promote. We can go out and promote those images to different places.

> *"Text is really the most important thing—in terms of search, at least."*

Here's something that's kind of a neat thing to do—shooting a video of some kind, it doesn't have to be well produced, but shooting a video that's of value to whomever's going to look at it, and taking screenshots of that. So here we are putting up the video itself on YouTube and other video-sharing sites, with links back to the client, but we're also taking screen captures of that video and putting those screen captures or images on the image-sharing sites. Those images are actually promoting the video.

Of all the different things that you can do these days, with videos, with blogs, with images, are there any that are more important than others?

Text is really the most important thing—in terms of search, at least. Depending on what channel you're promoting into, text is how search engines best understand the meaning of content. They can't read text in an image, they typically can't read any text in a Flash movie or a game or an interactive ad, but they can read standard text that you see on a web page. And they can also read the text that links one page to another.

That text is what gives the engine the ability to associate meaning with a particular document. So that when someone searches on something, like ping-pong balls, 40 million document types come back for ping-pong balls, and then a search engine, like Google, has over 200 different signals it looks at to determine how to sort those 40 million search results. And some of the most important signals are variances in text.

Beyond the basic text web site, what other media would you recommend a company get into? If they can't do everything, what things should they try and do first?

If a company can get good information about how to use a blog as a platform, that's one of the things that a company could do to give itself an advantage for the most bang for the buck. I don't mean journal entries from a CEO pontificating about their philosophy of the industry, or something like that. There's a time and place for that, but that's not what I'm talking about.

Most corporate web sites or even e-commerce sites are fairly static. Products might change, but for the most part, the information is fairly static, outside of maybe press releases or things of that nature. Adding a blog does a couple of things.

> *"Many blog content management systems are search engine–friendly out of the box."*

One, it's a content-management system, like many content-management systems, that are made for managing regular text content. But the difference is, many blog content management systems are search engine–friendly out of the box. They have certain features and functionality that search engines really like, because it makes it easy for the search engines to understand what the content is about. It's not that search engines go, "Hey, that's a blog; I'm going to favor it automatically,"—it's not that at all. What it is, is that the search engine looks at the link structure of the pages and then looks at how information is included in certain places in the document, and goes, "Wow, I know instantly what that document is all about," and they know what that website is all about. Whereas with some content-management systems that are made for the convenience of people as users, you and me looking up something on a web site, or from the administration side, they don't think of search engines as a third audience. So sometimes they make it difficult for a search engine to do what it needs to do in order to understand what that information is about. When a search engine's confused, then it certainly isn't going to present that web page as the best answer for a certain query.

Another characteristic of a blog that gives it an advantage is an RSS feed. In other words, when content is published on a blog, it can be subscribed to.

The presence of an RSS feed, even if it doesn't come with a blog (like with a press-release feed), allows that company web site to have this entry into blog and RSS search engines and directories, like Google Blog Search. A regular web site without an RSS feed will never get into Google Blog Search. Even a search web site that just uses its blog software to archive newsletters or press releases or any other information like that will give themselves an advantage in terms of creating access to a new channel of promotion. Because they have an RSS feed, it gives them visibility into a whole other place where people are spending their time looking up information.

That's also fresh content for the search engines, right?

That's right. We have a fairly popular blog at toprankblog.com, and when we post something, it's typically in Google Blog Search within a short amount of time. But what's really exciting is that it gets in Google's master database within an hour, hour and a half, which is kind of nuts, when you think about it. The speed of indexing new content often corresponds to the rate that sites add content.

With blogs, they are structured in a very easy-to-crawl, hierarchical, organizational-chart sort of way. That makes the search engine's job so much easier. If a company does anything, if you just make the job for the search engine bot easier, for finding the company's content. That's almost half the battle, in some cases.

There are certain things about a blog that make it easier for the search engine to index, as you said. Is there any other specific type of optimization that you need to do when you're putting together a blog?

Certainly, blog optimization is akin to optimization of any dynamically generated web pages, because there's a database and there are templates. The information or data that's contained within the database is pushed through these templates that output the web page that you and I see in a browser. There are optimization tactics that can be applied to the template, so that what gets published out to the browser contains keywords in the right places for search engines—for example, in the `<title>` tag, higher on the page. (Upward and to the left is kind of the guideline we use; because people read from left to right, search engines look at a document in that way, too.) Above the fold, or alternate text when you put your cursor over an image, those are also search engine signals. Simple things like that.

In a blog, you have the title of a blog post, which typically links to the full text of the post. It's important to make sure that the title of a blog post actually is a link; not all blog software, by default, makes that a link.

There are other things you can do to optimize a blog to be more social. One example of that would be adding social bookmark and social news-sharing buttons. In other words, you're inviting readers of a blog entry to bookmark that particular article, or to share it with other people.

> *"If it's interesting content, it will travel."*

You can do that, or publish it to a social news site where there are communities of like-minded individuals who consume news according to various topics. They can actually vote up or vote down stories that are submitted there. They can comment on those stories. If a story's voted on by a lot of people, it can hit a home page and drive a very significant amount of traffic and motivate other bloggers to write about that news item. It creates visibility to a whole other channel; if it's interesting content, it will travel.

Optimizing a blog socially includes things like adding little buttons for social bookmarking sites like StumbleUpon, which is a fantastic service, or Digg if it's a techie blog, or Propeller, Reddit, del.icio.us. Some of these social bookmarking services, when you bookmark something, they actually create a static web page with a link back to the source.

For example, for one of our clients, when you go to the digital photography part of their web site, you'll see near the bottom of the page this little indication to "share this" or "bookmark this." So if you're reading an article about how to take better photos and click that link, it'll open up a little window that lets you pick your favorite bookmarking service that you can save that article to, because maybe you want to read it later, or you want to share it with somebody else. Imagine you have thousands of articles out there and all of them have this little invitation. In essence, you have a linking machine that works 24/7.

The benefit of socializing content is that you're creating a service for users, allowing them to save your content in a way that's convenient to them, instead of having to go back to the web site. The other benefit is that by bookmarking something, can create a link back to the source. So if just a few people per article out of thousands of articles are bookmarking, hundreds of links can occur as a result.

And Google's PageRank is partly based on the number of links back to your site.

> *"Social networking is definitely a huge opportunity in terms of online marketing."*

You are correct. And the cool thing about it is that the users are making the decision to create that link. Search engines reward organic, natural behaviors, as opposed to just going out and buying a bunch of links, or hiding links, or doing things like that. What it's doing is using simple technology to make it easy for users to do things for themselves, with the added benefit of doing something for that web site.

The social bookmarking sites are just one aspect of the whole social networking phenomena. How does the rest of that play into things?

Social networking is definitely a huge opportunity in terms of online marketing. There are things that we've heard about, like Facebook and MySpace—in fact, Facebook is really blowing up.

Facebook started out more of a social platform, like MySpace, in comparison to LinkedIn, which is certainly more business-oriented. But I think we will see more and more business users using Facebook—primarily for social, but as applications get created, possibly for more business-oriented sorts of activities.

I know I've certainly seen business benefits happen by having a presence on Facebook. It happened to me just the other day; a gentleman saw one of my comments and said, "Wow, I have a client that really needs SEO; can you call me?" I called him up and it turned into a really cool thing, it created the opportunity for a connection that might not otherwise have ever happened.

Success from a business standpoint or marketing standpoint with social networks is centered around people being transparent and honest, and in putting information out there that gives an indication of what they're really like. In the case of LinkedIn, they're very structured about it, where they've got work history and so on. It's a lot more business-oriented. One of the neat features on LinkedIn is the Ask a Question feature. I've used that a number of times to get content for a blog or to do surveys, or even to promote content.

That's where a lot of the benefit of social networks comes from; the ability to promote information to communities of like-minded individuals. There's a certain amount of trust because you "friended" them, and they know you're not going to send them crap, or they won't be your friend anymore.

People can become filters. There's so much information out there, and one of the neat things about social networks is that every individual that's part of that social network is sort of a filter of information and can be a really great source of information for other people in their network, and vice versa.

> *"The only way to be successful is to engage and participate, not push."*

The challenge for marketers is to find a way to get in there. The only way they can be successful is to engage and participate, not push.

Could this also work against a business, if it was disingenuous or not transparent?

Yeah, especially those organizations that will go and create fake profiles just to artificially inflate how popular they are, or to represent evangelists for their brand when they're really not.

This leads to the concept of social networking optimization.

I'll use myself as an example. I use Twitter, which is a micro-blogging format, 100 or so characters. I follow maybe 50 people, and maybe there's only 100, 150 people who follow me. It's kind of an interesting way to follow what's going on, what people have on their minds.

There are two benefits I see to something like micro-blogging with Twitter. Number one, over time you really get a sense of what some people are like. From a business standpoint, I gain a lot more confidence in certain people who might be marketing partners, for example, because I'm getting little tidbits about what they're thinking about, and they're linking to things that support what they're thinking about.

The other advantage of something like Twitter or Pownce or Jaiku is from a promotion standpoint. Sometimes, when we're promoting content, part of deciding what content to promote is deciding if this is going to travel, is this going to fly, can we light up a network with this? Are people really going to be engaged and find value in this or not? If they will, then we might go to a Twitter profile that we've created and draw attention to a particular piece of content. Same thing on Facebook, messaging other members, or using StumbleUpon. You can message multiple members: "Hey, we're excited about this, maybe you will be, too."

> *"You've got to dip your toe in the water before you can swim."*

As you grow your networking, you're drawing a network of other people who are influential. The idea is not just to reach them, but for them to get excited about it and then in turn they pass it on within their center of influence. If they're a popular blogger, for example, that trend can trickle down.

For a business that wants to take advantage of all these things, the social networking, the blogs, and so on, what general advice would you give?

You've got to dip your toe in the water before you can swim.

For blogs, you've got to read blogs first. Do a search on Technorati or Google Blog Search to find some blogs in categories of interest or relevance to your own industry or company. Read a couple of them and get a sense of what it is that other people that might have a similar audience that you will are writing. After you've read a couple of blogs for a little while, get a sense of what that's like, then go ahead and create your own blog. It's very easy to set up a blog; it's not necessarily so easy to set one up that's going last for four years, like ours has.

Being prepared to allocate the resources to be a participant is what's important if you're going to play in the blogging or social media space. And that's a different animal than what folks are used to who do advertising or direct marketing.

In an organization, is this going to pull time away from something else, or do you need different people to do this than are doing your traditional marketing?

Brand managers, product managers, people with subject-matter expertise, should allocate a certain amount of their time to engaging with these different social communities. And the thing is, they'll get value out of doing that.

They could be collaborating with another business unit, two product managers or a couple of brand managers within the same larger organization could be collaborating. They could have their own Facebook group, for example, or they could set up their own social network through a white-label service like Ning.

One interesting thing about your Online Marketing Blog is that you include interviews with other industry people. It isn't just internal stuff.

About two years ago we decided that we're going to raise our profile in the industry, and we're going to use the blog to do that. At the time, I didn't know how exactly, but here's what we did. We looked at some other people who were doing well. One thing I noticed was people doing interviews. So I started doing interviews with prominent marketers, and of course folks that are marketers love to get interviewed.

So we do that, and I have other employees that'll blog every once in a while. We also blog conferences. We try to engage the audience by running reader polls that ask our audience to rate the best resources of various types.

Of course, those resources find out we're running a poll and they send all their community back over to our site to vote on it. And then when they win, they brag about it in their web pages and their press releases, all with a link back to us. It's absolutely wonderful, and it's a win-win-win situation.

We have this other feature called the BIGLIST, which is a review of SEO blogs. Consistently, every Friday we publish anywhere from one to ten new SEO blogs, those that we've found, with a little mini review. We say, "Hey, put our little badge on your blog, because you've just been named to the Big List." And a lot of them do! I really don't care if they link back to our site—we're doing fine there—what I'm most interested in is having the TopRank brand name be perpetuated to their readership.

That demonstrates the benefit of establishing yourself as an industry authority.

Yeah, that's right!

Sound Bites

Lee Odden has a lot of good advice for today's online marketers, not the least of which is the admonition to participate in online communities before you start marketing to them. Here are some other key points:

- Publish your media to different sites and channels to maximize the potential search engine hits—images to an image-sharing site, videos to YouTube, and so forth.
- All media are valuable, but none so much so as text, because of its importance to search engines.
- Most blog software is search-engine friendly out of the box and can provide a platform for delivering fresh content for the search bots.
- When content gets noticed and cited by multiple blogs, you get multiple links back to your main web site—which increases your site's PageRank.
- To succeed with social networking, you have to be transparent and honest.

Jill Whalen: High Rankings

17

> "*[Search engine optimization is] making your site the best it can be—for both the search engines and the users of the site.*"
>
> —Jill Whalen

Search engine optimization (SEO) is the key to making sure your site gets found by people searching at Google and other search engines for the information, products, or services that you offer. Jill Whalen has been doing SEO for more than a decade, which makes her as much an expert in the field as anyone out there. Her

firm, High Rankings, specializes in SEO services for companies big and small, and Jill herself is an in-demand speaker on the topic at numerous industry seminars and conferences.

Jill also writes the *High Rankings Advisor* search marketing newsletter, runs the High Rankings Search Engine Optimization Forum, and writes about SEO for various publications. In her spare time, such as it is, she co-founded a search marketing networking organization for New England (SEMNE)—which holds meetings every other month on various search marketing topics.

As you can see, Jill lives and breathes search engine optimization—which gives her some unique perspectives on the topic.

Optimizing Your Site for Google and Other Search Engines

Any business serious about marketing itself on the web has to get its hands around search engine optimization. That means optimizing the web site with just the right keywords in the right places—as Jill explains in the following interview.

What exactly is search engine optimization?

That's actually a tricky question. So many people have so many definitions of it that you could go to all kinds of sites online and find completely different definitions of it. My definition, that I've been using for many years now, is that it's making your site be the best it can be—for both the search engines and the users of the site.

That's a little bit different than what other people talk about. A lot of times other people are focused only on search engines, which just doesn't cut it these days.

How did you get involved in the field?

> *"SEO has changed... because the outside popularity of a web site is factored into how Google determines the relevancy of a page."*

I kind of just stumbled into it. About 14 years ago I had a parenting web site that I used to play around with and post parenting advice, and I wanted to figure out how to get it found in the search engines of the day, which were things like InfoSeek, Lycos, and Excite—engines that are pretty much not around anymore. I would look at what other sites were doing and what would make sites come up for certain words that I would type into those engines, then I'd look at the sites and look at their code and see what they did.

I realized, pretty early on, that it was the words on the page that really made a difference to why they would show up. It became relevant to the search query if those words were being used on the page. That's basically the way I've always been doing SEO.

That was very early on the web, obviously. How has this whole thing changed over the years?

It's changed significantly. It happens gradually, so I don't always notice it. Sometimes I think it hasn't changed as much as some people do; the more it changes, the more it stays the same.

Certainly, the search engines have changed. There was no such thing as Google back when I started this. Now Google is pretty much the only one that we even worry about anymore, because that's the one that everyone uses.

The way we do SEO has changed, to a certain extent, because the outside popularity of a web site is factored into how Google determines the relevancy of a page. They have what they call their PageRank algorithm, and that depends a lot on what other people are saying about your site. They try to determine what are the most popular sites out there, and they assume that the most popular ones are probably going to be good, because they're popular. To determine that popularity, they use links, because that's an easy way to figure it out; if people are linking to this site, it must be good. They count a link as a "vote" for the site.

So linking and getting links, and having a great site that people will link to and being popular, has become an important factor that we really didn't have as much of in the early days.

Why do you think Google has become so popular? What set it apart from the Excites and the Alta Vistas and all those sites from years past?

Originally, it was because it was better. I mean, it was *way* better.

At the time, before Google came about, Alta Vista was the best. I remember reading about it in '95; it came out of Digital Equipment Corp., which was local here in Massachusetts. I remember trying Alta Vista, and it was a big jump up from the other ones. It was really good.

Then, I remember when someone told me about Google. It was still on the Stanford site; it wasn't even at Google.com. I tried that one, and that was another leap forward. You could find what you were looking for so much easier. I remember telling my husband about it, because he was having to do different searches for work, and he could really see the difference, too.

That's how it spread. People were telling their friends about Google: "Try this; if you can't find what you're looking for with Alta Vista or the other engines, try this one." Suddenly you could find what you were looking for, fairly easily—or at least comparatively easily. That's kind of what brought it day-to-day respect.

The others also kind of lost it, too. Alta Vista wanted to become a portal and have all kinds of stuff on the home page. Google was simple. If you wanted to search you just went there, it was a search box, you did it, you found what you were looking for.

These days there's not as much difference in the quality of the results. It's more Google's game to lose, because people just love it.

Everyone is aiming at Google—Microsoft is, you still have Yahoo!—but they don't seem to be making much ground, do they?

No, because Google's gotten itself into the popular culture. You can't watch a TV show these days without them mentioning Google. It's kind of amazing to have watched it grow like this, especially the past few years.

Yahoo! and MSN, they're still not quite as good as Google in results. I try every now and then to do searches—real searches, not just for clients—I try them in Yahoo! or MSN. Oftentimes I'll find what I'm looking for, but sometimes not. Sometimes I feel I could be getting better stuff. I'll go to Google and, sure enough, I do get better stuff. I do think that they are still a step above. The others are okay, they work, but Google definitely shows the better of the sites.

From the standpoint of Google's search results, how has that changed over the past five or six years?

Of course, there's sponsored ads, on the right side and on the top [of the search results], that they didn't have in the very early years. Some people still don't realize that those are paid-for ads.

> *"Most of the time what we need to do is keyword research."*

Recently, they have a new thing called Universal Search. Now you do a search and you may see a little video clip pop up or a little picture in the search results, where you can click it and go straight to a video. That's partially because they bought YouTube, and they also have their own Google Video search engine. So they've integrated that into the search results. That's pretty new. They're trying to give people more variety in what they might see.

This incorporation of Universal Search—does it change how a business approaches search engine optimization?

It probably will. It is so new, people are scrambling to see what happens with it. They're changing it all the time, too, so at this point I wouldn't recommend companies to worry about it too much. You have to feel it out, see what happens with it.

If you do have video content that you make, or your marketing materials for PR purposes, then it probably is a good idea to submit them to YouTube, because those videos do tend to show in the search results now. Whether people should just start going out and making videos, that's yet to be seen. We'll have to see how it plays out.

Let's say you have a client who signs you up to work with their site. How do you approach the whole search engine optimization process?

Our process basically starts with a complete site audit, a complete review of the site. We review everything that they've got so far. Most of our clients already have a web site, so we look at that site, we see what it's doing right, what it's doing wrong, and let the client know. From there, that gives us a good idea of what needs to be done.

Most of the time what we need to do is keyword research, which is a really important aspect of SEO. Without knowing the keyword phrases that people are actually searching on in the engines, we don't know what to optimize for.

Back in the early days, when I was first doing this, we didn't have keyword research tools; we just basically had to guess. If I were looking for this, I'd type this into a search engine. So you'd optimize for your guesses and you might be right, you might be wrong. You might be number one for the phrase you optimized for, but you're not getting any traffic for it because nobody's searching for it.

> *"Make sure that the most important pages of the site are actually being linked to in your main navigation."*

So it's really important to use the tools that are available these days, like Keyword Discovery and Wordtracker. That's really the first thing, because keyword phrases are the cornerstone of anything that you do for search engines.

How do you optimize the site?

Once you know the keywords, then you have to figure out which pages of the site do these keywords belong on, because every page on your site can be a gateway to the rest of it. It's not like people are going to only come in through the home page of the site. You want to make sure you're not trying to do everything with the home page.

You need to look at the existing pages of your site and see where these keyword phrases can fit in, where do they make the most sense. What we do, and our processes are somewhat different from others, is we look at these different pages and then make a list from our keyword research. These key phrases will go on this page and these on this page, et cetera, et cetera.

From there, we optimize pages. That would mean you make sure that the keyword phrases were in things like <title> tags, <meta> description tags, and the content of the page.

There's also all kinds of things you need to do with the whole site architecture. Make sure that the most important pages of the site are actually being linked to in your main navigation, and not somehow buried. If they're in your main navigation, you're telling the search engine—and people—that these are the most important pages of the site. And they will tend to have a better shot at ranking higher, because of that.

You mentioned earlier that part of Google's PageRank is how many sites link to your site. How do you manage that in the optimization process?

That's a big piece of it. We like to make sure that we get the on-page stuff in good order first. So first you worry about that. We see so many people, they're all talking about links and all that, but they haven't got their pages correctly set up for search engines. You have to worry about that first.

> "What it really comes down to is being something that I call 'linkworthy.'"

Once you've got that as good as it can be, then you can worry about links. With existing sites that have been around for years, chances are you probably already have a lot of links. It's interesting; there's a lot of companies just assuming they have to do some kind of link-building campaign. But well-respected brands and larger companies, even small ones that have been on the web for a long time, don't necessarily need to go do anything to get links; they have them already, just by naturally being out there.

What it really comes down to is being something that I call "linkworthy." Having a site that *is* linkworthy. If you have a poor site, nothing on there that's informative, or you're selling just the same old products that hundreds or thousands of other sites are selling, you probably *aren't* going to get links. You aren't going to be popular. You can't just make any site be popular and get links if there's nothing unique to buy or interesting to do.

The key to getting links is being creative, adding value that others aren't doing in your space—and then getting the word out about it. You can make all those changes, do all those things, and if nobody knows about it, they're still not going to link to you. Then it comes back to traditional publicity. I recommend hiring a publicity firm, these days, because they can create a buzz about you and give you ideas of things you can do that are unique and interesting. Once they've talked about you, whether it's online or offline, it's going to generate links online eventually, because people start talking about it online, in various places, and that gets you links. That's what Google is looking for—the companies that are the best and the most popular.

It sounds like it comes down to business basics. You have to start with the good content, and then work from there.

It does. It really comes back around to that. People used to think that the web was somehow different from offline, that anyone could just slap up a web page and get results overnight. There might have been a few that got lucky somehow, but it's not like that. You have to build a real business online, and then it's hard work, it's making something good.

It's like any business; you can't just open up a store somewhere and expect to get business. It's all marketing, and it's really come full circle now, with people trying to understand that you have to market your web site—online and offline and any way that you can.

> *"A complete Flash site basically is a blank page to the search engines."*

You were talking earlier about keyword optimization and working on the keywords in various parts of the site. What about those sites that don't open up with text; they open up with this big Flash-produced extravaganza. Does that sort of thing rank with the search engines?

If the site's popular anyway, that popularity component can be enough, even though there are no words on the page. A complete Flash site basically is a blank page to the search engines. If the site's completely in Flash, they have no idea what the site's about. They will base it on links and the anchor text, which is the clickable part of a link that points to a page. If all the anchor text pointing to that particular page has, say, a certain keyword phrase, then that can help that page to rank well, even though it doesn't have any content that the search engines can read.

> *"The biggest mistake is not thinking about SEO as you do your design or redesign."*

Certainly, I wouldn't want to depend on just links. I would want to make sure that my site has information for the search engines, as well—as well as for people who don't want to look at the Flash page.

Sometimes it makes sense for some sites to be in all Flash. There's game sites and things like that, that's all they need to do. And that's fine. But the average business site, or anyone selling a service or product, they certainly don't need all that. It's not really good for people or for search engines.

I get the impression, looking at some sites, that they turned it all over to the designers and didn't have the marketing people involved at all.

That's usually the case. Then they come to me and say, "We're not getting found in the search engines at all. We just paid $100,000 for this web site, what can you do?" And I say, "Well, you better do a redesign." They don't want to hear that, usually.

This leads to another question. As you're working with companies across the board, what are the common mistakes that you find?

That's certainly one of them!

The biggest mistake is not thinking about SEO as you do your design or redesign. That's the most common thing. So many times they get through doing the redesign and they say, okay, now it's time to do SEO. It's like, no, you should have been talking about SEO as you were doing the redesign. You should be consulting with an SEO expert during that time, to make sure that the structure of the site is optimized—and everything that you put on the site is optimized

It's the whole keyword research thing. You don't want to do a redesign of the site without doing keyword research along with it, so you know what pages you need on your site. What are people looking for that you want them to find on your site? Then make sure you can show them exactly that. It's so much easier if you do it at the same time that you're doing your design.

That's probably the biggest mistake, and the most common. I don't think that's so painful, but people just don't get that. Instead they're putting Band-Aids on later, when they come and finally realize that they're not getting traffic.

The other big mistakes are sort of similar. They're just using graphics and not text that the search engines can read. They haven't done keyword research, so they don't know what people are searching for. They might make navigation that's not

> *"There are a lot of web site designers that don't really get how to do [SEO]."*

followable, so the search engines can't get to every page of the site. They might use JavaScript links or even a Flash menu that search engines can't follow. If [the search engines] can't get to all the pages of your site, then they don't know they exist, and you can't get linked with them.

Who's better at doing this—big companies or small companies?

It depends. It depends on who's working there, who's got some knowledge, and if they've thought about it.

Things have definitely changed, where the average person does at least know that SEO exists. They may not know exactly how to do it, but they do know it exists.

But there are a lot of web site designers that don't really get how to do it. That's a big problem, too. If 80 percent of the web site designers—and I'm just making a random number up—don't know how to do SEO very well, they're creating all these web sites out there that just won't have much luck in the search engines at all. That's a big problem.

I would suggest that any web designers try to partner with some SEO consultant, so that when they're redesigning and designing sites for their clients, they don't give them a useless page or web site that isn't going to get them much traffic or sales.

I've seen plenty of those, unfortunately. To wrap this up, what advice would you give a company that's putting up a new web site or redesigning their web site right now?

The big advice is to do keyword research. Then make sure, minimally, that you get about three different keyword phrases into those `<title>` tags. Not the `<meta>` keyword tag—don't worry about that one—but the `<title>` tag. It is given a ton of weight [by the search engines]. Sometimes just having some phrases in there, even if you can't get them into your copy, for whatever reason, or you're not ready to do that, at least get them into those `<title>` tags. That can often be a quick fix for a site that hasn't had any SEO at all.

Sound Bites

Search engine optimization might sound complicated, but as Jill Whalen explains, it doesn't need to be. The key thing is to think about SEO when you're designing the site (not after), and make sure the content on your site is "linkworthy."

Here are some more tips:

- If you design your site to provide value to your target users, that's a big first step in the optimization process.
- Links from other sites to your site are as important as the keywords you include on your site.
- Do your keyword research upfront to determine what words your visitors are likely searching for.
- Determine which pages of the site are best for which keywords.
- Put the appropriate keyword phrases in your site's underlying `<title>` and `<meta>` descriptive tags.
- Make sure that the most important pages of your site are linked to in your site's main navigation.

And, most important, don't undertake a site design or redesign without first taking SEO into account. Even the best-looking site design is worthless if no one can find your site via Google search!

Liana Evans: KeyRelevance

18

"If you optimize it and it's relevant for the keyword, it's probably going to rank."

—*Liana Evans*

Liana "Li" Evans is a search marketing guru. In fact, she's editor of the Search Marketing Gurus blog, which is one of the most respected such resources on the web; the blog features writing from Li and a variety of search marketing professionals, including Greg Meyers, Alex Cohen, Karl Ribas, Michael Abolafia, and Y.M. Ousley.

> **FACT SHEET: LIANA EVANS**
>
> Director of Internet Marketing, KeyRelevance (www.keyrelevance.com)
>
> Editor, Search Marketing Gurus Blog (www.searchmarketinggurus.com)

Li's day job is as director of marketing for KeyRelevance, a Dallas-based online marketing firm that she joined after leaving Commerce360, a similar company in the Philadelphia area. She is also an active contributor to a variety of search engine optimization forums, including those at Crea8site, High Rankings, Search Engine Watch, and Search Engine Guide. Li has also been a speaker at the Search Engine Strategies conference, WebmasterWorld's Pubcon conference, and Danny Sullivan's SMX (Search Marketing Expo).

Taking Advantage of Search Engine Marketing and Social Networking

While Li's long-held specialty is search engine marketing and optimization, she has a newfound passion for social networking. Read on to learn what advice Li has about both popular types of online marketing.

Let's talk a little about your background. How did you get started in the search business?

I have a technical background, so I can actually build databases and run programs and all different kinds of things. I had gone back to college and while I was at college in 1995 to 1996, I started building web sites on the side. Then I started figuring out how they started ranking at sites like Northern Lights and InfoSeek, all of the predecessors of Google. I found I had a real knack for that.

At the time, there was no such thing as search marketing. You couldn't make a living in search marketing. So I just did that on the side, while I was doing programming. Eventually, the market opened up and I fell right into it. I've been doing it full-time since 2003—but part-time since '95.

Obviously, you've been involved in the search industry pre-Google. How has search evolved over the years?

It's pretty interesting, because as time goes on, the search engines get a little bit smarter—not only about how people try to game search engines, but also about how people want things presented to them. Everybody says we're going to get to the way of artificial intelligence, but I still think that you'll need that human component in there.

They're trying to present it in a more human way, especially with the advent of universal search or blended search or whatever you want to call it. Now the four major search engines are trying to present you with more than ten blue links. They're showing videos, they're showing pictures, you can play songs in the actual results.

> *"It's hard…to see anything upsetting Google's apple cart at this point in time."*

I think it's just naturally evolved. First we figured, "Let's have a directory-like structure." Then it was, "Wait, let's do a little bit of search and present ten blue links." It's becoming more and more about what is relevant, not how to game the system. It's getting your content out to places where you can distribute it more. You can actually be in search engines with more real estate and be more relevant.

Do you see much of a future for some of Google's competitors? For example, I live in Indianapolis and just down the road from me is ChaCha, Scott Jones's company, which is trying to bring a human element into search. How do you think that's going to play out?

When it comes to ChaCha and Mahalo, I'm skeptical. It's like everything that comes out these days—it's the "Google killer." I'm very skeptical about that because I think Google and Yahoo!, those two, have become so ingrained in society. It's tough to see those things coming out and competing.

Unless they have something really spectacular, it's hard as a search marketer to see anything upsetting Google's apple cart at this point in time. That's not to say something won't, but I don't see that happening in the next year or two. Maybe five years from now, if there's some sort of dramatic technology change, then we might see some kind of change in the market. But with the way things are going now, Google is just so ingrained. You hear on TV, "Did you Google that person?"

It's tough to see something like Mahalo and ChaCha doing it. It would be neat to see it happen, but I don't think, realistically, it probably will.

What about the second-tier players today, Microsoft and Ask.com, for example—what can they do to compete with Google?

I think Ask and Microsoft are really making headway in that area. When Yahoo! launched their new platform, we have all four search engines with new ways of delivering the search results, that's a little bit more intuitive and more friendly. Whoever can make it the most friendly to the user, that's who's going to win.

It's also about being the most relevant, as well. For years and years and years, Google has been the most relevant. But if somebody else can come up with something that's showing as more relevant…

Ask, even though it has a very small percentage [of users] compared to Google, has been gaining in its market share. They're really small, but any small chunk off of Google is a pretty big thing. But it's really tough right now to see anybody like ChaCha or Mahalo taking over those places.

Microsoft definitely has the opportunity to, if they could get their algorithm to be a little bit more relevant. It's pretty much well known within our search circles that the MSN algorithm is the easiest to game, for people who do the spamming, the unethical things within search marketing. The spammers just target MSN, because it's so easy to do. Where Google is a little bit tougher; the same with Yahoo!

> *"It's really about looking at your audience and knowing your audience."*

I really, really like Ask's new presentation. I actually like Yahoo!'s new presentation, as well. Yahoo!'s being inclusive. If you're on Yahoo! and you're searching for anything and a video comes up, they don't just limit it to Yahoo!'s videos. They will play MetaCafe in their actual results, where Google is only showing Google and YouTube at this point in time.

In six weeks that might change, but whoever's serving the most relevant results—and that means being inclusive—that's who's going to win in the end.

It's hard for some people to think of Microsoft as the underdog, but they are in the search race. If you're a business allocating your search marketing budget, how much attention do you pay to the companies that aren't Google?

How I look at it is, who is your audience? You really have to know who your audience is. If your audience is female and over 50, you might not be getting a lot of traffic from Google; you might be getting more traffic from MSN or you might be getting more traffic from Yahoo! So that's how you decide. You really have to look at your metrics so you can see where they're coming from. That's how you should look at where you should be putting your budget.

It's not necessarily always Google that's going to be your number one. Eight times out of ten it probably is, but there's always those times when you have a very niche product that appeals to an audience that isn't Google. It could be MSN, it could be Yahoo!. It could even be Ask. It's really about looking at your audience and knowing your audience.

When you're talking about search engine optimization, is it different when you're optimizing for the different engines?

Not really. Basically, they all take the core values of everything that you do that is relevant to the page; they just apply different metrics to different things. One might weigh something a little bit more than the other. We just never know what that is.

For example, Google has PageRank. Everybody lives and dies by Google's PageRank, but that's not the only thing that they take into account in their algorithm. It's a big part of it, but they also take into account who's linking to you, they take into account what's on your page, they take into account how the people are linking to you.

Now, Yahoo! doesn't have PageRank. They probably have something very similar to PageRank, in their own inside metrics, but they don't post anything like Google PageRank. But they also have algorithms and they apply different things to it.

At the core, then, if you optimize it and it's relevant for the keyword, it's probably going to rank—even if it ranks different among the different search engines.

Just how do you go about optimizing a site for Google and the other search engines?

There's a lot of different key factors.

One of the things that I think is very important is that the content on your web site is on topic. That's the biggest thing that you want to make sure is being related. So if you're talking about blue widgets, your page should be all about blue widgets. It should be talking about how great the blue widgets are, what you can do with the blue widgets, those types of things.

Then there are different key elements on the page itself that you can optimize—like the `<title>` tag, you want to make sure you have some headers, even some pictures. But you want to make sure you're actually getting some content on there that the spiders can actually read and understand what the page is about.

Once you start combining all this stuff—the content with the on-page elements—then you start getting out there and say, "Hey, look at my page—it's about blue widgets," then people will start linking to it. If they want to talk about blue widgets, they'll say, "here's a great resource on blue widgets." If you naturally get links, that helps pull everything else in together.

The thing to do is look at links as being sort of like a vote of confidence that, hey, this site is about blue widgets. So take that along with how that link's formed, your `<title>` tag, and all the content on the page—that's how it's all put together.

If content is the most important thing to pay attention to, what's the least important thing?

A lot of people used to put a lot of stock in your `<meta>` tags. There's a few `<meta>` tags that you should have, and there's a few that really don't matter for competitive keywords.

> "The first impression you have to give a user is what your site is about."

For example, the `keywords` `<meta>` tag, people back in the day used to stuff that tag with sometimes over 500 or 1,000 keywords in there. They would think that that would get them to the top of the search engines. Well, the search engines have devalued that tag. So if you were writing a page about Viagra and you put "Viagra" in your `keywords` fifty times, that's not going to help you. If you put in "Viagara"—spelled not the right way—that *could* help you.

So the tag that probably doesn't have that much value is the `keywords` tag—but it still does have a little bit of use.

What tips might you give someone who's trying to optimize their site today?

Make sure you change your `<title>` tag and your `<meta>` `description` tag for each page. Here's why:

The first impression you have to give a user is what your site is about, and that's your listing in the search engine results. Even though the `<meta>` `description` tag is devalued, just like the `keywords` tag, it still helps the user to identify what the site is about and do they really want to click through and go to your site. You know the old adage about the first impression is everything? On the web, it's the same thing. If somebody is searching for those blue widgets and you have a great `<title>` tag that says "Blue widgets from a great company" or "Blue widgets on sale" or "We have the best blue widgets," you explain a little bit about what's on the page, that tells the user, "Hey, this page is pretty much what I'm looking for." So you're more likely to get somebody to click through and see the page.

Search isn't the only thing happening on the web right now, of course. You have the whole social networking thing happening— can you talk a little about that, and how that factors in?

I love social networking! Social media has such potential for businesses, because there are so many different aspects of social media.

A lot of people, when they think about social media, they think it's MySpace or Facebook or Digg, but it's not only that. Social media has actually been around a lot longer than anybody realizes. It's been around since the dawn of the message board. That's social networking; that's people talking back and forth to each other, creating their own content and pointing people to web sites that are on topic to what they're talking about. So the concept of social media has been around for a long time; it's just the wording, people calling it "social media," that's kind of new. It's been exploding within the last year and a half.

It gives a great opportunity for business people to have a conversation about their product or their service or who they are. What better way to engage a customer than to speak with them, or have them to talk to you on your web site? It gives web sites another outlet to help build

> *"[Social media is] another way to drive traffic to your site that's beyond the search engines."*

the conversation and help direct people to their web site to see if that's really what they want to find or use or discover. It's another great way to propagate your content.

When you're doing that, does that also factor into the search engine marketing?

Sure, it does. Take, for example, you might be a review site for movies, and you just started a blog about reviewing movies. Well, it might be a good thing to get involved with the forums at Rotten Tomatoes, because Rotten Tomatoes is all about movies. If you start interacting with that community, eventually you can start saying, "Hey, I just wrote a really good review about this movie that came out." You've now directed people to come and read it, and if they like it, they might turn around and link to it and drive more traffic to your site.

So it's another way to drive traffic to your site that's beyond the search engines. But it also has the added benefit that that link is on topic and it's going to point to your web site. Google's going to say, "Hey, that's a great on-topic link to the web site; they're giving it a vote of confidence; maybe this is a little bit more relevant."

It's twofold in that it gives another way of traffic but it also helps you in the search engine, to get that extra oomph, by getting the links in there.

So what advice would you give a company who wants to take advantage of social networking?

It's just like with what search engines you want to look at; it's knowing your audience. If I'm that movie blog, I know I want to go to Rotten Tomatoes, or I know I want to go to TV.com, or I might want to go to the IMDB [Internet Movie Database] forums, and start connecting with that community. Going to Digg probably wouldn't get me anywhere, because Digg isn't really a good social place to talk about movies. Or going to a diving community probably wouldn't be a good place to look at.

It's all about knowing your audience and knowing where your audience is and where they're having their discussions, where they're holding their conversations. When you know that, then you can join the conversation and you can really work with social media.

Let's talk a little about your company, KeyRelevance. What services do they offer to the online business?

We offer SEO (search engine optimization) and we mount PPC (pay per click) campaigns. We do online reputation management. We do social media strategies for clients. We do linking strategies for clients, as well. We're also doing some public relations on the web, helping clients optimize their press releases and making sure they get out there and they're discovered. It's a whole gamut of all different kinds of marketing stuff online that we do.

With all the different ways that a company can spend money online, what's the best way to divide up the budget?

It depends on how old your site is.

If it's a new site, then you have to put more money into PPC, because SEO will take a little bit of time before it actually takes hold and you can start to rank. So you want to look at ramping up with some PPC and then doing a little bit of social media and some linking strategy work. Then, in the background, you're going to be building your SEO.

If you are a site that has been established, then you can probably look at different keywords, re-look at your PPC campaign and look at where the opportunities are. If you're not ranking for some key terms, you can build on your SEO and spread that across social media and some linking strategies.

So it depends on the maturity of the site and how well you are ranking in your market areas. Even if you aren't [ranking], with a few changes you might be able to own those areas.

Is there anything you wanted to add for our readers?

One of the things that people overlook is that shopping comparison engines, like Shopping.com or Shopzilla, all accept feeds. So do Google and MSN, which let you upload your feeds to them for free; Yahoo! you have to pay for. Anybody who's not doing that who's in retail or they have some kind of news, they can upload this stuff for free, and it's another place to get your content out there. A lot of people don't realize that's available for them.

Any time a search engine is saying, "Hey, give us your content," give it to them! It's another place that somebody else can find you.

Sound Bites

From search engine optimization to social media—as Li Evans notes, it's all important. So what should you take away from this interview? Here are the key points:

- For the time being, Google, Yahoo!, Microsoft, and Ask are the most important search engines; the smaller players don't have much chance of breaking through the ranks.
- Google is the big dog, of course, but other engines might be better to reach particular types of users.
- Even though search engines rank different factors differently, the same basic SEO techniques will help your ranking across the board.
- When optimizing your site, focus on relevant content first and link building second.

- Also important: the `<title>` tag and `<meta>` description tags.
- Social media provides an opportunity for business people to engage their customers in conversation—if you choose relevant sites.

If you want more advice on an ongoing basis, check out Li's Search Marketing Gurus blog; it's a great source of relevant, high-quality information for all online marketing professionals.

Perry Marshall:
Perry S. Marshall & Associates

19

"You use Google to test everything and get the message right—and then you go to the other places."

—*Perry Marshall*

Perry Marshall is an entrepreneur, a published author, and a recognized Google AdWords expert. He's sold products on the web, he's started and sold companies, and he's offered all manner of consulting and educational services.

All of this makes Perry a good person to go to if you want to learn more about using Google AdWords to promote your business. In fact, Perry was using Google AdWords before it became a big thing, when Google was still an upstart search engine competing with the mighty Yahoo! behemoth.

> FACT SHEET:
> **PERRY MARSHALL**
>
> President, Perry S. Marshall & Associates (www.perrymarshall.com)
>
> Author, *The Definitive Guide to Google AdWords* (Entrepreneur Press, 2006)

Using Google AdWords for Market Testing

One of Perry's key messages is that AdWords isn't just for advertising; it's also for market testing. That is, you can use AdWords to quickly and easily fine-tune your marketing message, and then export that message to other advertising media. Read on to learn more.

Let's talk a little bit about you and what you do.

I am a specialist in a variety of direct marketing disciplines, but what I'm known for is Google AdWords.

AdWords started in 2000; it was Google's first significant source of revenue. What I quickly discovered, when they introduced that program, was that they had taken an idea that Overture (which is now Yahoo! Search Marketing) had started, and Google had actually done it right. I was amazed at how right they had done it.

They had created a system where you could almost instantly bid on a keyword and trigger an ad to be shown, and a person would then click to your web site and land on the exact page you wanted him to. But they'd added a couple of extra twists to it. One was they rewarded you for writing a better ad; ads that get clicked on move higher in the rankings and/or you can pay less money for the same click. And they let you test multiple ads against each other, so almost in real time you can find out which ads are more popular and which ads are less popular. They designed the system so that advertisers could evolve their marketing message to match the market. It was just extraordinary.

> *"If you can compete, buying commodity traffic…then you've got a good offer."*

For about a year, I considered this the best-kept secret. It was a little trickier to use than Overture's system and most people were still on Overture, but I got in there and started using it. I saw it as when you are going to market something on the Internet, this is normally—maybe not always—but this is normally going to be the place where you're going to start. This is going to be the place where you get your advertising message ironed out and working correctly.

About a year later I got invited to speak at a seminar about it. I started grabbing the bull by the horns and making it a big part of what I do.

So now you consult about AdWords. Do you also use AdWords yourself, in your business?

Oh yeah. Oh yeah. I give Google a lot of money!

That's not my MO; I really don't give a rip about Google per se. What I do give a rip about is people being able to profitably advertise their businesses. Then I deal with all the other stuff that comes after that first click—landing pages and copy and people's unique selling proposition and the offer they're making and the follow-up process, the testing process they use to increase their profitability. All that stuff I'm concerned with.

Let's talk about that a little bit. Let's say someone has a business where they're selling some stuff online. Walk them through the process; what would you recommend they do in terms of using Google AdWords to promote their business?

The assumption is what you sell is something that people are actively searching for. Now that is not always true. There are plenty of things that get sold every day that hardly anybody searches for online, like toilet paper. You know, hardly anybody searches for toilet paper on the Internet, because we all have a way that we buy it already and we all know where to get it. We all use it, but don't go typing in "toilet paper" on a search engine.

Another thing is, it's really hard to advertise to a problem that people don't know they have. Let's say that you're in nutrition and you happen to know that if people take this certain mineral that they would live ten years longer. Well, how many people are typing in "live ten years longer?" Some people are, but a very small percentage of people do that, compared to the number of people that could take it. I always have the example, if you had a pill that you could drop in somebody's gas tank and it would triple their gas mileage, everybody in the world would want it—but hardly anybody woke in the morning searching for it today.

But there are all kinds of things, like people are interested in tattoo pictures or interested in weight loss, or people are interested in finding a dentist or whatever, there's millions and millions of things that people search. And you can use the keyword tools that are available, like Wordtracker, to find out that 160,000 people searched for "paintball" last month—so, gee, there's a market there.

So that's the assumption. If a person is searching for that and there's a whole parade of people going through that are looking for something, then now you have a commodity market for traffic. It's whoever writes appealing ads and bids the most money and can make money on every single click, every single day—that's who gets to advertise.

Now there's a benchmark—and the benchmark is, Can you make your offer more popular than the other guy's offer? Can you compete with the other main players in that market? If you can compete, buying commodity traffic, with your offer, then you've got a good offer. Now you can take that offer to other places, like to e-zines and affiliates and banner ads and publicity and on the free search engine traffic, in addition to the paid search engine traffic.

So you're really talking about using Google as test marketing?

Yes. You use Google to test everything and get the message right—and then you go to the other places. That's why Google's the starting place.

How would you use Google to test a couple of different ad messages?

Have you ever heard of a book called *The 4-Hour Workweek*? [Timothy Ferriss, Crown, 2007] The guy that wrote that book, he had a bunch of different ideas for what to call his book. Some of them were completely different titles—I don't remember what they all were. One of them had something to do with sitting at the beach and making money; I don't know. But he took a bunch of different phrases and title ideas, and he bought keywords and he wrote Google ads, and "4-hour workweek" was the Google ad that got the most response. So that's what the book was called, and now it's a best-seller.

I can guarantee you, if that book had a different title, it would not be a best-seller. Tim Ferriss testing that Google ad was a crucial element to him making it big as an author.

> *"One of the very first things you should test is what domain name people actually like to read in your Google ads."*

In the old days, sometimes they used to do that with classified ads. They would run classified ads in newspapers and they would run these many-weeks-long, meticulous, slow tests. Now you can do it in hours or days instead of weeks or months. In fact, the title of my book, *The Definitive Guide to Google AdWords*, is the result of exactly that sort of a test. The words "definitive guide" outperformed a whole bunch of other things that I tried.

Once you've settled on your message, are there ways to go about improving your click-through rate?

You might start with a whole bunch of different title ideas, like "The Definitive Guide to Google AdWords" or "How to Be Successful with Google AdWords." I could come up with all sorts of titles, and then I come up with some winners, and then I refine the titles even more—changing one word instead of an entire phrase or idea, changing the capitalization, using punctuation or dashes or semicolons or exclamation marks, testing different URLs.

I own a whole bunch of different domain names; perrymarshall.com is one of them. But I also own adwordsstrategy.com and I own adwordsbook.com. I tried these different URLs, too, and I found out that some web site URLs are much more appealing to people than others. As a matter of fact, this has become one of the core things that I teach: When you start an online business, one of the very first things you should test is what domain name people actually like to read in your Google ads. It makes a substantial difference.

I worked with a startup company late last year [2006], and we found that with their original domain name, the cost to acquire a customer was 150 percent higher than with the best domain name I came up with. That's huge. That's probably the difference between survival and failure of the entire company. And that's just hinging on this one little thing.

Everybody who's started a business knows how delicate the thing was at some point, and how many hours of effort you would expend just to fix this one little thing that's going wrong today. If you could make your job 150 percent easier by changing one word in your business, which is the name of your web site, why wouldn't you? And then that rolls out into all the other things that you do in your marketing, every other way that you advertise.

When people are using AdWords in this fashion, what are some of the more common mistakes that you find?

The most common mistake is people who come up with a whole bunch of keywords, dump them into an ad group, write an ad, send people to the home page of their web site—and then they wonder why it's not working. If you don't really know anything about this, you would listen to that and go, "What's wrong with that?"

What's wrong with that is the lack of specificity. If you're a chiropractor, for example, then there's all kinds of keywords that you might possibly bid on. You might bid on "back pain," you might bid on "chiropractor Atlanta Georgia," you might bid on "knee pain" or "neck pain," you might bid on something like "chronic fatigue" or "fibromyalgia" or something like that. Well, "fibromyalgia" requires a different ad and a different landing page than "neck pain." You need a fibromyalgia ad, and a fibromyalgia landing page, and an explanation of why you would go to a chiropractor for fibromyalgia.

So you're really talking about multiple ads, multiple landing pages, to sell the same product or service?

Yes! That's just absolutely critical. If somebody's searching for a green silk tie, then you need a green silk tie ad, and a green silk tie landing page, and a picture of a green silk tie right there, so when they land there they go, "Yeah, that was exactly what I was looking for."

To compare it to a physical store, in a physical store you have to walk through the front door and you have to walk past all the suits and everything to get to the ties. But on the Internet you take them right to the ties and show them exactly what they want. After they put that in the shopping cart, then maybe you offer them other things.

How does all this tie into the concept of guerrilla marketing?

Jay Conrad Levinson made that term popular, and you compare it to warfare. There was this traditional way of fighting wars—your guys line up on this side and our guys line up on that side, then we point our guns at one another and somebody says, "Ready, set, go," and we shoot. Guerrilla marketing says, "Hey, they've got a hundred, we've only got ten, there's no way we're ever gonna win if we're matched up like that. So who says that we have to line up, and who says that we have to start when somebody says 'Go,' and who says that we have to fight on equal terms? Who says we can't hide in the trees? Who says we can't use Molotov cocktails?"

> "Direct marketing is a game that's played by people who buy advertising with their own money."

I'm not trying to be salacious here with some violence metaphor, but hey, business is brutal. You use any means necessary. So guerrilla marketing usually means direct-response marketing that is completely results accountable. It usually means using publicity and all the forms of free advertising that you can. It usually means getting viral word of mouth kind of stuff working for you. All of those things, the success of them hinges on the fundamental quality and reliability of your core marketing message—which you get right buying clicks and testing. It's a methodical process.

This sounds like a process that any size business can take advantage of?

Yeah—and the smaller businesses are, I think the more easily they're persuaded to do this. Big corporations, it's kind of hard to get them to, because everybody's got an idea and somebody else is paying the bill.

> *"We're going to get to a place where every one dollar we spend on traffic, we get two dollars back."*

I've always said that direct marketing is a game that's played by people who buy advertising with their own money. When you buy it with your money, that has a funny way of making you smarter a lot faster.

If somebody comes to you for help in this, what services do you offer them?

We've got a whole bunch of different things. We have a free email course and free tutorial, Five Days to Success with Google AdWords. We have a book called *The Definitive Guide to Google AdWords*, which we sell. I have a newsletter called The Perry Marshall Marketing Letter that's part of my Renaissance Club, which is a monthly subscription. I have several levels of coaching groups, where we do telephone coaching and we help walk people step-by-step through this whole process. I've got a course, for technical and business-to-business people, on using white papers as a lead-generation tool. We do various kinds of programs throughout the year, depending on what the schedule is, and you can check our web site for that.

And you attract people to all this via Google AdWords?

Yes, we do, absolutely—and a lot of other ways, too. AdWords is one of the primary ones, but we also have lots of affiliates who send us traffic, we also get free searches in traffic, because of the positioning of our web site on the Internet. I've got a book in the bookstores; I get customers from that. I do interviews like this one. It all kind of adds together.

You don't want to have a one-legged stool. A one-legged stool is better than a zero-legged stool, but once you have one leg, it's time to build another one and another one.

Is there any general advice you'd give to someone who's trying to improve their online marketing today?

I would encourage people to not get taken in by the hype. I suppose it's inevitable; pretty much anybody who gets interested in promoting their web site, making money online, and all of that, within a few weeks they're going to be on a dozen different email lists and they're going to be bombarded and blasted by all kinds of stuff. I would caution people to be careful to not get all enamored with the "idea of the week" bandwagon. There's a real seduction there, to get lured into "Oh, I gotta do this. Oh, I gotta do that." There's no real focus or strategy; it's just whatever somebody managed to sell you today.

People end up with a bookshelf full of CDs and manuals and a laptop full of e-books and stuff, but there's no disciplined strategy to move the ball forward step by step by step. This is actually very simple. What we're trying to do here is find a place where a person is definitely looking for something and has an itch to scratch, and we're going to understand exactly what that itch is and exactly how to scratch it. We're going to test different things, and we're going to get to a place where every one dollar we spend on traffic, we get two dollars back. That's the goal.

You don't need to do a dozen different strategies every week to make that work. You need two or three strategies, and [you need to] be consistent with them. All those other ideas will come into play in time, after you get your engine built.

Sound Bites

The concept of using Google AdWords for market testing was new to me before I talked to Perry Marshall. It makes sense; the speed with which you can create or change an ad and then see immediate results makes AdWords a very responsive testing mechanism. Just keep these points in mind:

- Create different AdWords ads with different combinations of keywords, and then compare the results.
- When you test different keywords, create unique ads and landing pages for each keyword.
- You can also use AdWords to test the pull of different URLs.

And don't forget Perry's parting words of advice—don't get seduced by every new idea that shows up in your inbox. Pick a basic strategy and stick to it—that consistency will pay off.

Kevin Lee:
Didit

20

"I think it comes back to Marketing 101. Who is your target audience? How are you trying to influence them?"

—Kevin Lee

Throughout this book we've heard from a lot of marketers with serious new technology credits. But now let's hear from someone firmly grounded in traditional marketing and advertising—and who has migrated this expertise to the online world. Kevin Lee started out working for traditional New York advertising agencies, like any good ad man of his generation. But he had, as he puts it, a "geeky" side, and eventually moved from Mad Ave to interactive advertising to online marketing. Today he's co-founder and executive chairman of Didit, one of the premier search engine marketing agencies today. Kevin is also a founding board member of the Search Engine Marketing Professional Organization (SEMPO); member of both the Interactive Advertising Bureau (IAB) and Direct Marketing Association (DMA); regular contributor to ClickZ; and author of *The Eyes Have It: How to Market in an Age of Divergent Consumers, Media Chaos and Advertising Anarchy*, a book highlighting the challenges faced by marketers within the digital media ecosystem where consumers control their consumption of both media and advertising. He is also as much on top of today's trends as anyone in the industry.

> **FACT SHEET: KEVIN LEE**
>
> Executive Chairman, Didit
> (www.didit.com)
>
> Author, *The Eyes Have It*
> (Easton Studio Press, 2007)

Migrating Traditional Advertising Online

More than anyone I've talked to, Kevin bridges the worlds of traditional advertising and online marketing. He speaks the language of advertising but with a technology accent; his views have particular relevance in terms of moving old-line advertisers into the online world.

How did you get started with online marketing?

It was interesting: after grad school I went to Madison Avenue and worked in mainstream advertising, which is an area of interest and an area of passion for me. Within those mainstream advertising agencies, I was considered to be the "geeky" one. So if it was technology-related, people would ask me questions about that. Whether it had to do with custom-tuning competitive ad spend reporting that was being computer generated or any technology-related question, I always got stuck with those. I considered this an area of pride, the fact that I was a little on the geeky side.

Then I had an opportunity to do some consulting for a much more nichey, high-tech ad agency that was doing some work in interactive marketing. This was in 1993. I gave my resignation at McCann-Erickson, which was one of the two agencies I had worked for (the other one was J. Walter Thompson). The managing director said, "You know, you haven't spent enough time working in the big agencies. You need more packaged-goods experience on your résumé. Besides, this interactive advertising stuff, it's completely unproven; are you really sure you want to go there now?"

I said, "It's interesting: you guys always had me working on the geeky stuff anyway. This will be an opportunity for me to combine some of my passion for advertising and marketing with what appears to be a natural predilection towards things technical." His words of wisdom were "you're making a big mistake," and the interesting irony was a year later I co-founded a small interactive shop, and then a year after that, co-founded Didit. At the time, obviously, the Internet was just getting started but I saw so much opportunity there that I was drawn to it as a way to combine my passion for advertising and marketing with my passion for technology.

Obviously, the big traditional agencies were slow to get hip to this. Are they getting it now?

They're certainly making a lot of acquisitions within interactive advertising, as well as within the search marketing space. Many of our competitors have been acquired either by holding-companies or by individual agencies that are under one of the big holding-company umbrellas. So they're trying to acquire the expertise by acquiring companies with this expertise—and that's not a bad stopgap. Whether or not they'll be able to adapt to the still-changing landscape and ecosystem of where marketing is going to go; I think that remains to be seen.

I've actually just finished writing a book of my own, called *The Eyes Have It*. It's all about the fragmentation of consumer consumption of media, the control over the advertising messages that consumers pay attention to, and how this dual fragmentation of the type of content

> *"Over time, [traditional] advertising will become less and less effective."*

that people are engaging with—whether it's video content, audio content, or written content—combined with the desire to pay attention only to advertising that is relevant, is really creating a bit of a quandary for the traditional agencies. In particular, it challenges the way that advertising and media is planned and purchased, which is, for lack of a better term, the "tonnage model." Media buyers and planners focus on getting the targeting ok; it doesn't have to be great—because if there's some waste in it, that's not that much of a big deal, especially if the media is not too expensive. The cost per thousand or GRP can be adjusted against the percentage of audience that fits my target and if more than half those exposed to the advertising are outside that target, the media buyer doesn't care.

My prediction, and the reason I wrote the book, is that over time, that kind of advertising will become less and less effective. The future will require narrowcast advertising, where the media is not only very narrowcast but the messages are far better tuned to specific sub-segments of the audience in order to be effective. Imagine the percentage of audience exposed to an ad for which the ad is relevant (and even interesting) skyrocketing from current levels to close to 100 percent.

Madison Avenue is quite concerned about this because accomplishing it takes a lot more man-hours, plus a technology infrastructure to buy and deploy narrowcast, targeted media. And of course, buying and deploying this media in a more effective manner may reduce the overall media budget. Agencies would much prefer to just advise clients to buy Super Bowl spots where they're going for a million bucks a pop; buy six or seven of these, and before you know it you have $6 million in billings. You don't really have to do much work. Whereas spending $6 million within a narrowcast media environment is a very different challenge—one that probably can't be supported within a standard "15 percent of billings agency" compensation model, either.

You mention that one way to make narrowcasting more efficient is to use technology, which brings up the point that the other companies that that have been acquiring online marketing firms are the technology companies—Google, Microsoft, and so on.

Absolutely, and those are the horses that we've attached our carts to at Didit. These media providers are morphing into digital ad networks and are our biggest strategic partners. That's where we spend most of our media, due to how we evolved and do our business, which is auction-based media and online media business.

The biggest area of auction-based media currently is paid search, where keywords are auctioned off in real time. This represents probably 80 percent of the media we currently manage.

> *"[Microsoft is positioning itself] for the transformation of the media and advertising world."*

There's other keyword-targeted media that we manage for clients as well, and a lot of investment is going into building more sophisticated media exchanges that go beyond the simple text link. Microsoft is a big player here, and one of the reasons it bought aQuantive and AdECN was that it wanted to really accelerate growth in this direction. And Google, of course, bought DoubleClick for similar purposes: to add sophistication to its already broadening media auction platform.

Plus we're seeing, especially with Google, the desire to move beyond the web in their domain. They're talking cell phones, they're talking radio; how does that play out?

It's a little early to know how that's going to play out. Google and Microsoft both see the fact that the [total] advertising and media spending pie is much larger than the online media spending pie, but they've got slightly different strategies with regards to getting their hands on more of it.

Google's strategy is, "Let's figure out how to remove friction from offline media in the same way that we've removed friction from the online media purchase process—by creating user interfaces that people can use to log in and decide which media they want to buy, upload the creative, decide what the targeting is, et cetera." They're saying that there's no reason that this couldn't work for print media and broadcast media—in particular, radio, but TV as well. Online video and audio is also replacing traditional TV and radio and Google's system is perfect for this market as well.

Microsoft has a broader vision which extends beyond just removing friction in an existing marketplace. Removing transaction costs and friction is an interesting evolutionary step, but it's more interesting if one can figure out how the media marketplace is going to change over the next five or ten years, with the help of the new advertising-industry players, including Microsoft. They're really positioning themselves for the transformation of the media and advertising world from a targeting perspective—i.e., moving away from broadcasting and into narrowcasting. Microsoft wants to be the way advertisers connect with consumers across several different screens and devices.

So Microsoft has been a huge investor in IPTV, which is TV delivered over any generic broadband connection that one might have; it doesn't matter whether it comes from your phone company or cable company; you can deliver TV in that way. Microsoft has been a huge investor in research and development in this area, and in mobile as well. It's even gotten to the point where, these days, if you buy a Treo phone, it now runs on Windows. At Microsoft, they're very much trying to put their tentacles into all the various touch points that consumers will have over the next several years.

And, of course, the Xbox—which I like to call Microsoft's "Trojan horse" into the living room. Yes, it's primarily a gaming platform but there's a lot more that the processor and hard drive in that Xbox can do besides play games. There's no reason why the role that the Xbox plays in the living room can't be expanded fairly dramatically should Microsoft feel like it's got a good installed base there.

If we look at traditional marketing, it was very human-based, very creative. But if we look at Google as an example of online marketing, Google's all about automation; they try to take the human being out of the process as much as possible. Is it all going to be one way or the other, or are we going to see a blend of automation and creativity in some fashion?

I think the creativity is still there. It may be manifesting itself in different ways, or maybe creativity is described in a different way. There are a couple of different kinds of creativity that still play a huge role in making the kinds of advertising that exist in Google, Yahoo!, Microsoft, more effective.

One is creativity with data and understanding how to read the data, how to take action based on data, how to formulate strategies based on data. There is absolutely room for creativity here, whether it's testing different kinds of ad creative against the same keyword and audience or testing ad creative and landing page combinations that maybe squeeze more leads per hundred visitors out of those hundred visitors, or, if you sell things, more dollars of profit per hundred orders. There's creativity there, but it's not creativity in the way that Madison Avenue would have perhaps described creativity in the past.

Data and visual/message creativity will merge because data has a lot to do with the way that ads are targeted. Putting the right message in front of the right audience will replace the current practice of putting the same message in front of the entire audience. Rich media and video advertising will still rely on creativity to convince the viewer—whether this viewer is a consumer or a B2B prospect—that they should actually pay attention to and engage with this ad, but the messages will be far more relevant and tuned to the customer segment. With text link ads, obviously, there's a limit to the level of creativity and the bounds of this creativity, but once you add rich media and video and even static visual advertising, you're starting to tap into some of those same creative centers that were important in traditional media.

> *"We're currently barraged with a lot of irrelevant advertising."*

Clearly, what differs now, and will become increasingly important, is that instead of having one creative message which everybody sees, for example the claim that Tide gets out grass stains really well, you're now going to start seeing creative which is targeting more narrow segments of a user base. So if Tide is going after the mother of the kids who play sports in grassy areas, they may also have a segment going after the bachelors who have their own grass stains to contend with. That message is different.

And now, or shortly, you'll be able to target much more effectively the ads that these different segments see. Where you and I are still stuck turning on a TV set and seeing Polident ads, that's really not an effective use of those ad dollars against us—at least not for me. I don't want to speak for you.

We're currently barraged with a lot of irrelevant advertising. The creativity will come from determining, now that we have 20 fairly large subsegments of our audience, that we may not want to actually have to use the same message for all these 20 sub-segments. As a marketer, the question becomes how do I, within a limited production budget, come up with 20 messages that I can use to grab the attention of these 20 really important sub-segments which have now decided that they're not going to pay attention to any advertising that they don't believe is relevant to them?

That's the situation with DVRs and TiVo right now; people are fast-forwarding through the commercials. How do advertisers deal with this quandary? Well, sometimes if the commercials are particularly relevant, maybe as you see them speed past you might actually let go of that fast-forward button for a second and pay attention. Or maybe it's ads that show up while you're fast-forwarding, and they're sold by the cable companies or by TiVo.

The future of advertising and media is going to look a lot different. We don't know exactly what it's going to look like; we just are fairly confident that creativity will have its place. But it's not going to be a one-size-fits-all creative; it's going to be creatively figuring out how to provide relevant messaging to each of the important segments of your audience.

> *"[Advertising is] about influencing the eventual purchase slightly in the favor of the advertiser."*

It seems to me that one of the key skills in doing that is analytical skills. Would that be right?

It is. Certainly, a big piece of the marketing and agency team is going to be made up of those analysts who help define what the segments are. They can sit in the meeting with the creative folks and decide how to actually move that segment of the audience down the buying funnel—influence them to include a particular brand in that final consideration.

That's really what advertising is all about. It's about influencing the eventual purchase slightly in the favor of the advertiser. You don't necessarily always move people from "I never heard of Lexus," to "I'm definitely buying a Lexus," but if you can influence each stage of that buying process a little bit more in your favor then you're actually doing something effective with your advertising. Doing this will require quantitative skills more so than it has in the past. You never had targeting levers to the same extent that you do now and you will in the future. Knowing which levers to pull requires analysis.

Once you've segmented your market as much as you can or as much as you want to, you're still faced with how to get your message out there—do you use search engine optimization, or pay per click, or rich media? How do you advise a company to determine their online marketing mix?

It's even more complex than just the online marketing mix. We're seeing that there's a huge interaction effect between the overall marketing mix and search.

> *"All the other elements of the marketing mix often stimulate search behavior."*

Search has become the next step that many consumers take when they become curious about something. Think about all the advertising that's out there to generate awareness or stimulate curiosity, or even alert somebody to the fact that they have a need. After seeing a TV ad, for instance, they might have, in the past, asked a family member or a friend, "What do you think about me dyeing my graying hair? Should I do that?" Now they might say, "I'm not going to bring that up with my family. I'm going to go to Google or Yahoo! or Microsoft and I'm going to look up before and after pictures. I'm going to figure out whether I should be doing this or not."

Media and PR and all the other elements of the marketing mix often stimulate search behavior. So search is simultaneously a marketing mix element and (to some extent) a success metric for your other media. Both the creative execution of the advertising as well as the accuracy of the media plan will likely show up in search buzz.

The phrase "integrated marketing" has been bounced around for probably a dozen years at this point, if not longer, but it really needs to start to take root within a company's marketing organization. There are clearly media interaction effects already, even when one sets search aside. When you add search to the mix, it's not only that media becomes more powerful with search, but that they're truly interacting with each other. Media mix models will be built to help guide the marketer with regard to allocation of media across channels.

Using the scenario that you put forth, that somebody has a need and that instead of asking a friend they're now going online and searching, it seems to me that social networking comes into this at some point, doesn't it?

It may well do that. Maybe the next thing you do, or congruent with your search behavior, you may log into Facebook, upload a picture of your graying temples, and say, "Hey, everybody vote on this: do you think I should dye my hair?" At which point, if this question gets posted to your Facebook network, wouldn't this be a particularly appropriate place for Grecian Formula or Just for Men to advertise?

So, yes, the ability to have that narrowcast message ride around to the appropriate individual and within an appropriate area is sort of the Holy Grail of advertising. Everybody wants the ecosystem to be efficient. The consumer wants to see more relevant ad messages, because if you're going to be inundated with them anyway, they might as well be relevant. The publishers know that marketers are willing to pay a little bit more for relevant advertising placement than less-relevant advertising placement, so they're actually going to make more money using whatever pricing methodology is going to be in place, whether it's CPM or CPC, et cetera.

And marketers knows that there's waste in their ad budgets, so they need to figure out how to more accurately target either the direct consumer or influencers to that consumer. (It could be the wife of the guy with the graying temples who's going to be an influencer!) If they

> *"I'm hoping that we move closer to the Holy Grail of advertising and media."*

can figure out how to target better, they can take that same budget that they were spending before and deploy it more efficiently—even if this means that the cost per thousand is higher. Because it's being used more efficiently, there's less waste; the cost per thousand improves, and everybody's happier. Efficiency in budget deployment translates into effective advertising.

I'm hoping that we move closer to that Holy Grail of advertising and media, which is driven by relevance and where everybody is actually happier—which is a fairly unusual shift within a market, where everybody wins.

Everybody could be happier, but it also seems like it is more work. How do you get the marketer's mindset away from the mass marketing, towards the narrowcasting?

It may take their competitors kicking their butts. Certain marketers will have a greater or lesser willingness to experiment here. It's not as if mass-marketing budgets will disappear overnight. Certain marketers will be more willing to experiment and the ones that are experimenting in that area and are seeing positive results will continue to shift budgets into areas that are working.

Nobody can really predict at this point what the level of acceleration will be. Everybody's placing bets; Google, Yahoo!, Microsoft, as well as the agency holding companies and a lot of the existing traditional media companies are all sort of recognizing that the ecosystem will change over time and they're starting to place their bets—sometimes in multiple places at the same time.

We don't know how quickly this will change. There could be a certain catalyst that occurs, where all of a sudden everybody's light bulbs go on at the same time and they say, "Wow, I can't believe that I missed this—this is the greatest thing since sliced bread." Or it may actually be a slow and steady evolution over time. The current ad clutter and decline in mass-media ad effectiveness will be a major driver of change.

> *"We advise our clients to always have budget available for experimentation."*

Paid search has only been around for ten years, and it's now maybe a $12- to $15-billion-per-year industry. That's not small. Interactive media's been around longer than that, and the total interactive marketing market is probably a little more than double what search is.

We don't know what the catalyst will be in mobile. We don't know what the catalyst will be in narrowcast TV. But there are a lot of fairly deep-pocketed players that are experimenting there. If it works, then marketers will experiment, too, along with the networks and publishers who are experimenting first.

We advise our clients to always have budget available for experimentation. With the speed at which the ecosystems are changing, you want to be an early mover. First-mover advantage can be very expensive, but early-mover advantage allows you to be early enough that you see a trend occurring and you can deploy resources against it. We are always advocating this. We are often the advisors there, advising where to place these test budgets to see if they work.

Any other advice you'd have for a company putting together their online marketing plan and budget?

The percentages of appropriate budget, in regards to online vs. offline, or search vs. other online, vary. They're all over the map as to what the appropriate levels are. We've got clients that are spending 70 percent or 80 percent of their overall marketing budgets online and we've got clients where they haven't hit 10 percent yet. Those might all be the appropriate numbers for each of those clients at this point in time.

I think it comes back to Marketing 101. Who is your target audience? How are you trying to influence them? Are you only looking at influencing them at the last stage of the buying cycle, when they're almost ready to buy, or are you doing a more holistic marketing plan?

The advice I give is: Don't think of your marketing budget in a very siloed manner any more; think about the marketing budget as more fluid. Once you start to think about those marketing budgets as more fluid, as the data comes in—and those analysts are going to become increasingly important, within agencies and within the advertising organizations, as well—then those analysts can look at the results and make a determination. For example, the data might indicate that one should say, " We really ought to take this much out of magazine or radio and deploy it in this other location, social media advertising or search advertising or IP-based TV advertising." Having the feedback loop there, to understand what's working and what's not, is going to be really critical. The idea of a branding campaign with brand metrics and a direct response campaign with DR metrics running in parallel is crazy. Each campaign delivers influence and if the influence leads to profit increases then that marketing is effective.

Sound Bites

With so many online marketers rising from the technology ranks, it's refreshing to find someone like Kevin Lee who has a history with traditional offline advertising. Someone needs to be able to bridge the gap between Madison Avenue advertising and online marketing; Kevin does a good job of it.

And just what advice does Kevin offer? Here's a short list:

- Consumers are beginning to pay attention only to advertising that's relevant to their needs.
- The way to reach consumers online is via narrowcasting a relevant message to each individual segment of your target audience; not by mass-marketing a general message that everyone sees.
- Creativity in online marketing involves the ability to analyze data and formulate strategies based on that analysis.
- Search needs to be considered in relation to other forms of advertising; everything interacts with everything else; nothing is a silo unto itself.
- Carve out a portion of your marketing budget for experimentation with new media and advertising types.

Paul O'Brien: Zvents

21

"General search engines can't solve everybody's unique needs, so vertical search engines in shopping or local are critical to the landscape."

—*Paul O'Brien*

In the age of global this and worldwide that, the concept of searching locally might escape your attention. But if you're a local or regional business, you don't need to advertise your wares to people on another coast or continent; you want to get your business in front of local customers, especially if they're searching for your goods or services online.

> **FACT SHEET: PAUL O'BRIEN**
>
> Director of Marketing, Zvents (www.zvents.com)
>
> Blogger, SEO'Brien Search and Online Marketing Blog (www.seobrien.com)

Paul O'Brien understands this situation. He's the director of marketing at Zvents, a local event search engine that's making a name for itself on the web. Before joining Zvents, Paul was head of interactive marketing for Hewlett-Packard's Home and Home Office Store; before that, he managed advertising solutions across several Yahoo! properties. Like many of the interviewees in this book, Paul also runs his own search and online marketing blog, SEO'Brien (www.seobrien.com); it's worth a read.

Exploiting Local Search

Paul knows a bit about search, and is applying that knowledge and experience to the local space. If you're marketing a local business, the advice he imparts could prove profitable.

For people who aren't familiar with it, what exactly is Zvents, and what does it do?

Zvents started a couple of years ago, in 2005, as an event index. The founders looked at the local landscape and realized that there wasn't enough information on the Internet about events, in a centralized location, where users could easily go and find things to do.

Almost a year ago [early 2007], they recognized that that challenge could not be addressed with merely a local platform for events, but that the real opportunity was in reinventing local search. Local search today is essentially static business listings where people can find businesses, but with very little engagement. As a result, there is very little reason for users to go back to that web site or destination to find out more information about that business or local listing. Adding the event context to business listings is what Zvents sees as a reinvention of the local search industry. Zvents puts context to those listings, creating engaging content to draw customers back to the business and back to Zvents in order to find more things to do. Events give customers a reason to continuously return to those businesses.

Customers, for example, look up REI because they're going shopping there; they have an intent to find a sporting goods store. What of the consumer who enjoys kayaking and doesn't know of their kayaking class next week? There are still more who search for camping and discover that next a week REI is sponsoring a camping trip. The gold mine in local search is getting people to repeatedly engage with those businesses and bring them back to participate in whatever may be going on.

If a person is using Google or Yahoo! or a similar search engine, it's relatively easy to find global stuff, but it seems like it's more difficult to find local businesses and local things. How is that landscape changing?

Inherently, Yahoo!, Google, MSN, and even a lot of the emerging start-ups were built as general web search engines. Though they're trying to change that with universal search (the federation of different search indexes into a single search result), at the end of the day, their audience still thinks of that platform as the place to find general information—all web sites or national weather, both very general listings. General search engines can't solve everybody's unique needs, so vertical search engines in shopping or local are critical to the landscape, giving folks a contextual resource.

Vertical search engines are naturally more effective with certain queries. Consider the consumer who says, "I'm not going to go to Google to find out what the price of a computer might be—I'm going to Shopping.com, or I'm going to BizRate."

The local landscape is the same way. Rather than using Google to find the address for the Chili's restaurant up the street, users get better results from YellowPages.com or Yahoo! Local. But that is still just an address; Zvents takes the local experience a step further, helping users not only to find Chili's up the street, but to discover that the restaurant features live music.

So if you're running a local business, just what should you be doing to promote yourself on the web, locally?

I think that the search marketing industry today is too focused on local search, in the context of finding the business: IYP [Internet Yellow Pages], the incumbents, the business listings. So as marketers read about how to optimize for local listings, they see the recommendations that explain how to put your address on your web site, how to put your address on every page of your web site, how to include your location in your page titles and page headers. They're really addressing the needs of Superpages.com and YellowPages.com and to some extent Google.

There are three legs to the local story. There's *what happened*, which is news. Certainly, on a local level, there's an opportunity for businesses to take advantage of that, by issuing press releases and running paid search campaigns at a local level, to take advantage of news related to their business and respond to other things going on that their customers might be interested in.

There's the *where to buy* listing, the second leg of that three-legged local story. I want to buy a computer; where do I go buy a computer? Where do I go shopping for men's clothes this weekend? Where do I go buy a car this weekend?

> *"There's a difference between optimizing web sites and optimizing for local search."*

But the third pillar is what Zvents is creating for the industry, and that's *what's going on*. What's going on fits nicely into the three-pillars strategy, because news about this weekend is, in fact, an upcoming event. If Barack Obama is coming to town, it's news because it's something to do or see this weekend. After Barack Obama is in town, it is again news about the fact that he was in town.

From a merchant's standpoint, the fact that I'm going to buy a car this weekend is a merchant listing, it's a business listing. But a sale at the local Lexus or Mercedes dealer is an event; perhaps the new models are arriving. As a consumer, if I'm looking for something to do in the context of shopping for a car, I'm much more likely to go shop where there's a compelling reason for me to do so.

Should the local merchant, then, be focusing on the search engines, on directories, or on some form of localized advertising?

Certainly more the former—local businesses are just scratching the surface of what search can deliver, but in the context of local, that includes directories.

There's a difference between optimizing web sites and optimizing for local search, in that when you're optimizing web sites, directories are not as important a consideration. When I optimize a web site, I largely ignore Yahoo!'s web directory, because the search engines are increasingly discounting the significance of web directories. Knowing that they're edited by people, they aren't necessarily going to be always accurate, they're not necessarily always up-to-date and users don't turn to directories the same way they do in the local space.

> *"Local businesses need to be thinking about the context in which they present themselves to their customer set."*

In the local space, though, directories *are* critical. The Yellow Page listings, the places that the local business need to go to submit their business address and their phone number, are critical. They are both sources of information for the search engines and destinations for users to find information about a business. When you've got those two things working much more effectively for local businesses than for web sites, certainly directories and search engines should be thought of as part and parcel, one and the same thing.

Local advertising, I think, is increasingly less…it's not that it's less relevant; it's that search is replacing it. From 2006 to 2007 local advertising online increased around 20 percent while local search advertising grew 30 percent. If you think about what Google is doing with AdSense or what ad vendors like AdBrite are doing with local targeting, local advertising is really becoming a layer or subset of a search campaign. At a local level, if you think about your business in the context of its location and the keywords associated with it for a search campaign, that applies very nicely to what you can do with advertising—in a much more targeted fashion. Instead of buying billboards or placements in your newspaper (which, for that matter, though they are local, they are still mass-reach and are not targeted), you can buy a keyword-based local ad campaign—not a search campaign, an ad campaign—to make sure that that display advertising is reaching your audience, your enthusiastic, engaged customer, at a "local" level.

Let's talk a little bit about local search. What's different about optimizing a site for local search, than you might otherwise do?

Not much. There are some other considerations in regard to keywords, but when it comes to optimizing the site itself, the structure of the site, the organization of the site, the process is essentially the same.

At a keyword level, though, local businesses need to be thinking about the context in which they present themselves to their customer set. Their customers are offline. Their customers are searching for their business within their city—which may also have a metropolitan area or a regional area associated with it. For example, businesses in San Francisco or San Jose or Palo Alto also need to ensure that their web sites use keywords like "Bay Area," "Silicon Valley," "San Mateo," "Berkeley," "South Bay," "East Bay," "West Bay," "peninsula." Local businesses need to refer to different things that folks might be looking for other than just the name of the city in which they are located, because not everyone is going to think of their business as being in Palo Alto. The goal is to reach as many folks as possible, which includes all of those other connotations to the local context.

It's simply a broader consideration of the keyword set, to make sure that you're taking into account abbreviations, local nomenclature for the region. It's putting yourself in the shoes of the local offline customer as much as you do the online customer when you're optimizing for a web site.

Do we know how people are finding local businesses these days? Are they still using offline media like the Yellow Pages? How much of that has shifted online?

I don't have any specific numbers in terms of how many folks are still using offline. I can only speak anecdotally; I haven't looked at a Yellow Pages in years. I'm sure most of my peers are the same way. I do know, and this is really what attracted me to the opportunity at Zvents, that those ad dollars are shifting online much more quickly than any other advertising space has shifted in recent history. We're dealing with, roughly, a $60 billion ad market dominated by newspapers and Yellow Pages but shifting online at a rate unseen in recent history. Most of that money is directed to search engines—not online display, not online email, but to search engines. That Zvents recognized a unique opportunity in local search, created both a fascinating opportunity for me, in terms of the development of the technology, but also a new and unique opportunity to support advertisers.

How important is mobile search going to be in the context of all this?

Perhaps more so. Critically so.

As the technology catches up, and it's doing so still slowly relative to Europe and Asia given the hurdles created by the mobile providers, users will increasingly use mobile to search locally while finding things to do, when it comes to Zvents, with that handheld device. Zvents has a very exceptional Apple iPhone application, which helps present how the mobile experience will evolve. It's a very seamless transition between the search experience and a map experience which allows folks to see exactly what's going on near them.

> *"If you're not in the search engines, your business doesn't exist."*

The challenge with mobile, though, is that it makes most search optimization by businesses that much more important, because of the display area that's available to search results and advertisers. What's exciting for search engines is that it makes really good search technology that much more important. What I mean is that, ineffective search engines can depend on five or ten or fifteen different listings on a web results page to insure that they've got something that the user is looking for.

When it comes to mobile, there's only enough room to present two or three results to a search query due to the limited amount of space. Only exceptional search technologies, like Google and Zvents, can respond with exactly what the consumer is looking for, delivering a positive, engaging, memorable experience that will prompt that user to continue to use mobile.

What general advice would you give to local businesses today, planning their online marketing?

In regard to local businesses, online in particular, the one thing that I think is still most significantly overlooked is search optimization. Not search marketing, but search optimization. It is critical to prioritize the structure of your web site, the use of local keywords, the presentation of calendars and event content and store locators, through search engine friendly, exposed, basic HTML—and not buried within Flash or JavaScript.

The bottom line is it doesn't matter how exciting your offers are, it doesn't matter how compelling your marketing or your opportunities might be. If the search engines can't index you, they can't crawl your web site and absorb your content to include it in their own index well. Ninety percent of everybody on the Internet uses search; if you're not in the search engines, your business doesn't exist—you're not in front of the customer. It's much the same way that 20 or 30 years ago, if you weren't in the Yellow Pages, people didn't know how to get hold of you. The same is true of search now.

So focus on the priorities. Define the priorities for your business and focus on things like search optimization before doing anything else. You need to attract an audience before you can figure out how to compel them to convert, how to convince them to buy, or interact with your business.

So what excites you the most about what's happening in search today?

What I'm really excited about is the future of local, in particular, and the opportunity that it brings with mobile.

What I find most coincidental with your timing of this interview is that the local and mobile spaces are converging at a very rapid pace. You've got Nokia acquiring NAVTEQ. You've got TomTom expressing some interest in Tele Atlas. So mobile, in the case of Nokia, is recognizing the importance of owning the most significant local map player in the industry. That says a lot for the future of those two industries converging, and those two industries really becoming the future of the Internet, in a sense, becoming the future of the web and the way that folks interact with businesses.

> *"On [GPS] devices, local search becomes much more relevant."*

I think that within the next six months or the next year, there is going to be a big shift in where marketers will need to spend their advertising dollars. They'll be better able to take advantage of opportunities with NAVTEQ and Nokia, with Zvents— and certainly with Google, who is making some interesting moves into mobile as we speak.

You mentioned TomTom. Do you see GPS playing a part in this?

Absolutely. One of the things we're most excited about here is that at a local level, the industry typically thinks of local as an address. But at the map level, what's important is that every business has associated with it a latitude and longitude designation that allows Zvents and other mapping technologies to present that information in any environment where the platform requires a latitude and longitude for a business—like GPS.

What it means is that on Magellan devices, on Garmin devices, local search becomes much more relevant, because the platform can then present results in a map interface. Not in a search-results experience, but literally right on the map.

One of the things that we've done is to present search results through a Google Maps application. Zvents, about six months ago [early 2007], launched an application wherein users can search for a type of event—live concerts, for example—and the map will exhibit the exact location of upcoming live concerts. As users drag the map up and down, north and south, or east and west, the results update in real time to show you anything going on—directly on that map.

Certainly, the same can be done on GPS devices, with auto-updating as people move through locations in their cars, bikes, or even while walking around. A GPS device with Zvents could show that there's a shopping sale right around the corner—up the block is a farmer's market this weekend that you didn't know about.

I think this is a wonderful opportunity that's really going to emerge next year [2008], with NAVTEQ being much more prominent in this space. It will give marketers a completely new platform on which to promote themselves. I can see a company like Starbucks being much more prominent with their logos on maps, to show folks that there's a Starbucks coffee shop right around the corner.

There'll be a Starbucks logo at every intersection of the map, I think.

Yes, there sure would be.

How soon do you think it will be before we find GPS integrated into mobile phones?

I think that it's a couple of years off. It's certainly coming, but I think there's an adoption curve that still needs to run its course. There's some standardization of mobile technology that needs to occur, as the providers figure out 3G or whichever technology is that on which they're going to rely and depend.

There are lots of start-ups that are playing in this space, trying to take the network out of the equation and develop applications that are of equal value on any cellular provider. We've also just witnessed Google's announcement of Android, a Linux-based open-development software platform for mobile phones, which will undoubtedly accomplish the same thing. Since they are start-ups now, it's going to take them a year to get on their feet and a year or more for the technology to catch up to the point where a handheld device, as small and with as much real estate on the display as the iPhone, can integrate seamlessly with a GPS device.

So look to 2009 for this to explode, but that means now marketers need to be thinking about it, figuring out how it fits into their portfolio.

Sound Bites

If you want to convert local shoppers into customers, you need to take advantage of local search. As Paul O'Brien points out, that means doing the following things:

- Optimize your site for local search—make sure you include locality information as part of your keyword set.

- Focus on local directories as much as you do the big search engines.
- Think beyond the business listing. You'll retain your customers with a business listing but attract customers with search engines like Zvents.
- Make sure you have a version of your site available that's optimized for mobile devices.
- Include latitude and longitude information for inclusion in upcoming GPS-enabled devices.

Ron Belanger: Yahoo!

22

"More and more marketers are starting to realize that, in a lot of cases, this should be their first buy. It's easy to do, it's easy to measure results, it's not that difficult to learn, and there's a low barrier to entry."

—*Ron Belanger*

Yahoo! was one of the first major search sites on the web, and it remains a major player to this day. Not surprisingly, Yahoo! is at the forefront of next-generation search, with a new universal search results page and interesting forays into social search.

> **FACT SHEET: RON BELANGER**
>
> Vice President of Agency Development, Yahoo! Search Marketing
> (searchmarketing.yahoo.com)

What Yahoo! thinks about the future of search and search marketing matters to everyone interested in the topic. For that reason, Ron Belanger is a man whose opinions matter. Ron is the vice president of agency development for Yahoo!, where he's responsible for building relationships with Yahoo!'s advertising clients—in particular, the big advertising agencies.

Ron has been around the search field for a number of years. Prior to joining Yahoo!, Ron was vice president of search and affiliate marketing at Carat Interactive, where he worked with clients such as America Online, Microsoft, Hyatt Hotels, Radio Shack, Hyundai, and Kodak. While he was at Carat, Ron co-authored the industry's "premier course on search marketing" (in conjunction with iMedia Learning).

The State of the Search Industry Today, According to Yahoo!

While Ron's focus is on getting big advertisers more involved in search engine advertising, he's also well aware of the issues and challenges facing smaller businesses online. Our interview covers a variety of related topics, and provides much useful information and advice for online marketers of all sizes.

Let's talk about you a bit, Ron. How did you get to where you are today at Yahoo!?

I've been in the search marketing business for going on eight years now. This industry really grew up on the service side, in a kind of boutique agency business. I worked for a small search engine marketing firm in the greater Boston area. I was in the technology space at the time, working for one of eBay's competitors—back when they had competitors—called FairMarket. I was doing business consulting, guiding clients into how to use this new medium.

I heard about this search marketing craze, and I had a connection there with the CEO, and decided I'd go check it out. This was in late 1999, early 2000. I thought, boy, this really sounds neat. I didn't really think of it as something that would get as big as it got; it just sounded, from a technology and business perspective, kind of a neat thing to dive into.

I joined this small company out in that area, learned the trade, and kind of grew up with the business. At that point, the business was very fragmented. There were a number of search engines that are no longer really around. The bulk of search engine optimization at that point was paid search, which was just coming into its own.

After doing that for a number of years, what started to happen was that some of the larger ad agencies started to realize that hey, this could be an area where we could potentially invest for the future. We feel that money's going to increasingly tip to not only digital, but to the search thing; it seems to be working.

So I got a call from one of the bigger media agencies, named Carat Interactive. They said, "Hey, how would you like to come on board here and help us build a search practice to complement some of our media buying?" It sounded like a great opportunity for me to take what I'd learned at the little search shop and upgrade it, if you will. So I went over there and built a practice.

When I arrived, there were two people who were search marketing managers. They had maybe two or three small accounts. During the time I was there, we built that group into one of the largest service lines in the agency—about 50 employees; we had staff in seven offices. They made a bet that this would be a high-growth area, and it certainly was. That was fun.

In my time in the search business, I'd developed some relationships with the search engines themselves—Yahoo! and Google and Microsoft and the others. I always saw culturally and philosophically where Yahoo! was headed, the way they thought about search, and the way they treated clients. And as a

> "*It's easy to do, it's easy to measure results, it's not that difficult to learn, and there's a low barrier to entry.*"

user, I always had a bias towards Yahoo!. So when it came time for me to do something different, I thought, boy, wouldn't it be neat to take what I've learned running an ad agency and take that to Yahoo! and help others learn?

So I got this job here [at Yahoo!] where I'm helping agencies globally try to figure this stuff out. Some are far down the path, some are just raising their hand, asking for it. I have a team of people that have been bringing ad agencies into the new millennium. Quite a lot of fun.

It does kind of amaze me how big search engine marketing has become, in such a short period of time.

It's going to be what this year, an $11- or $12 billion industry? Two or three years ago, I think it was $3- or $3.5 billion. It's pretty incredible.

I think what's fueling a lot of the growth is that more and more marketers are starting to realize that, in a lot of cases, this should be their first buy. It's easy to do, it's easy to measure results, it's not that difficult to learn, and there's a low barrier to entry.

You think about, even on the local spot cable level, [what it takes] just to make something rudimentary—the product costs, the delivery time, four to six weeks. In search, you can get an ad up in four to six minutes. It's a very unintimidating advertising medium.

Our early-on adopters were these online retail guys—the Amazons and eBays of the world—who saw it as a direct response, instant customer acquisition vehicle. Now what you're seeing is not only enterprise clients, like Procter & Gamble, Johnson & Johnson, and Unilever using search as a way to expand their marketing mix, but you're also seeing it go downstream. You're seeing the pizza places and the plumbers, the folks that traditionally made their entire bet in the Yellow Pages; they're embracing search now.

> *"You need to be able to take advantage of…high-impact moments."*

I think what you're seeing with some of this growth is more and more of the search inventory and more and more of the available keywords are being purchased and are being actively managed. It's just incredible how quickly this industry has grown.

The money that's being spent on search advertising—is that new money for most of these advertisers, or is it money that's shifted?

A lot of it is [new money]. It seems like almost every day or every week we have successfully talked to a customer about trying search for the first time, or moving it beyond direct response into general "always on" advertising. In a lot of cases these are new budgets; these are folks who are looking to more actively embrace the digital medium, because it's completely changeable, completely measureable. It's easy to determine what you're willing to pay for an action or transaction.

It's all kinds of marketers, even consumer packaged goods. We've done big search deals with Hellman's Mayonnaise, Dove beauty products, a number of these industries that when I first joined the search business, you'd never think these would be advertisers—that 70 characters of text on a white page could possibly compete with print ads and 30-second television spots. So in a lot of cases, it is new money.

Traditionally, search marketing has been used as more of a direct-marketing vehicle, but is it also being used for brand marketing?

Absolutely. These budgets that we're getting from clients like Unilever and Procter & Gamble, these are brand-marketing dollars. These are folks who understand that a marketing dialog is much more complete than it was in years past.

To build a healthy dialog and healthy relationship between advertiser and consumer, you need to be able to take advantage of what we call high-impact moments. This is when a consumer is raising their hand, essentially saying, I'm in a mode now where I'm interested in receiving a marketing message or receiving a communication from you.

If you think of the CPG [consumer packaged goods] space, think of a new mom or new parents, a couple who just found out they're going to have a baby. We use that example all the time as somebody who's hungry for information and hungry for new brands. They may be seven or nine months away from making their first purchase, for example, but they're in discovery mode, with that experience they're going through as they learn which brands and products their family is going to rely on. Those are great junction points for these brand marketers to begin a dialog, even though they may not see the first dollar for six or seven months.

How would a consumer-brand company use search marketing as part of their mix?

One of the obvious areas is for those brands that have an affinity for something consumers have an affinity for. A good example would be celebrity endorsements. If you're spending all this money on a Tiger Woods or a movie star, that type of thing, and you have consumers who are interested in that individual, that seems like a great area to intersect consumer interest with brand-affiliation message.

We've seen the case of Tiger Woods, with his affiliation with Buick. They were buying keywords. For those individuals looking for information on Tiger Woods, they say to the consumers, "Hey, we've made an investment in this celebrity; we're interested in the same types of things you are." It builds an intimacy and it builds a relationship with the consumer, in which they're able to ascribe brand values to that celebrity.

Another thing would be looking at need states, and what products or brands do you have that fill certain needs. In the medical and pharmaceutical industry, that's pretty easy. If you've been diagnosed with high cholesterol or high blood pressure or a number of ailments, that's a great way to get educational advertising information in front of consumers; "Hey, we have a potential solution to what you're looking for." Another need state would be going to college for the first time or investing for retirement for the first time.

You think about how people use search. A lot of times they're actually looking to be introduced to brands, products, and services. A lot of times their needs are new needs that they haven't had before. They don't have a resource or an oracle, if you will, to go to, so they're using the Yahoo!s and Googles of the world to answer their questions.

Boy, what a great way to introduce your brand or introduce your solution to consumers! Even though a lot of times these transactions will happen in a brick-and-mortar store or in a bank or over a telephone—just because a transaction doesn't happen on a web site that doesn't mean that's not a great place to introduce your message.

How does a company track the performance of a more brand-oriented approach like that?

There are a number of models being worked on today. One of the more basic ones is call tracking, where we've worked with companies where they've set up different 800 numbers for their different search campaigns—one 800 number for Yahoo!, one for the other competitors. A lot of times web sites or customer surveys will ask consumers, "How did you hear about us?"

> *"Most of the larger engines…have the ability for marketers to really laser-target an audience.*

One of the things we're excited about is, in the entertainment business on opening weekend, it's customary to go to theaters and ask, "How did you hear about this film? What drove you here?" Well, search is now a check box in the stodgy old entertainment industry. They're actually asking, "Hey, am I driving butts into seats using search, because of the buzz we've created?"

In an interesting kind of way, because search came out of the box so strong, with a response-driven direct-response kind of measurement, we almost hampered ourselves a little bit. It seemed like if you weren't selling a widget off a web site, to get that conversion tag marked, then how do we know this is effective?

I think we're slowly trying to learn from other advertising models. We've done brand studies with customers, saying, "Has this helped with moving your brand perception?" It's certainly a business problem that the advertising community, the agencies especially, are working on, to get full media mix modeling out there to understand what is the true impact of search campaigns, and how does it work synergistically with other mediums.

How does a smaller company, a local company, use the search medium as part of their marketing mix?

What's happened from a technology and segmentation perspective is most of the larger engines, certainly Yahoo!, have the ability for marketers to really laser-target an audience. Early on, it was tough for a regional plumber or a local bank to compete with search, because you were competing on a national stage. Now, for example, on Yahoo! you can target down to the DMA [designated market area].

Say that you only want to target to the greater Chicago DMA. Then we serve that ad to users within that area—and we know that for a number of reasons. One, in a lot of cases they specified a locality in their search query; that's an obvious way of doing it. The second one would be understanding the users based on data they've shared with us—their home page, what is their hometown weather, what is their local sports team. We understand a number of things about a user based on what they tell us, and on registration data, as well. If somebody raised their hand and said, "I live in Boston, Massachusetts," we'll know that if that individual is looking for a plumber, he's looking for a plumber in that area.

We've gotten a lot better at only serving search ads to a local audience, when the advertiser specifies that. I think that development has opened up or de-risked, if you will, the ability to do search on the big players [Yahoo!, Google, etc.].

What we're seeing is [companies] who have relied solely on the Yellow Pages, their audience is aging. When they come to the web and they come to Yahoo! and our competitors and start using local search, we're seeing a fuller gamut of consumers. If you're under 25, the only thing you use the Yellow Pages for is maybe to reach the top shelf in your kitchen.

A friend of mine says that he keeps a copy of the Yellow Pages in his car. I wondered if that was just to weight it down in the snow in the wintertime.

I like that. [laughs]

That brings up another question. What about mobile search?

Our Yahoo! Go platform is the biggest mobile platform out there, and we absolutely allow advertisers to buy on mobile search. I think it's a slightly different need state, and I think it's ultimately going to appeal to a slightly different type of advertiser.

If you think about what you use mobile search largely for, it's movies, restaurants, very immediate needs, regionally based. So part of what we're doing now is getting the message out there to those advertisers who maybe have not been as hip to search—your local coffee shop or dry cleaners or what have you. There's definitely still a lot of evangelism to do, but there is an increasing amount of demand, from a consumer perspective, for mobile search. What we're challenged with now is how do we bridge the gap between these existing search queries and trying to get advertisers in front of them?

> *"Social search, if you think about it, really democratizes search results."*

The train has left the station on that one, for sure. It's just like we had to do with search in the last ten years, evangelize the heck out of that. We're going to have to do the same here on the mobile stage.

Everybody knows about paid search and organic search, but now there's social search. How is that important?

I think, personally, that it's one of the biggest revolutions in search. The search business hasn't changed a heck of a lot in the eight years I've been doing it. With the paid and the organic, there have been certain refinements, and we've gotten better at crawling different kinds of data, but social search, if you think about it, really democratizes search results. It takes the power out of the hands of search advertisers and web masters and puts it into everyone's hands.

Historically you've been limited in your answer set. If you do a query for model kits or jazz drumming, you're only going to find results of people that have either gone through the headache and hassle of building a web site on that topic, or for folks who, for whatever reason, have a financial incentive to take out ads on sponsored search.

What social search does is it allows every user—and we have half a billion people globally who use Yahoo!—these guys now become a repository of collective knowledge. So anyone with information from a secret fishing spot to Grandma's apple pie recipe now becomes able to answer and provide responses for people's queries. What that does is opens up the aperture of what kind of data you can find, probably 100 times, 1,000 times, 10,000 times.

What's interesting, as a student of the space, as I've been for awhile, is to ask, "How is the marketing and advertising community going to respond to this? And how is this going to change the dynamic of the search result page?" I think, because it's so new, that we're still seeing that play out.

What about a company that wants to take advantage of that— what kind of strategy should they put together?

It's funny. I've been talking at conferences a lot about this, recently. I think there's a hesitation, because it's a relatively nascent area of the business. A lot of marketers are saying, "Let's see how this thing plays out."

But what we're saying is, just dive in and get your feet wet. We talk about Yahoo! Answers, which is our social site. If you're a brand manager or if you're an advertising agency, why not participate in the dialog? Certainly advertise to the consumer that, this is the voice of the brand or I'm a representative of the company. By all means, if customers are dialoging and inquiring about your brands, your products or services, why not jump in, create a brand avatar, get in there and get involved with some of these great Q&A sessions?

In other cases, it's a great way just to listen to what people are saying. This is part of a search strategy, is what we're saying. Use the tools out there to collect some general feedback. Are people responding well to the new flavor? What are they thinking about the new hybrid? It's a great consumer-feedback-collection mechanism.

I think the third thing is that it allows you to find what we call those passionistas, brand advocates if you will, people who are kind of megaphoning about your brand. Boy, these are people that are our best customers; a lot of times we spend so much money to try to find and please and repeat them. Social search gives you the ability to find these people pretty quickly. Why not invite them into your marketing dialog? Put one of their quotes on your web site or invite them into a special peer group. To me it's an incredible opportunity for marketers to get much more intimate with what your consumers are saying—as opposed to costly panels, small sample sizes, overpaid consultants, and all this other stuff. It's just some great data out there.

Aside from the social search, what else is new and on the horizon?

Another area of search that hasn't changed a tremendous amount is the search engine result page itself—paid ads on the top and right, and some truncated site descriptions below that. What you're seeing—certainly with us, and I've seen some neat treatments on AOL search results pages, even Google to a certain degree—is starting to get a little more creative with what does a search results page look like.

We're doing some things now. If you search for any current film that's playing in theaters, you're going to get a special module that we serve up on the search results page, which allows consumers to watch the trailer, find show times, get reviews, chat about the movie, right on that search page. It's producing an additional content element to it.

> *"The search results page itself is changing rapidly."*

I think it was Google that did something with the last *Bourne* movie, where there was special treatment on that page, where consumers were able to dig in and learn more about the film. We've done a few special branded treatments. We did one with Special K and we did one with Hellman's Mayonnaise, where next to the top search listing we put a little branded logo as part of a special treatment. You're seeing universal search, some video treatments, some pictures.

I think the search results page itself is changing rapidly. We're getting away from that traditional black-and-white text on page, and getting more rich media, more content. So that's a pretty exciting thing to be on the forefront of—to figure out how are we going to make this into people's search engine marketing practices.

Are consumers embracing these changes or are they wary about the all-text page disappearing?

I think that's why you've seen it go much slower than it probably would have. Here at Yahoo!, we have a pretty strong separation between the advertising group and the technology folks that keep the search page sacred, if you will. It's always kind of a yin and yang battle between what the advertisers are willing to sell and what the technologists are willing to let appear on the page. The only things that sneak out the front door are those that we've seen that consumers respond well to and advertisers respond well to. There are probably a number of things that I'm sure the advertising community would love to get on there that will never see the light of day.

So that's the balance, keeping the search page relevant so the consumers increasingly find it valuable. And, of course, finding it valuable for advertisers, as well.

Let's talk a little bit more about Yahoo!. What services does Yahoo! offer a company putting together its online marketing plan?

It depends on who you are. Obviously, for enterprise-level customers and large agencies we have teams of people and training. We'll go in there and educate them about the industry in general. Then we'll take it to the next level and say, "If you're willing to set up a practice or are willing to try this, we have resources available to walk you through it, train your people, and offer you some best-practice guidance."

But there are hundreds and thousands of mom-and-pop advertisers out there that don't have that ability. For those folks, we have a number of online tutorials and learning modules on advertising.yahoo.com. If you are one of these mom-and-pops that have been doing the Yellow Pages for 20 years and you want to try something else in a very low-risk, easy-to-learn way, you can figure this stuff out.

There are also some trade organizations that are playing kind of Geneva to the Yahoo!s and Googles. There's SEMPO [Search Engine Marketing Professional Organization], which has some great research and tutorials. The DMA [Direct Marketing Association] just came out with a search course, as well, which is targeted more at the individual level. I think it's priced pretty reasonably, a few hundred bucks; it's a deep dive into learning the ins and outs of the trade for people who either want to develop a practice or just do it themselves. And we're continually sponsoring events in various markets as an outreach to advertisers, to get them hip to search. So there are a number of outreach efforts, both partisan and bi-partisan, out there for folks who are interested in raising their hands.

When a company is trying to decide how much of their budgets or efforts should go into search engine optimization versus how much should go into paid search, what kind of advice can you offer them?

The technology behind search engine optimization tends to be fairly static, meaning a site optimized well today will likely be optimized well in six months. We would absolutely say if you're building a site, take care of the SEO first, because that's going to pay dividends down the road and obviously there's no CPC [cost per click] involved.

> *"What many marketers find is that their budget is…only constrained by the performance of the results."*

We publish some standards on our web site which educate webmasters to the types of things we look for and we don't look for. In other words, these are the kind of things that, if you were to put on your site, it may hamper your ability to be found in Yahoo! search. We're very public about the kind of stuff you should and shouldn't be doing with SEO.

Once you're comfortable with that, the nice thing about paid search is that there's really no minimum. What we recommend is, dip your toe in the water, get an account live, and fund it with a few hundred bucks. You can certainly throttle your daily spend, what you're willing to spend on the CPC, until you learn the trade.

What many marketers find is that their budget is, in a lot of cases, only constrained by the performance of the results. We have direct-marketing clients, when we ask "What's your search budget?" they tell us, "How much traffic do you have?" It's not a like a TV upfront where I'm going to do $3 million on CBS, or I'm going to do $2 million in *People* magazine. For these direct marketers, as long as this traffic is converting, they'll buy it all day long.

For brand marketers who are using it to reinforce their message, those are generally budgeted on an annual or quarterly basis. It's generally done as a percentage of overall media mix. Some people say, based on all my touch points with consumers and based on the available inventory, I'm going to dedicate X to search. For better or for worse, that's still a relatively small part of the advertising pie, something we're working hard to open up.

What other general advice would you give to a company that's looking to improve its search advertising efforts?

It's one of those industries where people are pretty passionate about it, so there are a number of great resources out there to learn, especially if you're new to it. There are some great conferences out there—there are a number of web sites. We have a search marketing blog [www.ysmblog.com] where we publish our best practices. Google does a good job with theirs, in terms of telling folks some ins and outs. From the publishers themselves you get some great data, some of the trade groups and associations are a great place to learn.

Then a lot of it is old-fashioned A-B testing. You need to invest the time to understand what's the right mix of SEO and SEM [search engine marketing], based on your clients, what's the right allocation of budgets across search engines. And then test what are the right keywords, the right copy, and the right landing page to produce that optimal mix for folks. It's one of those practice areas where you're always learning and you're always evolving, based on market needs.

> *"This is something where you can start very, very small and incrementalize it as you go on."*

Is there anything else you'd like to add for our readers?

I guess my message to them would be that this is one of the lowest-risk, lowest-barrier-to-entry advertising mediums available. So if there are folks who are sitting on the fence, saying "I wish I were hipper to this stuff than I am," my advice is to dive in—a hundred bucks here, a hundred bucks there, dive in and learn it. Unlike a TV commitment or the back page of *Rolling Stone* magazine, it's not one of these things where you're betting on a horse race, and if it doesn't work, your advertising budget is out for the year. This is something where you can start very, very small and incrementalize it as you go on. Even those folks that are late to the game can just jump on in and learn as you go.

Sound Bites

Ron Belanger was a gracious and informed interviewee, and his knowledge and advice is much appreciated. What can you take away from Ron's experience? Here's a short list:

- It started out as a direct marketing medium, but today more and more traditional marketers—including brand marketers—are beginning to utilize search engine advertising.

- Use search advertising to take advantage of high-impact moments where a customer is interested in receiving a product or marketing message.
- Search marketing isn't just for national advertisers; local businesses can use search marketing to target down to the individual market level.
- Social search lets you locate and communicate with passionistas—your most passionate brand advocates.

And don't forget Ron's most important advice: Search advertising is a low-barrier, low-risk medium. It costs you very little to get started, and the potential results are huge. So dip your toe in the water and start advertising!

David Fischer: Google

23

"What we want, in time, is to offer all advertisers a very advanced set of features but in a way that's incredibly easy to use, so our system can help optimize advertisers' performance without causing too much work."

—David Fischer

When it comes to online marketing and advertising, almost every marketer mentions Google AdWords. AdWords is the preeminent search advertising service, the big dog that almost every online advertiser users.

> **FACT SHEET: DAVID FISCHER**
>
> Vice President, Online
> Sales & Operations, Google
> (www.google.com)

It makes sense, then, to include Google in this book. That inclusion takes the form of an interview with David Fischer, who is VP of Google's Online Sales & Operations. In this post, David is responsible for Google's North American online advertising program, which includes AdWords, AdSense, and Google Checkout.

Before David came to Google, he served as deputy chief of staff of the U.S. Treasury Department, where he was an advisor to the secretary of the treasury and worked on a variety of economic policy issues. Prior to that, he was an associate editor at *U.S. News & World Report*; not surprisingly, he covered the economics and business beat.

Google AdWords: Yesterday, Today, and Tomorrow

If you're advertising online, Google AdWords will be part of your media mix—probably a major part. To that end, it's important to know what Google has planned for AdWords, as well as how to get the most from this essential advertising service. David provides the information on both counts.

It seems like almost every online marketer is using AdWords as part of his advertising mix. What has made AdWords so essential?

> *"AdWords creates a level playing field for advertisers."*

We think of AdWords as a fantastic vehicle to serve advertisers, one advertiser at a time. Since AdWords launched in 2002, it's certainly scaled dramatically, both in the U.S. and around the world, but the main way we approach it at Google is to think about the needs of an advertiser. One of the important principles behind AdWords is we want it to work for advertisers from the largest Fortune 500 company to the smallest mom-and-pop shop in your neighborhood, and for that to be true in the U.S. and in every country around the world. Part of what's incredibly powerful is that we've built a platform that works for a huge range of advertisers, and we think that's been a key to its success.

You answered my next question, which was going to be, is AdWords targeted at the bigger advertiser or the smaller advertiser? You say it's targeted at both?

That's right, it's targeted at both. One of the things that I find most exciting about AdWords is that when you do a search for a given product, you might get the largest players out there advertising right alongside a small local retailer. AdWords creates a level playing field for advertisers. If they're selling the same products, they can show up on the same search results; at that point, it's whoever has the better product or can run their business more efficiently who can win.

That's incredibly empowering. If you think about prior to online advertising, prior to AdWords, if you were a small local business, you had very limited ways to reach out and get your message out to a broad audience—particularly to a national or international audience. With the targeting that AdWords allows, you now have the ability to reach out to an audience that's looking for exactly what you're selling. That's created a large number of success stories of small advertisers who have harnessed the power of the Internet and of AdWords to build successful businesses—often from scratch.

How could a small, even a local business utilize AdWords to target local results?

One of the important things to keep in mind is that small and medium businesses are still at a pretty nascent stage overall, in terms of online advertising. Many people are surprised to find out that over half of local businesses in the U.S. still don't have a web site. So at Google we start from the position of how can we help these businesses succeed, and make our success contingent on their success.

What we've built up is this system that starts with the very basics. It starts with the question, "Do you have a web site?" And for small businesses, local businesses that don't have a web site, we can help them get a basic web site. They enter basic information about their business, about what they're selling, if they have a storefront, where that's located; information about their hours, payment information, and so on.

Then we enable them to advertise, even if you're a particular niche business. One of my favorites, there's a guy out here in the San Francisco Bay area who came up with a design for pants, where he decided instead of corduroy pants that go vertically, he was going to create something called Cordarounds, and sell horizontally striped corduroys. He started a small business [located at www.cordarounds.com], and it still is a small business, but he found a way through AdWords to get his message out. He's a really clever guy; his marketing collateral is incredibly clever. He's mentioned in several of his newsletters how Google has helped him get his message out and find people who are looking for the pants that he's selling.

We get stories like that all across the country and all across the world. One of the most rewarding points of my five years at Google came about three years ago or so, when I happened to be in Las Vegas for a conference. I went out to meet with one of our advertisers, a woman named Ge'Lena Vavra. She had started out selling her husband's clothes out of their garage, to make some space, and had had so much success with that online that she went to some of the big hotels in Las Vegas and bought some of the things they were selling on closeout and started selling those online. She eventually moved on and formed relationships with some of the top Italian designers, and is now at the point where she runs a thriving online business selling men's Italian fashions. [Her website is www.vavraitaly.com.] She actually bought and owns a warehouse in Las Vegas. When her customers come to town, they can come and get fitted there.

These are the types of stories where someone who has a great entrepreneurial spirit, starts with an idea, and builds up a business. They can take it as far as their abilities will take them, through the distribution and the ability to target the right audience they can get through AdWords and other forms of online advertising.

When you're talking about the services that you offer small merchants, how does Google Checkout fit into that?

Checkout is really an extension of our advertising system, in that the goal is enabling businesses of all sizes to succeed. Google Checkout is an online payment system that enables a customer to come and buy something online, through their Google Account that they might already have set up for whatever Google products they might be using—Gmail or Google Analytics or AdWords or so on. As a buyer, the customer just enters in his credit card information and Google Checkout creates a very fast checkout process. When I go to a merchant that accepts Google Checkout, I can simply click on the Google Checkout button and enter my password, and it already has all of my shipping information, my preferences, and so on. It creates a very fast buying process.

> *"A product's success is going to be driven by creating a great user experience."*

For a merchant, for the seller, it likewise gives them the opportunity to better track their customers' experience online, to get information ultimately as an advertiser. As a merchant, what I want is to have the most efficient and the most profitable business that I can, which Checkout works in a number of ways to do. It allows you to work with Google all the way from the point of acquiring a lead for your business through AdWords, through completing the checkout process and purchasing. If you can track all that information and understand for every person who comes to visit your web site what percentage of them result in a sale, what each of those sales is worth to you, and so on, you can compute exactly how profitable your business is and use that data to optimize your web site's performance.

We are big believers at Google that a product's success is going to be driven by creating a great user experience. So for us, all the benefits I mentioned on the buyer's side therefore transfer to the merchant. By giving them Google Checkout, a way to shop and to transact really easily, it creates a better experience that we believe will ultimately lead to more sales for them.

Let's get back to the AdWords advertising. You mentioned that a small merchant's listing can be right next to a big merchant's listing. What determines whose listings pop up on top?

When an advertiser comes in and sets up an AdWords account with us, there are a few important variables that are going to determine how their campaigns run, and ultimately will make them successful.

The first is targeting—that is, deciding where their ads will show up. The easiest way to think about this is to put yourself in the shoes of a searcher and think about what is someone who is looking for my product or service likely to be searching within Google. In the example I mentioned a minute ago about the woman selling online Italian clothing, it might be the names of a number of Italian designers, or "men's Italian shoes" or "men's Italian shirts" or whatever else might be relevant. So you choose the right place to show up.

Again, that can be something that is focused on incredible niche businesses. One of the things that strikes you about Google is you can do a search on a product's SKU number, or you can search on a particular product name; if you put in very detailed information, you get phenomenal results, both in the organic search results and in the AdWords advertising results. The reason is, if someone enters a plasma TV model number, there's a real good chance they're looking to buy that TV. That's an incredibly qualified lead. So the first key is picking the right keywords.

The next thing, in regards to the way the ads appear on our page, we look at two main factors. The first thing, simply, is based on price. It's important to understand that Google runs an auction. So we don't set the prices for our advertising program; we let our advertisers do it themselves; we let the market decide. To take a given keyword, let's say "running shoes," if I'm looking for new running shoes and I enter that keyword, there are a lot of merchants out there that are going to be interested in having their ads show up there and showing me what they have to sell. They will set a price that they're willing to pay, per click. (AdWords is primarily a cost-per-click program.)

The second variable that comes into where ads appear and in what order is something that we call Quality Score. What the Quality Score does is bring in a number of factors that, together, add up to how well that ad is performing and is likely to perform. For example, one important metric that goes into Quality Score is click-through rate—that is, the percentage of times that your ad appears that it's actually clicked on. That's letting our searchers, our users, be the judge of what's a high-quality ad. In this system, if an ad is showing up and getting more clicks than another ad, then we judge that as being that searchers are finding that ad to be more relevant. And we want to reward more relevant ads, because we want to create a great user experience.

There are other factors that go into Quality Score. We look at the landing page that the ad leads to and make sure that that's relevant to the content of the ad itself. And so on, a number of factors. What we actually do is factor in both your bid and the Quality Score, and together that determines the ranking on a page. That's important for a number of reasons.

> "I always encourage advertisers to start out by thinking about their business and understanding their metrics."

One, as I mentioned already, we don't actually set the prices; we let our advertisers and the market set the prices. Second, we want quality to be just as important as pricing. So if you have two advertisers and one of them has a Quality Score that's more than twice that of the other, that advertiser could actually bid half as much and still appear on the page above the advertiser with the lower Quality Score. That's really important, because we think that for the long term, both for our advertisers and, most important, for our users, it's better to factor in quality than to just worry about price and revenue.

So you really can't buy your way to the top, then.

No, that's correct.

How does an advertiser determine how much to bid, on a cost-per-click basis?

I always encourage advertisers to start out by thinking about their business and understanding their metrics. The more an advertiser understands about their own goals, their own metrics, their own profitability, how much they want to pay and are willing to pay for a lead, then the better off they'll be. So it has to start with an understanding of your own business.

The next thing is our system will suggest, along the way, proposed bids that will give you a sense of what kind of traffic, how many clicks you might get, and what sort of ranking you might get—whether you might be the first ad on the page or the fifth ad on the page and so on. That's going to depend on the keywords that you run on.

I mentioned the example earlier of running shoes. Well, if you just choose "running shoes," that's a pretty broad keyword, so you're probably going to have a lot more advertisers. If you serve a particular geographic area—if, for example, you only served the Bay area—then you might run the keywords "Bay area running shoes." Or you might choose just to target the region that you operate in, or a particular part of the country. You can target everything from a particular city to a geographic region—the entire Bay area or the New York City metropolitan area, and so on—or you can target by state, or the entire country, or all speakers of a given language around the world.

Likewise, with your keywords you can get a lot more specific. Like I said, you can choose a specific make and model of a product, of a running shoe or of a TV, or you can run on very broad keywords. Typically, being more specific is going to be more effective, and it's also typically going to be more cost-effective.

We've focused so far on the search advertising, but what else is Google doing in terms of other forms of advertising—banner ads, video ads, or whatever?

Google is expanding AdWords to cover more different ad formats, both online and offline. In terms of online, in addition to the text ad format that we've talked about, Google also offers image ads that allow you to run either static images or dynamic image ads on web sites. We also allow video ads that you can run on video sites like YouTube or on other web pages; if you have a particular video ad, whether that comes from a TV format or something you've made just for online, you can run that using exactly the same platform and the same AdWords system.

We've also recently introduced a new ad format that we're excited about, called gadget ads. The easiest way to think about what they are is they give advertisers a mini-site within a web page. If you think about a web page on about a given topic, let's say a site that's targeted to runners and has a bunch of information around running trails in a certain area and reviews of running shoes and so on, then as an advertiser you could create a little gadget that would sit off on one part of that page. It might have information about your product; you can embed videos in there, you can have more information about your store, and you could create some dynamic games or whatever you want. We've had advertisers using that to embed videos, to show customer videos of customer testimonials, any number of things. What it does is puts in the hands of advertisers control over a dynamic advertising experience within a web site.

> *"We want advertisers to understand exactly how well they're performing, and to ensure that their advertising experience is a positive one."*

Those are all online advertising experiences. Google has also taken AdWords and expanded it into the offline formats. By offline we mean anything that's basically not there on the Internet. For example, we've recently been running a closed trial of TV advertising. We're also testing mobile ads, letting advertisers show their ads on mobile devices, when people search that way. We're running the same AdWords model that allows you to target a particular audience and particular region and bringing that to TV or to radio advertising or to print advertising, to put as much control as possible into the hands of advertisers—and also to provide them accountability.

One thing we haven't talked about yet is that the AdWords system gives you real-time reporting that shows you how many people see your ad, how many people click on your ad. If you use either conversion tracking or Google Analytics or our Checkout product, you can figure out how many people buy a product as a result of those ads. We want advertisers to understand exactly how well they're performing, and to ensure that their advertising experience is a positive one. There's the old saying about advertising spending, that I know that I'm wasting half of my ad budget, I just don't know which half. We want to help solve that problem and let advertisers know that.

When you're moving into mobile and especially into offline advertising, you have competitors that you didn't have before. What's been the response to your movement into these areas?

It reminds me of the early stages of AdWords, where it's a new product with a different model than what a lot of marketers and advertisers are traditionally used to. We've certainly found some early adopters who are very excited and getting involved and having positive results. But it takes time, both for an advertiser to figure out how to work effectively with us, but especially for us. One of the things that Google always tries to do is to develop innovative new products that create value for its users—in this case, for our advertisers. Then we put the product out there and see what works and what doesn't, and constantly innovate and change. We're in that early stage right now for most of these offline products, so we're seeing a bunch of early successes and also getting a lot of valuable feedback about things that we will surely improve over the coming months.

I know it's hard to generalize; every company's different. But given all the different media and formats where you can spend your advertising budget, how does a company these days go about allocating the mix?

It's a great question. Let's start with where Google wants to help advertisers go. Advertisers and businesses care about their success and their profitability. Frankly, one worries so much about how you're getting your leads and where you're getting your sales—whether it be from online advertising, from offline advertising, from TV, from radio, from online video, whatever it might be—that you want to know what's going to be most cost-effective for you, and that's what you're going to want to do.

> *"You want to know what's going to be most cost-effective for you."*

By creating a single platform—that is, increasingly enabling all these different media formats—Google is aggressively moving in that direction, to try to bring that level of accountability and understanding to advertisers. That's the way we ultimately want advertisers to think about that.

Now, how do you do that today? We're not quite at that point today, where you can automatically say, "Hey, Google, here's my budget; go out and figure out how to maximize my profits with this budget," and our systems will automatically calculate for you how do divide up that budget. We're still working to get there.

But you can today come in and see that, even within AdWords today, which particular forms of advertising, which sites, which keywords, which campaigns within your AdWords account, are generating higher returns on your investment. What we always encourage advertisers to do is look at the reporting we provide, figure out what's working and do more of that, and if something's not working, stop doing that—and allocate your budget towards what's working. We have a number of tools what we call the Budget Optimizer and Conversion Optimizer, a number of things that are built in, that advertisers can turn on and let your system automatically allocate their budget to the most effective parts of their AdWords account, so that we can try to ensure that they maximize profitability.

If you had a crystal ball, what's the whole online advertising thing going to look like three to five years from now?

I think one of the most important changes that can come in online advertising in general is to allow advertisers to fully benefit from the enormous scale and reach of the Internet—and, frankly, from all the offline formats we've discussed—with minimal to no amounts of work and thought around that.

One of the incredible values that AdWords offers today is within the year in the U.S., Google reaches 66 percent of all Internet users, and through our AdSense for Content network, reaches 76 percent of all Internet users. That's amazing reach, but that's also a lot of [other] sites to think about, and a huge number of opportunities in terms of reaching that audience.

Some advertisers today advertise with us and use a baseline set of features, and some use many, many advanced features. What we want, in time, is to offer all advertisers a very advanced set of features but in a way that's incredibly easy to use, so our system can help optimize advertisers' performance without causing too much work. Ultimately what we want is very pinpoint and accurate precision at massive scale—and to put that power in the hands of our advertisers.

Sound Bites

If you're going to allocate a big chunk of your online advertising budget to Google AdWords, it helps to know what Google is up to with its online advertising service. To that end, here are some of the important points noted by Google's David Fischer:

- Google reaches 66 percent of all Internet users.
- The AdWords program is designed for both large and small advertisers—and, in effect, levels the playing field between the two.
- Google Checkout supplements AdWords by providing an easy-to-use online checkout and payment system to AdWords advertisers.
- To ensure your AdWords ad achieves high placement, make sure it's properly targeted with the appropriate keywords.
- Placement is further determined via an ad's Quality Score—which itself is influenced by the click-through rate, the relevancy of the landing page, and so on.

Going forward, Google isn't just for web advertisers. In addition to its traditional text search ads (as well as newer web-based video and gadget ads), Google is migrating its services to other media—including radio, television, and print advertising. An ad system that rewards quality and relevancy isn't a bad thing, even if it is a new thing in the old media. Watch and wait to see what kind of reception Google receives.

Phil Terry: Creative Good

24

"Our job is to facilitate our clients' direct experience of their customers."

—*Phil Terry*

Creative Good is a consulting firm that focuses on the customer experience, often at the very highest executive levels of a company. The driving force behind Creative Good is Phil Terry, a Renaissance man who tries to focus his clients on the big picture—that is, how to change a company's culture to be more customer-centric.

> **FACT SHEET: PHIL TERRY**
>
> CEO, Creative Good
> (www.creativegood.com)
>
> Co-Founder, Good Experience
> (www.goodexperience.com)

Phil's partner Mark Hurst started Creative Good in 1997 and they both went on to "later" start Good Experience, a company best known for its Gel (Good Experience Live) conference and its self-named email newsletter that also focuses on the customer experience. (I've been a subscriber to the Good Experience newsletter for several years now.) Phil also founded and runs The Councils, a leadership network that brings together more than 400 senior executives to build better, more customer-centric businesses.

In other words, Phil is all about customer-centricity—which is the key to all successful marketing, online or off.

Developing a Customer-Centric Mindset

Phil was initially reluctant to be interviewed for this book; he thought that readers would be more interested in the people that actually execute the strategies than in the consultant who advises them. Based on what I knew about Phil and his company, however, I obviously thought otherwise. As you'll read in the following interview, Phil has a unique and useful perspective on how businesses should create a great customer experience. It's all about developing customer-centric thinking, starting at the very top of the org chart and working down through the organization.

What is the state of the customer experience on the web today?

It's mediocre, at best. Basics still don't work—most customers and users of the web can't find what they are looking for and can't complete their transaction when they have found it. This reality points, at least in part, to the fact that we're in the middle of what I think is a very long transition between epochs of business.

In 1954, Peter Drucker released a book, one of the seminal books, *The Practice of Management*. In that book he posited that the fundamental purpose of a business is to create customers; that's what you're there to do, primarily.

In the mid twentieth century, businesses were pretty much management-controlled bureaucracies where the customer had very little voice in anything. It was still very much, "You can have whatever color you like as long as it's black." Peter Drucker saw the next epoch—saw what was on the horizon. And he was right: the fundamental purpose of a business is to create customers.

Interestingly, I believe that this has been true for hundreds of years. In fact, I consider the first star in the customer-centric pantheon to be Josiah Wedgwood, who in the late 18th century pioneered a lot of what we now consider to be basic practices in marketing and business design; he went into the homes of the gentry and observed how they were using their flatware, their tableware, where it was stored, where they kept it, how they used it, what they didn't use, and what they did use. That was critical.

In London, he opened the very first showroom where he pioneered the use of glass cabinet displays; even more to the point, he made his showroom a "fashionable meeting place for ladies." He understood what Starbucks understands now, 300 years later, that you want to create a place. And he did that.

[Wedgwood] was also the first direct marketer and catalog marketer. He sent one free piece of his latest set to the royalty and aristocracy of Germany along with a letter that said, "Here's your free piece and here's your catalog; feel free to order." And he had something like a 50 percent conversion rate.

Wedgwood innovated based on his ability to focus on and understand his customer. He understood that he himself had to spend actual time with his customers, generate insights from those observations, and then integrate those insights into everything that he was doing—obviously the design of his products, but also how he thought about his overall business, his marketing strategy, and his operations.

I would argue there have been other important stars over the last several hundred years, but for the most part—certainly after the second industrial revolution—businesses lost touch with the importance of the customer, the centrality of the customer, the fact that their whole purpose is to create customers. In the early 1950s, Drucker saw that customer-centricity was actually going to become a driving force for business success in the coming 50 to 100 years.

We're in the middle of that period right now. Over the next 50 years, companies will survive or die based on their ability to integrate insights from their customers into everything that they do. Unfortunately, the way business evolution works, as all evolution works, is that those who don't understand or don't have those genes just basically wither away; they don't continue on to the next epoch.

I first started using the web when it was a text-based interface at CERN in Europe. I didn't understand the importance that it would have later, but I stuck with it. When the visual web with the graphical browser came out by the mid '90s and grew in popularity I saw an opportunity. Because the web was a direct interactive medium, I sensed that it would be the lead of this customer-centric evolution.

> *"You can…measure the impact fairly quickly from the investment you make in customer experience."*

Why? When you do business on the web, any investment you make in understanding your customers better and changing your interface, the products and services that you're offering, or your fundamental strategies, gives you an immediate measurable payoff. You can for the first time measure the impact from the investment you make in customer experience.

I'm proud to say that we were one of the first firms to identify, in the retail space, conversion rate—which seems unbelievably obvious today. We asked one of our early clients "Do you know how many of your visitors are buying?" And they didn't, so we figured it out, we did the research, and then I started evangelizing conversion rate as a key retail metric in all my industry speeches and writings.

A cornerstone of our methodology is we're not the gurus; our job is to facilitate our clients' direct experience of their customers. If we help our clients directly experience their customers, then they will make a cultural shift far more powerful than what simply comes from reading a report. We don't want our work to simply be a report that gathers dust or just another opinion at the table. What we want to do is make room for the customer at the table. We don't necessarily want a seat for ourselves, but for the customer. That's the change that we're looking to make.

Unfortunately, many companies do not have a seat at the table for their customers. Several Harvard Business School professors wrote an important article, called "Bringing Customers into the Board Room"[David Court, John A. Quelch, Blair Crawford, Gail McGovern, *Harvard Business Review*, 2004] that made this point. The hook of the article was that in many American boardrooms, there is no seat for the customer; there is no board-level committee dedicated to marketing and customer issues. Instead, most executives have the problem of having reams of data that they don't know what to do with, yet no actionable insights to work off of. I completely agree with that.

Companies need to make a seat at their tables for their customers. Ironically, to do that, executives need to get out of their seats and out from behind their tables and directly observe their customers. A few days of well-designed qualitative research, especially in the field and homes where the customers live, can be an almost world-changing event for the client executives. Back to that early client, we figured out the conversion rate and then we went out into the field, and we brought the executives with us. What they saw made their jaws drop. No report or expert opinion could have had the same impact as getting them out from behind their desks.

By the way, I mentioned Drucker before; if you boil down all of Peter Drucker's books—and, as you know, he wrote many books over 50 years— the most common theme or recommendation he has for executives is, "Get out from behind your desk."

[Drucker's] a mentor of mine, although he doesn't know me—and, of course, he's now dead. And he didn't know me when he was alive. As we'll discuss later, I recommend that executives adopt mentors, living or dead, whether they know them or not.

You talk about getting the guy out from behind the desk, but a lot of corporate culture today is very internally focused. How do you get the guy out of the corner office and into the field?

As consultants, it's easier for us than it is for internal executives. We make it a stipulation of our contract. If you're going to hire us, you have to commit to coming out from behind your desk and participating in this field research. And by the way, the most senior people have to commit to doing it—or don't hire us. We won't agree to the project. It's a serious requirement.

Unfortunately—and this is so common with our clients—people tend to focus more on internal politics than on their customers. Internal politics and inward-focused culture is the number-one obstacle to creating a good customer experience. I think you must have heard that

> *"Internal politics and culture is the number-one obstacle to creating a good customer experience."*

from other people, and one of the only ways I know how to break it is to get executives in front of customers.

I've experienced it personally, yes.

So this dynamic of internal fighting being the obstacle to good customer experience is well known, right? This is one of the areas that I focused on it early in our consulting practice. If we're going to touch the customer experience, we have to have some impact on the organization behind the customer interface. We are not organizational consultants. No, we do something that is simpler and possibly more powerful. We get those fighting executives out into the field together and convert their internal politics into a shared external view of the business. It's not enough that we know something. Our clients have to experience it and know it themselves if we're going to stop their internal bickering and get them to focus on their customers.

We are serious about having an impact and I've allowed that mission to guide the design of our business. For example, our consulting operation is small. It's small by choice. We want to be in the position where we do not have to see work. Because our goal is to have a big impact, we're very selective with whom we work. We want to make sure the environment is right for us to have an impact. As a result, we turn down clients where it's clear that there's not a serious commitment to change. We don't participate in RFP [request for proposal] processes and we don't sell hard. We want to have an impact that's not measured by our own profitability at Creative Good, but measured by the impact that we have on our clients—and *their* profitability.

What does a company need to do to be customer-driven over the long term?

To make long-term change, companies need to have a consistent process of observing customers and their behavior. I don't mean focus groups, and I don't mean usability tests. I mean open-ended behavioral sessions like the simple listening-lab method we created and use.

I also don't mean that this should be done at the end of a new strategy- or product-development cycle, but rather at the beginning, to inform the new product development.

> *"Are you long-term or short-term in your orientation?"*

Companies can implement a customer-driven approach internally. We encourage them to do it; we train them to do it; we hope that they do it. We hope that they build a discipline around it. Part of that discipline is you can't just have a side group that does it and brings the results back to the executives. No, the executives need to make a personal commitment to spend time.

I saw a typical CEO keynote recently. The CEO of a major retailer got up and used a lot of the typical tricks in the bag of the corporate communications and marketing department. He showed a video that looked like a high-quality TV commercial. He used the word "customer" a lot. There was pounding music. It was all high energy. After the dog-and-pony show and during the Q&A, one of the attendees in the crowd asked him a very important question: "How much time do you personally spend in the field with your customers?"

His answer, typical of most corporate CEOs, was, "I don't spend any time with individual customers. I don't have time to do that."

Well, that was an honest answer and one that would accurately describe the priorities of most CEOs. That's a problem, and it's the 20th-century way of running a company. This particular CEO helped lead a turnaround of the business, so he's doing some things that are right. But will he have a long-term impact?

A lot of the difference between what we advocate and what is done in the business world comes down to a very simple question: "Are you long-term or short-term in your orientation?" Frankly, there are a lot of things you can do with financial statements to juice them up in the short term. I'm not talking about fraud or anything immoral. Then there is another set of things you can do if your orientation is more long-term. The problem is, how do you get to a long-term orientation?

Warren Buffett, who's another one of my mentors who doesn't know me, obviously has a long-term orientation, and at Berkshire Hathaway he's built a shareholder base that is also long-term. He's done that through years of work; it took a long time to build a long-term base of shareholders. How did he do it? Most importantly, he did not split the stock, so the stock price has increased. Now an A share of Berkshire Hathaway is more than $100,000. You don't join the Berkshire Hathaway shareholder base on a whim and you don't leave it on a whim either. If that stock goes up by 10 percent, it's not necessarily going to attract the short-term buyers and sellers. And if it goes down by 10 percent—or there's an off quarter—then it is not necessarily going to attract short sellers.

Do a majority of business executives follow Warren Buffett's long-term philosophy? Absolutely not. And he's completely open to the whole world about his approach. We also don't try to hide anything or patent our consulting ideas or framework. We're not interested in that, at all. We're interested in being part of leading a long-term change in how business is done.

Getting back to your question, "How do you make this change happen internally? How do you affect the culture? What are some of the things that we recommend? What are the basic practices?" Again, the first step is to create a culture of continuous customer observation, from the CEO down. You can't have a CEO tell you, "No, I can't do that, I don't have time for that." What they're essentially say-

> *"So, first, get out from behind your desk and visit customers—and also employees."*

ing is "I'm spending time with Wall Street analysts. I'm spending time in these other areas. I'm at conferences often." Usually, that's what behind it, and that's a certain way to play the game.

Hewlett Packard, I think, is an interesting counter case to the conventional approach. Take their CEO [Mark Hurd], who came in after Carly Fiorina. He said, "Okay, the first 18 months here, I'm not going to any conferences and I'm not going to do any press interviews. What am I going to do? Get on the road and spend time with my employees and my customers." And that's what he did. He learned some very important things that he used to shape and change that company. I'm not saying every decision he's made has been good; there's still challenges that HP is facing. But HP rocketed ahead of Dell—who could've predicted that, at the time he took over?

There are many examples around us showing how to make customer-centric organizational and cultural changes. But they're not quick fixes, and they require commitment and long-term vision.

So, first, get out from behind your desk and visit customers—and also employees; they're an important part of this equation. When I talk about customer-centric, in many ways I'm talking about people-centric, whether it's your customers, your employees, your partners, whatever.

Second, you need to create a culture where executives feel comfortable asking each other—as well as peers outside their company—for help. Asking for help is a powerful discipline that the best business leaders cultivate but that most executives do not. Cultivating an environment inside the company where executives are encouraged to ask for help creates the context for learning from your customers, from each other and from other industries. You can then constantly use that learning to provoke and inspire new perspectives. Building a culture that encourages asking for help prevents the tendency for companies to calcify.

The world is changing; both in small and big ways. Whatever works today is not necessarily what's going to work tomorrow. Companies need to be flexible to changing customer, competitive and technology dynamics. Seven years ago we weren't even talking about search engine optimization. Eight years ago, in online retail, checkout was the big issue. Checkout isn't the main problem anymore (although many sites still have poor checkout processes).

Third—and this is much more tactical but surprisingly powerful—build an engine around the Net Promoter (www.netpromoter.com) survey methodology. I was skeptical of surveys before Fred Reichheld came out with the Net Promoter approach. It took me a couple of years before his methodolgy won me over. It's a simple approach; that's one of the winning things about it. You don't need a bunch of PhDs to decipher it for you, or to spend a lot of money on actual administration. But if you use this methodology in conjunction with behavioral research and a culture focused on asking for help, it's very powerful; together, these three things can really help you create a machine of customer-centricity.

It appears to me that everything you've described, in terms of trying to turn around the culture, would seem to favor a smaller company over a larger one?

It favors a company that builds customer-centricity into its DNA from the beginning over a company that does not, whatever its size. What you do at the beginning has a huge impact over time. By the way, this is consistent with chaos theory and probability theory and so on. The small design changes you make at the beginning, over time—and as something grows— have big and sometimes unpredictable impact.

Look at a company like Amazon. Over the years, all our retail clients say to us, "Can't we just do what Amazon's doing?" Imitation is an important part of human development, whether it be childhood or business development. I don't have anything against imitation, but it

> *"If there's going to be imitation, they're imitating the wrong thing…for the wrong reasons."*

should be creative imitation and imitating with an understanding what it is that you're imitating. What companies often want to do is imitate the tactics rather than the root causes.

For example, people always want to imitate Amazon's personalization approaches, their product pages, or their checkout path. But the bigger issue that people miss is the culture that Jeff Bezos initially created at Amazon and which led to the development of those things—and will lead to the further development and changes and abandonment of some of those things over time.

Why don't people want to talk about copying the root causes? Well, it's much harder!

It turns out that copying the tactics is also hard because it doesn't work. A rule of thumb that I've found when people copy tactics is that they often copy the things that don't work, not the things that do. It's just sort of a rule; call it "Phil's Rule," if you will. If there's going to be imitation, they're imitating the wrong thing—and they're imitating the wrong thing for the wrong reasons. That's why it often doesn't work.

I think it's really important to look at what competitors are doing. Companies don't do it enough. On the other hand, you need to understand why they've done those things—the root causes—and then think about your own culture and customers. Many times, what Amazon does is not relevant to another retailer, who is thinking about copying them. Or what Amazon is doing *is* relevant, but you need to make a quarter-inch turn or be inspired by it, and then change it in big or small ways to make it part of how you create your own business to better serve your own customers.

There's a big difference between just copying something and being inspired by it.

Right. And again, copying something exactly is not a bad thing to do as part of the process of being inspired by it—in your own internal ways, to deconstruct it. But creative imitation is what's important.

> *"Be patient and persevere. Understand the importance of small changes over the long term."*

Let me also take a moment to clarify something else about customer-centricity. I want to make it very clear that I'm not advocating that companies ask their customers what they want. Customers often don't know what they want, and it's not customers' job to innovate for you. What I am advocating is to observe their behavior, and from that develop insights that help you understand what unmet needs or obstacles exist, which can then inspire you to create solutions.

Often the objection I get, when people hear I'm into customer-centricity, is that focus groups don't work. Well, that's right. Focus groups should be banned; starting today, there should be no more focus groups. I'm very clear on that point.

The smart people in academic psychology have taught for years that focus groups are not only a waste of time but also produce wrong results, because of the group dynamic and the gap between opinions and actions. Focus groups should be banned tomorrow, and the world would be a better place. (And that money could be redistributed to shareholders—or to customers, through price cuts!)

To kind of wrap things up, what advice would you give to a marketing executive who wants to push some of these principles within the organization?

I would say, be patient and persevere. Understand the importance of small changes over the long term. And focus on these three things:

First, get their fellow colleagues out from behind their desks to observe and learn from customers.

Second, build a culture supportive of asking for help. Learn to encourage yourself and your colleagues to ask for help from all kinds of sources—from smart people—alive or dead, from peers outside your business, executives inside your company. Read outside the mainstream. Do not allow your information flow to be totally determined by what everyone else is reading, it will hurt your ability to be creative and to think creatively about your customers and the design of your business.

Third, integrate the Net Promoter survey methodology and turn it into an operating system.

Fourth, develop a discipline of asking for help from all kinds of sources—from smart dead people, mentors alive or dead (whether they know you or not), peers outside your business, executives inside your company. Read outside the mainstream; if your information flow is totally determined by what everyone else is reading, it will hurt your ability to be creative and to think creatively about your customers and the design of your business. That is what I would recommend.

Finally, I offer to your readers a free service. I host a free phone-based reading group—the Reading Odyssey (www.readingodyssey.com)—or executives who want to read in a way that challenges their thinking and helps inspire creativity. We read classics like Herodotus, Thucydides, Plato, the Old Testament, by phone, with some of the leading academic scholars participating. We also read current books like Danny Meyer's *Setting the Table* and Peter Bevelin's *Seeking Wisdom*.

In fact, if there's one book I would recommend that every one of your book readers should read, it would be *Seeking Wisdom* [Peter Bevelin, PCA Publications, 3rd edition, 2007]. This is a book that basically explains the advice of Warren Buffett's partner, Charlie Munger, about the importance of building what Munger calls "a latticework of frameworks." The book reviews the big ideas of biology, physics, astronomy, mathematics, probability, psychology, business history, and so on, and teaches the reader to use them together in integrated ways to approach and think about the world and to make decisions that benefit your customers, your employees, and your shareholders.

It sounds like you're arguing for a liberal arts education over a strictly business education.

Absolutely.

Sound Bites

How do you create a great customer experience on your web site? As Phil Terry explained, it all starts with the mindset of the people at the top of the organizational chart. It's not about copying what your competitors do. It's not about conducting focus groups and usability studies; it's about everyone in your company, from top to bottom, watching and talking to your customers directly. You have to know your customers so you can think like your customers.

That means, of course, getting out from behind your desk and hitting the street. It also means getting your boss and your boss' boss out of their corner offices and in front of your customers. And it means enhancing your normal business inputs with a well-rounded flow of information from other disciplines. (Your customers, after all, don't read your industry trade journals.)

What's the takeaway from Phil's interview? It's high-level stuff:

- Get people out from behind their desks.
- Observe what your customers are doing—and talk to them directly.
- Integrate Net Promoter survey methodology.

- Develop a culture where executives feel comfortable asking for help from other executives in the company—and their peers outside the company.
- Be patient, persevere, and have a long-term orientation to everything you do.

You want to instill a customer-centric mindset early in your company's development, and at the highest levels of the company. Change has to be real, and it has to come from within. That may be difficult to envision when you're working in the trenches day by day, but it's something a consultant like Phil can see from the outside. Take his advice, and a great customer experience will follow.

Patrick Duparcq: Kellogg School of Management, Northwestern University

25

"Interactive and digital technology doesn't necessarily do a lot of things new, but it does all things better, faster, more cost efficiently."

—*Patrick Duparcq*

To better understand how all the different factors discussed in this book affect online marketing, I wanted to wrap things up with more of a big picture overviewto rise above the details of blog marketing or search engine optimization and look at what's happening out there at a 30,000-foot level.

> **FACT SHEET: PATRICK DUPARCQ**
>
> Professor of Marketing, Kellogg School of Management, Northwestern University
> (www.kellogg.northwestern.edu)

To provide that big-picture overview I turned to the world of academia—in particular to the renowned Kellogg School of Management at Northwestern University, and to professor Patrick Duparcq. Patrick has been at the Kellogg School since 1997, where he teaches several online marketing–related classes. He closely tracks what goes on in internet marketing, e-commerce and mobile marketing, but more generally has his radar tuned in to all digital technology developments that impact marketing. Previously, he taught marketing at Purdue University's Krannert School of Management, and served as director of that school's Center for E-Business Education and Research. Patrick also keeps his ear to the ground by consulting with several technology startups and major Fortune 500 corporations.

Technology and Marketing: The Big Picture

Yes, search engine marketing and optimization are important. Yes, email and blog marketing are important. Yes, social networking is important. But these are today's trends; they're not necessarily what will be important next year or the year after. What will be important in the future? Read on to learn Patrick's views on technology trends, as well as what skills you need to keep on top of online marketing going forward.

When it comes to online marketing, how useful are traditional marketing skills?

I would say very useful. Maybe even more important than ever! One of the biggest mistakes that people made in the '90s was to look at online marketing as an entire new phenomenon that required rewriting all the rules. It sort of depends on what perspective you take. Obviously, different technology platforms provide different forms of customer interaction: you communicate differently on TV (or in print) than you communicate with people online. But that is going to the microscopic detail and the tactics of what you do. If, however, you think about *why* the interaction takes place, or about which audience you select to target, or what the content of the message should be, the approach is fundamentally the same as in any marketing approach. It's just better, more accurate, and more cost-effective.

Those sound marketing principles apply whether the platform of interaction is the physical world, the world in print, radio, TV, the internet, or mobile devices. The platform changes, but the principle remains. I think in the '90s, too many people were too caught up in the technology and were forgetting the 30,000-feet view of where this fits in.

> *"Clearly, it's important to keep an overall view of sound marketing principles."*

It is especially important, I think, for online marketing (or even for mobile marketing, which I consider the next wave), because it's a medium, more than any other medium, that actually ties together all the other media. If anything, it makes marketing principles apply even stronger. What you do online has an impact on what you do in traditional (brick-and-mortar) retailing. Online activities, in most cases, will make traditional channels work more efficiently. They create store traffic, and bring in customers that are better informed about what they want.

Conversely, physical-world customers, which often don't leave much personal information behind in the store (other than maybe a credit card number or in the best case a store loyalty card identifier), will—given a chance—interact with the merchant online and provide a plethora of information: which product they like, what attributes are most important, price sensitivity, and much more. Likewise, ads in printed media or TV commercials will often lead to a spike in online visits for that brand, providing both a stronger and richer interaction with prospective customers, and an indication of the advertising effectiveness in the medium from which the visitor was sent to the web site. There's a lot of interaction. Technology is the glue that binds different platforms together.

Clearly, it's important to keep an overall view of sound marketing principles. The Internet integrates across platforms and approaches.

The questions mostly remain the same. What do we want to accomplish? How do we best reach our customers? How do we position our product? What services can be attached to our product to make it more valuable to our customers? How can the insights we gained from frequent and deep online customer interaction help us in product development? Same story, different platforms, different speeds, better outcomes.

Certainly in the early days of the Internet I saw a lot of companies that were doing marketing without marketing people.

Absolutely. Many marketers felt intimidated by the technology (granted, it was not always user-friendly in the early days). Or they didn't see or believe that this could ever be a legitimate marketing channel, so they didn't get involved. Not unlike the current hesitation with respect to mobile marketing. Internet marketing in the early days was driven by IT people, like, "Look at how cool this is that we can do." But don't blame the IT people; technology is what they're trained to do, not crafting marketing strategies. Technology for the sake of technology, without a strategy that drives it, rarely does anything for a company. Always ask (like in the old song), "What is it good for?" And hopefully the answer is *not* "absolutely nothing!"

As you say, the traditional marketing skills are essential online. Are there any new skills that people need to learn?

Yes—maybe not as much at the strategic level, but definitely at the tactical level. Marketers just have so many more ways to interact with customers nowadays. But it's a two-edged sword: customers also have a lot more alternatives and a lot more ways to punish companies if they don't deliver on their promises.

If you don't deliver, word spreads like wildfire among your customers. So you better have it right the first time. Community involvement and reading blogs has become an integral part of a customer's information search before buying a product. In some product categories, information from blogs and communities represents more than 50 percent of the information on which customer choice is finally based. As a marketer, this means you better develop the skills to learn from communities and blogs (or use a specialized company like Nielsen's BuzzMetrics to do it for you). Same principle (listening to customers), different skill.

More important even than acquiring new skills is to strengthen the application of existing sound marketing principles. That holds for being customer-oriented, understanding the customer, or even for approaches such as product differentiation.

In the past, if a company was the only game in town, it didn't have to differentiate its product very much, because that was the only thing that was available. If the next supplier of products is a thousand miles away, then it's really hard for customers to find out (a) that that supplier exists, and (b) what the product is all about. In other words, the customer is *stuck* with you and you don't have to worry too much anyway.

But if at any point in time customers become more aware of all products that are available, not only locally and regionally and nationally but worldwide, then you can't really get away with saying, "Well, that's not possible" or "That's too difficult." People really know what is available and what is possible.

The principle isn't new—we always understood the importance of being customer-oriented, the principle of product differentiation and of rigorous competitive analysis. But companies that don't practice and apply these principles religiously will get harshly penalized for it.

Another example is business integration. Just about every textbook on marketing talks about how the marketing function should be integrated with other functions, like finance, accounting, manufacturing, and so on. Before the Internet, it was much more difficult to do that; often functions were assumed in different parts of the company, sometimes in different locations. Other companies had the same challenges. So we all acknowledged the importance of cross-functional integration and how it would theoretically get you a better-run marketing operation, but no one was really practicing it.

Today, technology allows companies to integrate the marketing function much better with all others. Marketing knows what manufacturing is doing, manufacturing knows what marketing is doing, and in the end we come up with better products. It's always going to be a challenge, but the excuses and arguments for *not* doing it are a lot less convincing.

The principles haven't changed, but in the way we execute marketing principles we just have to become a lot more agile. We really have to play much more according to the rules that we always understood, but we weren't penalized for it before.

This brings up the question of education. For a student going through school today, looking to make online marketing a career, what different courses are available?

There are lots of options on different levels. Most disciplines in business have understood the growing importance of technology in our business world. The Internet is currently the most dominant technology, and many functional areas have started to incorporate insights and the realities of today's more technologically enabled world in their courses. That's not only true of marketing; it's also true in human resource management, it's definitely true in logistics, it's true in most of the disciplines. I don't think you can take any course in any business school anymore without ever talking about the Internet.

This integrated view assumes that by now we understand the reality of the Internet, how it modifies or enhances different aspects of a discipline and we'll just incorporate that in all our courses. For me, that just doesn't cut it. It is very hard to find enough time in a basic principles course to provide the depth of detail and insights and the myriad of new possibilities offered by technological innovations and still have enough time to cover the basics. There just isn't time enough to do that.

I applaud that many schools offer specialized courses that specifically focus on the use of the Internet on a particular discipline. In marketing you'll find courses on Internet marketing, e-commerce, online consumer behavior, online retailing, etc., but also newer areas like mobile marketing. Offering at least some dedicated courses related to the use of technology in different aspects of marketing is the right way to go, in my opinion.

What about for an existing marketer—somebody who's 35 or 40 years old and has been thrown headfirst into all this online stuff? How can they get up to speed?

Do a lot of reading; there are excellent articles in the business press and the academic press.

For example, look at research by Gartner, Forrester, or eMarketer to see what they consider to be the next big thing.

> "The most important thing is to be aware of what's available—and then not to forget all the basic marketing principles involved."

And there are excellent courses that universities offer, relating to getting up to speed on how to use technology in different disciplines. Just about every business school would offer either full-time or part-time programs in which these things are covered. Or they would offer short-term seminars, going from half a day to three days, to cover these aspects. Also, don't be shy to surround yourself with younger 20-something professionals who live and breathe technology. Students graduating in 2008 have never known a world without the Internet or mobile phones. And as always, listen to your customers! If you're willing to learn, they're willing to teach you and tell you what online functionalities they want, and how they prefer to be approached.

I often tell my students that the most important thing is to be aware of what's available—and then not to forget all the basic marketing principles involved. When I go out to companies and I talk to them, often what I find is that they're not even aware of what's all possible, how technology can be used in a number of functions—not only in marketing, but also in logistics and human resource management and other functional areas.

About a month or so ago, I ran into a company that developed online training tools for companies. The first application they wrote sort of mimicked what they were doing in a regular setting, either through printed materials or through seminars. The approach pretty much consisted of doing the old thing, but on a new platform.

But with a deep understanding of available technologies and consumer comfort levels with the use of technology, they now incorporate principles of social networking, blogs, wikis, and other Web 2.0 approaches in their learning platforms. Their customers are large corporations with a need for more effective employee and partner training. Users of the learning environment learn about particular aspects of sales or engineering, not just the basics, but also share some of the basics and their experiences with the people in their organization that have similar interests. We all know that that's how we learn the best.

We learn the best if we ask people who speak the same language, at the same level that we are, if we ask them for input and help. The example I usually give is when my assistant needs to know how to do something in PowerPoint, he's probably not going to go to the Microsoft web site, because that's too technical. He's probably not going to call the computer-support people in the organization, because the language they speak is foreign to him ("technical mumbo-jumbo"). What he does is ask his colleagues, "How do you do that?"

Community building and social networking will become increasingly important in selling products and selling and distributing ideas.

Focusing on the technology, as you know, is like shooting at a moving target; whatever you teach today is going to be different five years from now. Right now the hot buzz phrase is social networking and everything associated with that, but what's coming next? What are the big trends that you see happening?

I prefer to start with a very high-level view, the 30,000-feet view—or maybe even the orbital view. So what is next?

At the highest level, the question you're asking is what the impact is of technology on business, and what is the next major technology that will significantly change how we view and organize our business? In my opinion, it's mobility—mobile marketing and mobile applications. Think about it. Marketers constantly struggle for customers' attention, eyeballs, ears. But any platform at best gets only a fraction of a customer's attention 24 hours a day. A typical Gen Y (teens to late twenties, those born between 1981 and 1995) customer will read a newspaper for about 10 minutes a day, watch TV for less than 2 hours a day, listen to radio for about an hour a day, and is online for about 2 hours a day. Beyond that, this customer is out of reach. Except for the mobile phones. Mobile phone are very personal and always with the customer. In addition to making phone calls, users use messaging (SMS), watch TV, listen to music, browse the web, request product info (e.g., through QR codes), and increasingly use the phone's navigation capabilities. That is a *huge* opportunity for marketers, and if we do it right, we'll have more access to customers than ever before. As usual, there are dangers involved. Unless we learn to play by the customers' rules and not abuse our ability to easily reach customers, we may just kill this tremendous opportunity before it matures.

I also believe that we'll see an increasing number of e-enabled products: appliances, entertainment devices, home security, and cars. Once the Internet connectivity is omnipresent (wired, wireless, through power-lines) and connectivity hardware costs falls below a certain level, you'll see some creative new ways to provide service or convenience directly to the product.

> ## *"Often…technologies bring things full circle."*

If you come down to a much lower level, before anything mobile, but just focus on the people who are stuck in front of a computer screen, social networking will only increase in importance. More will happen through blogs, communities, virtual worlds (like Second Life) and viral campaigns. Also, I believe that computers, Internet, and home entertainment will be much more integrated than they are today. Internet-enabled radio and TV (pure IPTV or Internet-enhanced TV) are finally breaking through. Imagine the commercials on radio and TV as focused on your interests as Google's sponsored links are now!

The thing that gets me about social networking is that it's not new. Social networking existed before the Internet, with bulletin boards and such, right?

Absolutely—and even further back. It's not new because it's part of the human condition—it's what people have always done. Don't you ask your friends, family, or neighbors about their experience with a new product before you go buy it yourself? What's really powerful about the Internet is that it scales just about any basic human interaction to a global level: more choice, more competition, more interaction. The Internet is the human condition on steroids!

It's actually interesting to look at the "what's old is new again" thing. I often observe that technologies bring things full circle. We do what we've done a hundred years ago, but we do them faster and more efficiently—and reach more people. Social networking is one of those things. Another example is online grocery retailing and delivery. I never thought of Peapod or OnlineGrocer as very revolutionary. When I was a kid, there was a milkman, a newspaper man, and a grocer with large truck delivering at home. Nothing new. Of course, the online grocers know exactly what you want. There's no guesswork anymore. It's more efficient. What was old almost always comes back in a later technology cycle, but in a more efficient way.

If you think about technologies that are important for marketers, they mostly all have to do with improving communications and increasing reach, affordability, interaction, identification (you know who you reach). As I mentioned earlier, mobility is *really* the next big thing because it increased the reach to 24/7. Historically, look at how marketers have connected to customers and start more than 600 years ago, before the printing press was invented. The only interaction you had as a marketer was probably as a manufacturer of a product itself, whenever a customer came in you would talk to him, educate him, and hope he would buy the product. The process was effective because the manufacturer knew exactly what the customer wanted. In later times, mass manufacturing and mass marketing have separated manufacturers and customers from each other. With the Internet, we return to being up-close and personal with our customers.

With the printed media, you could reach a much wider audience, but the impact of the message is less dramatic or engaging compared to an in-person interaction. Also, after the printed message is delivered, you sort of lost them, because people forget things. Move forward to radio and TV, and with TV you have a much higher reach, you have their attention longer, and you can do it in a multimedia format that has a higher impact. But again, you may only have their attention for two or three hours a day.

On the Internet, we can deliver a message to customers in just about any form-factor we choose: just text as in a printed medium format (web page), or audio and video as on radio and TV, or conversational and interactive as on the phone. Plus it's addressable; you can actually observe what people are looking at and learn about consumer behavior. That's something we couldn't do before with print media

> *"The mobile platform…gives you everything an Internet-connected computer can do, but people have it with them all the time."*

and radio and TV. We can get post-exposure recall data from Nielsen and stuff like that, but it's only a sample and it only relates to recalling advertising. Online we capture the entire browsing behavior of a visitor.

Yet, the Internet leaves some "reachability gaps" too. In-between the time someone looks and surfs online and their next visit you kinda lost them again. Where the interaction stops, churn starts. You can't have people sitting in front of a computer screen all the time. They may spend two hours a day in front of the computer, but that's only 2 out of 24.

The mobile platform really gives you everything an Internet-connected computer can do, but people have it with them all the time. Customers look up information at the time they need it (for example, in a store), not hours or days in anticipation. That makes it much more powerful. The interaction becomes contextual—i.e., relevant to the present situation. You never lose them; you potentially have nonstop connectivity to that person, wherever they go, whenever they go. Moreover, in addition to being able to provide everything on the mobile platform that you can do on a desktop or a laptop [PC], you have location-based information that allows you to provide even more contextual information—information about shoes if a customer is in the shoe store and about groceries if they're in the grocery store—and allow them to do comparative shopping while on the go.

The cynics would say it will never happen on that mobile phone, that the screen is too small, it's not convenient, or that the data connection is too expensive or not fast enough. Funny enough, that's exactly what cynics and disbelievers said in 1995 about the Internet. I'd say, "Web marketers, don't get stuck in the Web!"

Love it or hate it, but the iPhone has just accelerated that process significantly. And it's happening for the same reason that the Apple Macintosh made computing more accessible, why Mosaic and Netscape browsers made the Internet more accessible to users, and how the iPod made digital music on the go more popular. It's all about the interface.

In essence, Apple has put all other cell phone manufacturers on notice that from now on, unless they make a much better user interface for the customer, people are increasingly going to switch to phones that can do what the iPhone does.

People who never before would have considered browsing the web on their phone, now happily have become mobile Internet users. And if they interact more with their phone for a variety of reasons (browsing, mobile TV, music, navigation), it just legitimizes the platform and makes it more feasible as a marketing medium. Or as marketers like to put it: there will be a lot more eyeballs focused on the phone.

It seems to me that another aspect of mobility—as well as, to some degree, with the Internet and computing—is the whole concept of narrowcasting a message, as opposed to mass-marketing a message.

Absolutely. Narrowcasting, of course, is not new, either. Narrowcasting is about customer intimacy. We gave it up in the past because it's more expensive. But it's also more effective. When you have technology that makes it affordable, narrowcasting is almost always preferred to broadcasting. Here's again where technology has allowed us to come full circle. We can now do narrowcasting, but do it fast and efficiently, and not go bankrupt while doing it.

That's often what interactive and digital technology brings into the equation. It doesn't necessarily do a lot of things new, but it does all things better, faster, more cost-efficiently; it's very scalable.

> *"You have to stay five years ahead of the curve."*

The Internet already allowed us to do narrowcasting, and we do that better every year. Early Internet marketing was still predominantly broadcasting. But we've become much more sophisticated at personalized and localized advertising—we can easily target down to the city block these days and we have the technology to do even better on a cell phone. Exact geographic location can be determined through triangulation, if there is no GPS chip in it, but increasingly more and more phones will have GPS built in. Nokia's acquisition of Chicago-based NAVTEQ just indicates that that trend is really happening and well underway.

Expect more narrowcasting and contextual marketing based on as much who that customer is as where a customer is.

Knowing the way the trends are going—towards mobility, towards narrowcasting, the integration of everything—what advice would you give to somebody entering the marketing world

today? What do they need to know, what do they need to do to keep up with all this?

Very good question. I guess there is probably a long answer and a short answer—although I don't know what the short answer would be.

If you're involved in day-to-day marketing in a company, you just need to know the tools of marketing today very well. Be very well informed about what other companies are doing, what your competitors are doing. Read the business publications, read your books, read my books, and so on.

> *"When you do something new and innovative...customers will grant you a lot of leeway."*

If you're more involved in strategic planning, you have to stay five years ahead of the curve. The tricky thing about technology is its integration in business processes. You may be able to buy technology overnight—let's buy a new server, or let's buy an SMS server, let's buy anything under the sun. You can do that fairly fast—but to incorporate a technology in how you do business, that takes time. I would say it takes easily two to three years' time to get to know the technology, to understand what it can do for you, to properly integrate it in business processes and then roll it out and keep improving it.

If you're not thinking about what's going to be important five years from now, by definition you're already three years behind. All of a sudden you're waking up to something you notice your competitors are doing, and then you have to decide whether to buy it, and then you have to start thinking about how it can be used for your company. It takes easily two to three years.

The danger is you're going to be three to five years behind everybody else, but is there any danger in being the first out there or being ahead of everybody else?

When you're looking into a crystal ball, it's definitely difficult to assess the magnitude of all the pros and cons. But let's not be silly. You can realistically try out and test a technology without betting the company on it. In essence that's what any cash-strapped startup company does!

On the downside, yes, the technology may not be mature; I would definitely not spend very aggressively on technology that is not proven yet.

On the upside, if you are the first to do something that is really useful for customers, first of all you'll get a lot of incredible media coverage that is not to be undervalued. The problem in the mid '90s was, that was the only thing they were thinking of—let's do something totally cool and all the media coverage will keep us afloat. Of course, in the '90s that worked because people were so crazy, people with lots of money but no under-standing of business were just throwing money at these people. As an entrepreneur, I would have done the same. I don't think it's sound business, but if by doing it you get people throwing money at you, by all means do it! That's not going to work anymore today.

You will get good media coverage; that is on the upside. If you're really lucky, you may lock in the market and enjoy first-mover advantages. Also, when you do something new and innovative, even though it may not be perfect yet, if you're the first one to do it, customers will grant you a lot of leeway. They will be very forgiving.

Look at the iPhone. It's an incredible, beautiful phone. It has a wonderful user interface. It got incredible media coverage. It has a lot of people buy-ing it. Yet all the people who buy that phone can read the same reviews that you and I read and conclude that this is probably not the best possible phone you can buy; it has a lot of negatives. But if you provide people value in a feature of a product that is really important to them, they will forgive you a lot.

The user interface, we all know, is the weakest thing on every phone. It's unbelievable that it took Apple to really push that forward, because it's not rocket science. We understand these technologies, we have the technology. Very few things in the iPhone are really new, but Apple has packaged them together, has bundled them in such an appealing package. People who were only making phone calls and avoiding or neglecting all extra features on their phone (WAP, web, SMS, music) are now fully engaged in the entire mobile application spectrum of music, games, navigation, web surfing, and video watching. *That* is what we call an inflection point! Mobile marketing will start moving very fast from now.

How do you tie all this together?

In the end it's all about understanding where technology impacts business and how we use technology. When you look at all the technologies from a thousand years ago to now, you can see a number of commonalities. With every new generation of technology that gets inserted in the business equation, you have a number of things that happen.

First of all, customers become more powerful. Every technology makes customers more powerful.

Further, technology reduces the importance of distance. That was true with the printing press, it was true with the combustion engine, the railroad system, radio, TV, the Internet, and even more with mobility—every next technology reduces the importance of distance.

Usually, new technologies increase the fixed costs of operating a business and they usually reduce variable costs. Take a look at the book-writing process. Before the printing press was invented, it was very cheap on fixed costs—ink and a goose feather or something, and some parchment paper. Very cheap. But the variable costs of that process were huge—the hours and hours or years and years it took to write just one copy of a manuscript.

In the age of the Internet, variable costs are nearly zero, or often actually *are* zero. Whether an online article is viewed by one person or a million people, it's not going to make a difference. With significant increases you probably need a few more powerful servers, but by and large, the variable costs are zero; the fixed costs are much higher (computers, servers, and bandwidth versus parchment, ink, and goose feathers).

> ## "We literally compete with the entire world now."

Of course, it also depends on the industry and type and scale of a business. In traditional retailing you have to rent or buy a storefront; in other words you have to have a physical presence. If you compare that with creating a web site, it's going to allow you to do it much cheaper. You can create a fully functional online retail site for a small business with say 250 SKUs and credit card processing for under $10,000 with minimal monthly maintenance fees. So I can't say across the board that fixed costs are always higher. But trend-wise through history, the more technology gets injected in business, the fixed costs go up, the variable costs go down, consumers become more powerful, distance becomes less important, and competition becomes more important.

We literally compete with the entire world now, either actively or passively. Even if you're a little company selling something in downtown Chicago with no interest in global marketing, your customers will still know what's available in the world. If you cannot provide the product they want, even with the convenience of going to a local store and picking it up, they will seriously consider ordering it online from someone who can provide it to them.

A smart marketer would take advantage of that. If you have international competition, that also means you can compete internationally, right?

Well, yes, but not every company has the wherewithal and the infrastructure setup to really compete internationally. Technology definitely lowered the hurdles. It lowers the importance of distance, but it doesn't make it totally inconsequential. There is still logistics involved, currency exchange risks, service. Easier, yes, but not without some remaining complexities. There is a little store here on Broadway in Chicago that sells candy. I don't think they'll find it easy selling candy to the Chinese (but the Chinese may try to sell candy to them!).

Even if you have no interest in doing business overseas—or even buying your product from an overseas supplier—just the mere fact that people know what is available or possible will have an impact on how demanding consumers are. People say that not every product is equally appropriate for online sales. Well, that is true, but Internet marketing is not only about selling online. It is also about education, informing and supporting people. Or helping them in the selection process and providing them with a physical location where they can buy the product.

That demonstrates what you said about giving more information and power to the consumer.

Absolutely!

Sound Bites

That ended our formal interview, but Patrick and I talked for another half hour or so, covering everything from the decreasing importance of email to the possibility of mobile phones replacing notebook computers. (Patrick thinks mobile phones will continue to add more digital and computer-related functions; I'm not so sure.) It was refreshing to talk to someone who isn't invested in any single technology or medium, who has the liberty of looking at the entire industry and not just a single segment, who doesn't have to deal with the minutiae of day-to-day marketing management.

In taking the 30,000-foot approach, Patrick was able to highlight some of the larger trends in Internet and technology marketing. Here are some of the most important things he noted:

- Every new technology makes customers more powerful.
- New technology reduces the importance of distance; you're now competing globally, whether you want to or not.
- When you implement new technology, your variable costs go down in relation to your fixed costs.
- The next big trends? Mobility and context- and location-sensitive narrowcasting.
- No matter what the trends, traditional marketing skills will remain important—if not increase in importance.

It's key to not just keep abreast of these trends, but to get in front of them. As Patrick told me, "I personally make sure that I stay ahead of the curve about five years." Sure, social networks are hot today, but if you're just now jumping on the bandwagon you're already several years behind the curve. Take the time to pull your head out of the day-to-day fray and look at the bigger, longer-term trends; it's the only way you'll keep your business on the cutting edge going forward.

Index

Heroes are everywhere.

Interviews with 25 Successful Online Marketing Gurus

online marketing heroes

Michael Miller

978-0-470-24204-9

Interviews with 30 of the World's Top Bloggers

blogging heroes

Michael A. Banks

978-0-470-19739-4

Interviews with 30 Web 2.0 Influencers

web 2.0 heroes

Bradley L. Jones

978-0-470-24199-8

WILEY
Now you know.

Available wherever books are sold, or order online at wiley.com